WHITEWASHING
America

Whitewashing America

MATERIAL CULTURE AND RACE IN THE ANTEBELLUM IMAGINATION

Bridget T. Heneghan

UNIVERSITY PRESS OF MISSISSIPPI
JACKSON

www.upress.state.ms.us

The University Press of Mississippi is a member of the Association of American University Presses.

Copyright © 2003 by University Press of Mississippi
All rights reserved
Manufactured in the United States of America

11 10 09 08 07 06 05 04 03   4 3 2 1

Library of Congress Cataloging-in-Publication Data

Heneghan, Bridget T.
  Whitewashing America : material culture and race in the antebellum imagination / Bridget T. Heneghan.
p. cm.
Includes bibliographical references and index.
   ISBN 13: 978-1-934110-99-7   ISBN 10: 1-934110-99-X
   1. American fiction—19th century—History and criticism. 2. Race in literature. 3. American literature—White authors—History and criticism. 4. Material culture—United States—History—19th century. 5. Human skin color in literature. 6. Material culture in literature. 7. Segregation in literature. 8. Slavery in literature. 9. Racism in literature. 10. White in literature. I. Title.
   PS374.R32H465 2003
   813.009'355—dc21   2003002247

British Library Cataloging-in-Publication Data available

Print-on-Demand Edition

TO MY FAMILY

CONTENTS

Acknowledgments ix

Introduction xi

1. The Pot Calling the Kettle
   White Goods and the Construction of Race in Antebellum America 3

2. Living on White Bread
   Class Considerations and the Refinement of Whiteness 44

3. Unmentionable Things Unmentioned
   Constructing Femininity with White Things 86

4. See Spot Run
   White Things in the Rhetoric of Racial, Moral, and Hygienic Purity 129

Epilogue 165

Notes 171

Works Cited 183

Index 199

ACKNOWLEDGMENTS

This book began as a dissertation—indeed, a seminar paper—with Nancy Walker, who inspired many and made merely imagined things seem matter-of-fact realities. I'd like to thank her for the beginnings, then, even though she cannot see the ending. I owe an unpayable debt to the other faculty who contributed incisive commentary and professional guidance for the dissertation as well as the book: Teresa Goddu, Cecelia Tichi, Michael Kreyling, and Larry McKee. These are included among the scholars who generously lent their time to critique specific chapters; I am grateful as well to Suzanne Bost, Deandra Little, Alison Piepmeier, and Lynn Myrick for their timely help. I would also thank Lori Merish, who with an article in the early 1990s showed me that my lifelong love of both archaeology and literature could, in fact, be put to use, and whose work continues to challenge me. For their technical support, I must thank Kathryn DuRant Johnson and Dan Gage, always within reach of a telephone's beckon and ready with their expertise. For innumerable daily enablings, I will be forever grateful to Dori Mikus, Janis May, Natalie Baggett, Carolyn Levinson, and Sara Corbit.

I also want to thank my family. Thanks to my parents, Jim and Glenna McKivergan. Thanks to Tom and Gail Heneghan, for the time. Thanks to Connor and Máille, most especially, for perspective, and to Shaun Heneghan, for everything.

A different version of chapter 1 appears as "The Pot Calling the Kettle: White Goods and the Construction of Race in Antebellum America" in *Nineteenth Century Studies* 17. I must thank the journal and the editor, David Hanson, for working with me at length, as well as the reviewers, especially John Michael Vlach, who volunteered his name and his office time to helping me refine my ideas.

At the University Press of Mississippi, Craig Gill has untiringly guided me through the process, and his contributions and correspondences were always a joy. Especial thanks, also, to the anonymous reviewer who applied such constructive, insightful, and concrete criticism to my initial draft.

INTRODUCTION

In Nathaniel Hawthorne's *The Blithedale Romance* (1852), the narrator Coverdale marks the beginning of a Transcendentalist experiment with a simple tea ceremony. Although the experimenters aim for a classless society, Coverdale cannot elude the material markers of class even at the outset: in a show of "equal brotherhood and sisterhood," the group that considers itself "people of superior cultivations and refinement" gathers at the rustic dinner table with the hosts, "unpolished farmers" (23). Coverdale critiques the sincerity of Blithedale's expressed goals when he boasts that they "saw fit to drink [their] tea out of earthen cups to-night, and in earthen company" only because they are secure in the knowledge that "it was at [their] option to use pictured porcelain and handle silver forks again, tomorrow" (23). Although the narrator recognizes the hypocrisy involved, he cannot escape the social distinctions marked by the simple dishes used. His direct connection between the "earthen" company and its "earthen" cups, as well as their contrast to the refined diners accustomed to "pictured porcelain" encapsulates an antebellum use of material goods that identified and created social identities. By the time Hawthorne wrote *The Blithedale Romance* in 1852, an evolution in dishware had developed to encourage the connections made by Coverdale—a link between class and race and the things one used. In the middle of the eighteenth century, American colonists generally ate from buff-colored "earthen" ceramics—coarse earthenwares or stonewares that could be manufactured locally. More refined dishes could be obtained only as imports. As European potters attempted to imitate the refined porcelain of China, dishes became whiter by degrees. After the 1750s, yellowware became available, which was later replaced by creamware. By the 1790s, British manufacturers were circulating creamware worldwide. By the end of the century, pearlware replaced creamware; whiteware was developed between 1820 and 1830 (Majewski and O'Brien 22). The closest English approach to porcelain was achieved in 1850 with white ironstone dishes; and imported Chinese porcelain with a blue willow design remained the most expensive and "cultivated" of ceramics at the time *The Blithedale Romance* was published. The coarser, darker ceramics remained in circulation, but mainly for working or storage vessels, or for the lower classes. Silas Foster, the Blithedale farmer, maintains an "earthen" identity clearly belonging to a lower class than the Transcendentalist characters because his dishes belong to an outdated style and buff color that, along with his "sun-burnt" complexion, visually segregate him from his guests (36).

Frederick Douglass contributes to the racial conversation of dining ware in *Narrative of the Life of a Slave* (1845): at his childhood plantation, the slave children eat from a "large wooden tray or trough," with oyster shells or "pieces of shingle" or their bare hands for silverware, "like so many pigs" (72). In Douglass's description, the difference between the pictured porcelain handled by gentlemen and the wooden trough used by slave children establishes the latter as nearly another species. Slaves in general were issued dark, undecorated earthenware dishes in the early nineteenth century.[1] As wealthy consumers purchased whiter and whiter ceramics, lower-class diners could afford only outdated creamware and yellowware, and slaves ate from coarse, dark earthenware or wooden trenchers. Douglass and Hawthorne record, in these examples, the way race and class could be read from simple eating vessels—how, in fact, these social messages could not be avoided. And the dishes themselves painted their users—black slaves used wooden or dark ceramic dishes, earthen laborers used earthen cups, sallow lower-class factory workers used yellowware, and the truly "white" consumers used white porcelain.

Archaeologist James Deetz notes a "whitening of America" occurring in the material record that extends far beyond just the dishes used, however. Beginning at the time of the American Revolution and increasing until the Civil War, American consumers began preferring whiter, more finished products over dark-colored natural goods.[2] Deetz notes the emerging popularity of whiteness in ceramics, house paint, and gravestones beginning in the late eighteenth century; the early decades of the nineteenth century show this trend spreading to landscaping, interior design, women's clothing, and literary heroines as well. From the beginning of the trend in the late eighteenth century, these "whitening" things also became more specialized, segmented, refined, and standardized as manufacturing technology mastered mass-production. As dishes became whiter, dish sets included more specific types and more exacting etiquette; houses began to be whitewashed and divided into more private, use-specific rooms with mathematically measured architecture;[3] and gravestones shifted from rough-hewn slates and dark materials to smoothened, white marble with engraved angels and urns (Deetz, "Material Culture" 223).

By contrast, slave housing was commonly rough log cabins or unspecialized sheds. The dishes issued to slaves were mostly handed-down pieces from the masters' sets or coarse earthenware vessels, or possibly wooden or tin dishes as described by Frederick Douglass and Booker T. Washington. The paths set on plantations may have been racially informed also—for example, Douglass's birthplace and the historical homestead Morven had white paths leading to the mansions' front doors and dark paths in the back, for slave use. While the upper classes ordered white marble tombstones, slaves were often buried without markers, or perhaps with temporary wooden ones. In the North, white houses found contrast against the increasingly segregated lower classes that came to live and labor in the less visible spaces—alleys, basements, the backs of yards. White goods contributed to the upper and middle classes' attempt to deny its dependence on labor, to expel the "blackness" of slavery and servitude and impose an imaginary segregation even were integration was absolute.

The white things of the early nineteenth century signified more than racial concerns—including the traditional understandings of moral purity, as well as refinement and democracy, cleanliness, femininity, and order. Market trends with white products were also a response to European fashion and the availability of building materials. Henry Glassie suggests that the architectural choices made in the eighteenth and nineteenth century followed a discernible pattern and pointed to a cultural shift from natural to artificial after about 1760 (Folk Housing 160–161). This change, he argues, is a response to social crises, a show of democracy and control (156). Deetz finds these choices made also in ceramics, cuts of meat, and gravestone engravings which can be dated to the turn of the nineteenth century—signaling, also, a move towards artificial and cultural over natural ("Material Culture"). But the coincidence of popularity for white things in so many realms of everyday life, as well as the even more emphatic preference seen in the South generally and plantations specifically, suggests that blackness and slavery informed these choices and even determined the categories from which choices might be made. The existence of slavery, which established a permanent black lower class, demanded that even when a New England housewife far separated from slavery sought to appear upper class, she was fleeing the blackness of this bottom rung. As the nineteenth century wore on, fictional representations of slavery reached northerners through minstrel plays as well as slave stories, and the image of the black slave as carefree, undisciplined, dirty, and sexualized required a flight from these associations as well. The choices that in the eighteenth century may have been towards democracy and control over nature became in the nineteenth century—with the increase in slave populations and dependence on slave labor—a choice towards civilization compared to the savage slave, a unified democracy of white people, and control over nature as well as those who labored in it. White things radiated refinement, order, discipline: but in doing so, they also radiated race.

While the proliferation of elite items—porcelain, classical architecture, and imported gravestones—began as an attempt by the upper class to mark its distinction, mass-production made such goods more available to an aspiring middle class. Advertisements for white luxury goods, whether printed on the pages of *Godey's Lady's Book* or displayed on the dinner tables or in the china cabinets of the elite, also helped to disseminate the trend. The advent of professional architecture spawned numerous guidebooks for home and landscape design; guidebooks on manners and managing a home were popular as "gift books" in the early nineteenth century. For those without access to the elite dining room, novels described ideal domestic scenes and behaviors that included the details of white china, white decor, and white-clad women—or criticized their absence. As increasing imitation among the lower classes called for constant refinement of upper-class definitions, the image created by material goods drew closer and closer to that of the upper-class white woman. Decorations and trim on white houses and ceramics came to mirror female clothing fashions, and the cemetery became a feminized space of flowers, angels, and meditation. As the main consumers of the family, upper- and middle-class white women were responsible for purchasing these white goods. They were responsible for teaching the etiquette that white dishes enforced, and they bore the burden of the ideal purity and spirituality of fiction's white heroines.

The white things that flooded households and landscapes in the nineteenth century created an essentially conservative message, telling consumers that the exploitation and miscegenation in slavery were ignorable; that the wage slavery of emerging industrialism was justifiable; that the stricter delineation of gender roles channeled a "greater" power to disfranchised women; and that all of these were mitigated by the sanctified, otherworldly sphere of the home. As the most expensive available, the whitest items—white paint, marble, and porcelain—distinguished the wealthy. These ceramics became common in sets in the late eighteenth century; these sets increased in specialization, elaborateness, and number of vessels throughout the nineteenth century. As pieces of ever-expanding collections, the many types of salad plates, bread plates, and dessert plates demanded training in etiquette which marked the "civilized" from the masses, but which also trained imitative lower classes in the type of standardized detail work needed in the factory. In favoring these goods, consumers built a definition of "whiteness" that naturalized its pairing with wealth, discipline, and purity, ultimately reserving these qualities for the racially "white" only.

The significance of these white things—both the cultural work they might do and the ways people from varying social positions responded to their messages—can best be examined when placed in a four-dimensional setting. Material culture studies treat the thing in its social and historical context, often identifying popular conceptions and uses of a thing. Historical archaeology finds the thing as a concrete, three-dimensional object and places it in its geographical and functional context: archaeology can identify who uses things, where they use them, and with what frequency. Literature invests the "thing" with an action context, depicting the thing as it exists in time: in the literature of the early nineteenth century, the white thing is used, discussed, interpreted, discarded. My approach draws from the contributions of each of these, as I design the thing to be a physical entity through archaeology, with a traceable history and future, as well as an individual agent in literature, guided by its cultural biography but not determined by it. As I attempt to bridge the disciplines, I project from the archaeological and historical findings a sort of "life story" for the white "thing," exploring its role as commodity and social signifier. As I move to the white thing's appearance in literature, I examine the extent to which the story shows these cultural meanings at work. Its "life" in that story, whereby it becomes an individual agent, helps reveal the author's manipulations and possible uses for it. With an awareness of the cultural work being done, we can distinguish the work of this particular thing from that of others of its kind.

My contextualization of the white thing draws upon the thoughts and labor of historical archaeologists beginning with Deetz, but extending throughout the specialties with southern and northern gravestones, ceramics, architecture and folk housing, landscape archaeology, and more ideological post-processual work. In the field of material culture studies, I begin with the observations of Robyn Wiegman and Karen Halttunen, who establish in their work an early nineteenth-century American culture that turned to visual, commodified clues to explain the conflict between newly emerging social distinctions. In *American Anatomies* (1996), Robyn Wiegman argues that one of the products of the Enlightenment was a dependence on visual traits in structuring scientific categories. Appearance as a determining factor in identity came from science's emphasis of empirical impressions. In her argument, color became "the primary organizing principle" for distinguishing groups of people by the late seventeenth century, initiating an eventual formation of "black" as a race. "[M]aking the African 'black,'" she contends, "reduces the racial meanings attached to flesh to a binary structure of vision" (24, 4). Thus race, indicated first by black or white skin, established a social division that had not before existed.

But other divisions were also arising to be designated. The visual tendencies of empiricism colluded with a preference for binaries that characterizes a society in crisis, and the flood of manufactured goods suddenly available became vehicles for marking these divisions. Studying the clothing fashions of *Godey's Lady's Book* in the nineteenth century, Karen Halttunen begins with the claim that in "early industrial America ... preindustrial methods of coding the urban stranger were breaking down before modern methods could replace them" (42). A visible display took the place of detailed biographical knowledge of a person. In Halttunen's argument, clothes became a way of asserting class and gender distinctions, providing fine gradations in femininity, sentiment, and wealth—and causing anxiety about the possibilities of misrepresentation and deceit. Other visual markers also provided this bulwark—house fronts and household architecture, furniture, ceremonial dining and teas—and the use of these things, bound by strict rules, helped to filter out imposters who lacked the proper social training. As goods became more refined through new manufacturing techniques, their consumption became an ideological claim: first, for the new over the old, progressive over traditional. But the appearance and association of these new products suggested, even further, an embrace of new ways of viewing social categories—masculine and feminine, upper and lower class, white and black.

The power of white things relied upon more than their simple visual presentation, however: these dishes, houses, and gravestones were things—solid objects to be put to functional use, to be exchanged and valued, to be cared for, repaired, saved, and stored. The concrete presence of a thing does not simply resonate meaning; it acts upon a body. As Stanley Johannesen explains, the form and mechanics of a chest of drawers introduces "an entirely novel repertory of thought and action in putting things away and retrieving them again: the stooping, pulling, shutting; the employment of elbow, backside, knee, belly, forehead, foot; the bracing, balancing, tugging, slamming: all unknown to the medieval householder in this variety" (218). The body introduced to a chest of drawers is, in effect, a different body from the one using hooks or shelves; and the mind is at least as changed, forced to organize articles into small square categories, to decide upon the propriety of hidden-ness, if clothes, dishes, or junk belong in the drawers, to subdivide by drawer, and even further to fold, compress, and display within. In the examples from Hawthorne and Douglass, the literary works use material things to demonstrate both how social categories are formed and reinforced and how their use influences both user and audience. Douglass defines the brutality of slave treatment through the wooden trough the children eat from, but also by the way they eat from it—"He that ate fastest got most; he that was strongest secured the best place" (*Narrative* 72). Hawthorne's "brawny" farmer uses earthenware dishes, but he also behaves "less like a civilized Christian than the worst kind of ogre" when he "pour[s] out his own tea, and gulp[s] it down," when he uses the same knife for buttering toast as for slicing ham, and when he drinks directly from the water pitcher (*Blithedale* 30).

When I examine the white thing in both literature and archaeology, I expand upon the textual and social approaches by treating it as a subject, an inanimate personality, rather than an object. I respond to it as a material entity first, a solid object that will be used until it is finally discarded and unearthed by an archaeologist or preserved in a museum. This material use places demands on the body of its user, whether consumer, author, or reader; it exists textually for the reader's mind and physically in the reader's cabinets. The biography of the thing—the social history—describes where it comes from, who made it, and how it was obtained. In an industrial society, however, the makers of manufactured products and their designs are the least important aspect of the thing's life. The thing as commodity—its cost, scarcity, and usefulness—only activates its social life.[4] Afterwards, the use of the thing defines its social life or its identifying personality: how it is used, and how it in turn acts upon the user, visually and anatomically.

A precise approach to the thing as the object of material culture studies has been debated since the field's early days. Anne Yentsch and Mary Beaudry review its progress in archaeological scholarship: in the 1990s, Ian Hodder suggested viewing the thing as a "text," to be read as sign or symbol. In 1995 Gottdeiner treated things as signs, and their use as "a staged performance" (Yentsch and Beaudry 233). Glassie suggests more specificity: things should not be viewed as mere texts, but as "[P]oetry, explosive with vague profundity" ("Studying Material Culture" 255). His analogy to poetry works on one level because even a simple plate cannot be "read" and universally understood: its design, form, and message may be studied, internalized, misinterpreted, or recontextualized. At the same time, any text is almost pure symbol. It exists in the perpetual present tense, and only in perception. Arjun Appadurai's study seeks to liberate this dependent existence, assigning to things a "social life" and an agency. The essays in *The Social Life of Things* address "those commodities whose consumption is most intricately tied up with critical social messages [and which] are likely to be *least* responsive to crude shifts in supply or price but most responsive to political manipulation at the societal level" (33). Such long-lived commodities must be basic to everyday life, but the shifts as well as the political manipulation can be revealing. The life span of the "whitening" trend ranges from the Revolutionary War to the Civil War and beyond, with variations in design and degree but also a steady adherence to increased specialization and racial contrast. These things are exploited by literature, political propaganda, advertisements, and periodicals as salient social markers.

But the life history of a thing is only part of its story, and several material culture scholars have attempted to bridge the gaps between its past and its future, or its textual and its material significance, or its passive, deposited existence and its active "life" in everyday use. In historical archaeology, this gap is addressed as the tension between processual and post-processual approaches. The former treats a single site such as a plantation with intensive collection of data and an adherence to scientific method (Renfrew). The post-processual approach, on the other hand, can gather select data from many sites to make an argument about symbolic significance that is more culturally widespread. It takes logical liberties with a site defined not by a provenience, a yardstick, and straight sidewalls, but by an idea: for example, any middle-class dining room table. This leap requires an imaginative bridge, however, variously voiced as "an ethnographic interrogation of documents to construct 'action contexts' " (Yentsch and Beaudry,

"Material Culture" 225); as a concern for "'specifically existing moments'" and "real people"(Meskell 19); or as an attempt to imagine the artifact in a "lost physical context which is always no more than a fiction of [the scholar's] own wit" and is "usually inappropriately" shaped "out of our own culture" (Glassie, "Studying" 257, 256).

Reconciliation of this tension is best achieved, argues Henry Glassie, when the artifact is "[e]nvisioned as a composition, a set of parts, and as a thing in context, a part of sets. . . . The next step is to loop composition and context into a single reciprocal system" (Glassie, "Studying" 259). This describes the thing's nexus of associations as part of an assemblage, the conception of which distinguishes my use of material culture from other studies. Historical archaeology makes an important contribution to material culture studies, especially as reflected in the literary record, because it studies not individual objects or products, nor specific historical events, but rather an assemblage—a category of things shaped by appearance, use, or location.[5] The white thing as investigated by archaeology is not, then, merely representative, but part of a collection that expands into other dining rooms, is witnessed by other classes of people, and must be negotiated into a culturally reliable signifier. The whiteness of the whale in *Moby Dick* can symbolize an abstracted whiteness which has undulated through infinite meanings throughout the decades,[6] but Moby Dick had also a physical presence in readers' homes, as Melville reminds us: the whale oil was used for lamps, the bones were used in corsets and skirt hoops.[7]

A literary text can invest the white thing with such an imaginary "action context," one deliberately developed by a contemporary author who is imbedded in the thing's own culture. The thing gains a social life that acts within the fictional and ideological confines of the author's creation, but also across the terrain of many literary works. I have treated in this study many literary texts with a brief, focused attention, and even more only glancingly, but these texts are exemplary rather than exhaustive. White things pervaded antebellum everyday life and also pervaded fictional settings—although the one does not guarantee the other. The recent works linking material culture studies with literature in the nineteenth century offer finely focused bridges from one to the other: the continuing project of this aspect of material culture, I would argue, is the creation of as many bridges and entrées as possible, building truly interdisciplinary understandings, with the concrete concept of the "thing" as the bridge. Arjun Appadurai and Igor Kopytoff, with their collection in *The*

Social Life of Things (1986), view the thing as a commodity and place it in a historical context as capable of making social change. Bill Brown provides a most clearly elaborated relationship that is, in fact, a mutually beneficial exchange between historical things and literature. In it, literature can reveal what has actually happened in history, and history can "recuperate" the meaning of a given thing in a literary passage.[8] Lori Merish's *Sentimental Materialism* (2000) and Gillian Brown's *Domestic Individualism* (1990) successfully integrate the material object and the literary text in order to reveal social constructs, investigating theoretically what I attempt to demonstrate archaeologically. Merish's *Sentimental Materialism* begins with a philosophical history in order to uncover a material basis to the gendered and racial constructions presented in literature. In *Domestic Individualism*, Brown investigates the workings of gender among antebellum literary texts and material things such as house design and fashion. Having built theoretical bridges themselves, these scholars leave blueprints rather than paths—different starting points require new methodologies. My work moves from the physical to the fictional, weighing ideals and realities in the thing's representation. In this way, my study is able to integrate the general and the particular when considering social phenomena, especially the construction of whiteness. The thing as a product to be consumed and the thing as an invention of the author both undergo investigation; with this approach, the literary text cannot remain ahistorical, nor can the product remain unspeaking and anonymous.

"NO IDEAS BUT IN THINGS"

Things were the building blocks of antebellum culture, and white things helped to build the binary definitions that supported notions of class, gender, and race.[9] They accomplished this work mainly through their color and their relationship to their users. In the visual economy of emergent industrialism, the consumers' relationship to their things was demonstrated daily in ritualized performances, even within their own households. From a mainstream, middle-class white perspective, from the archaeological record and from literary examples, only those who had fashionable white goods could have been variously styled as racially "white"—because white goods were the popular elite products and markers of upper- or middle-class refinement and because mainly the properly respectable, middle-class, or sentimental characters were allowed a fictive white skin. These standards left some Caucasians as nonwhite, and the records afford them buff-colored, yellow, and red dishes, unpainted houses, and sallow, red, or swarthy complexions. White-skinned slaves—mulattos, quadroons, octoroons—could also in this way be deemed "black," since "race" was based on material goods as well as skin color. The racial caveat, of course, was that one white thing remain that could not be attained by African Americans or other racial minorities—white skin.[10] Arguments about white slavery or wage slavery assigned the slave's legalized lack of upward mobility to working-class whites, and the lost potential was regarded as a darker evil than mere poverty—although most laborers would reject the label as applied to themselves.

The thing, or brute, appears not to participate in the material economy at all, neither possessing nor desiring, nor able to acquire things. In antebellum America, the term "thing" virtually vibrated with tension as it became a battleground for both pro-slavery and abolitionist arguments. Both sides generally agreed that a *person* should not be owned; therefore, the definition of "thing" and a slave's status in relation to it became the site on which slavery's rationalizations were contested. James Fenimore Cooper appends a footnote to this effect in *Notions of the Americans*, advising that slavery and politics do not mix because "the slaves have no more to do with the government than inanimate objects" (qtd. in Doolen 153). The single distinction between a slave and a brute—a thing to be owned with no agency of its own—is the desire to participate in the material economy. Therefore, pro-slavery writing attempted to portray slaves as content and carefree, erasing their humanizing ambition.

Outside of pro-slavery rhetoric, slaves could desire freedom or literacy or material comforts beyond what was given them, and this desire alone made them active participants in the system. This, in addition, helped to justify the rest of the system: those who did not "desire" in the American way insulted it; on the other hand, slaves might embody naked desire, unfettered by attainment or potential. Thus, when Frederick Douglass claims in the pivotal statement of his *Narrative*, "You have seen how a man was made a slave; you shall see how a slave was made a man," he posits a rise of several levels. He has been brutalized by the slave driver Covey until he passes his Sundays in a "beast-like stupor" and is therefore less than a slave.[11] When he begins to desire freedom again, he regains his personhood; but when he fights Covey, he begins to see that he might be able to attain his freedom, and with this potential arises "a sense of [his] own manhood" (113). Manhood—humanity with the addition of "masculinity"—was a participation in the material economy that included the ability to have, to desire, and to obtain.[12]

My definition of "feminine" as materially built depends upon two claims: that femininity was only afforded to middle- and upper-class white women, who depended upon something other than their own marketplace labor for their livelihoods, and that the "feminine" must pretend not to desire this material comfort, only maintaining it for the sake of their family or other sentimental interests.[13] While this claim was variously contested, it was generally resolved by denying the possibility of a working-class "femininity." Female factory workers were upheld in the early part of the century as unexpectedly feminine, by their cleanliness and fine clothes, but even more by their lack of necessity and their eagerness to marry and retire to household work—manufacturing interests claimed that women generally worked for adventure and spending money before marriage, and not for subsistence. Female performers and writers had a tenuous claim on femininity, so long as they followed a very strict rhetoric delimiting their performance, such as Harriet Beecher Stowe's claiming that *Uncle Tom's Cabin* arrived as an inspiration from God, or female reformers' embracing the nation as a sort of extended family, rightfully under the influence of their spiritualizing interest.

For the most part, upper- and middle-class women were excluded from earning a living and simultaneously retaining feminine respectability; but while they could not earn things, they were required at least to possess enough to demonstrate industry and self-discipline in the use of their things. Femininity, therefore, required a preparation for upward mobility, while masculinity required its own version of ambition, discipline, and hard work. The aristocrat and the minister were incidental industrial products. Aristocrats, such as Hepzibah's immediate family in Hawthorne's *House of the Seven Gables*, wealthy plantation owners, or possibly the bachelors in Melville's "Paradise of Bachelors" would have been constrained from entering the workforce by their own class pretensions, but could enjoy their wealth without visibly laboring to earn it. Those choosing not to "get" troubled the material economy; leisure was morally suspect in the nineteenth century. Ministers, philosophers, and scholars might have chosen to direct their energies towards spiritual or intellectual pursuits; though they demonstrated through their education an access to goods, they also lost status from this perceived insult to materialism. Both the philosopher class and the aristocracy became "feminized" when they shunned material production: we can see reaction to this taint perhaps in the ritualized masculinity of southern chivalry and in the fierce assertions of masculinity posed by Transcendentalists in the figure of Man Thinking.[14]

Furthermore, the posture of "not desiring" entailed extreme care to negate the possible insult to capitalism. Feminine women and ministers could only maintain status through an all-pervading claim to spirituality, so that it became not a denial of materialism but an ambition to heaven as greater—and heaven was then furnished with the properties of the home, which women could desire without restraint. This claim came at the cost of an unforgiving moral purity, however; the greedy minister or the fallen, "compromised" woman, belying their non-spiritual desire, could not be allowed to remain in their place.

Lower-class Caucasian citizens remained in a racially liminal position—neither white nor black—and their goods and skin were suitably colored. Gender applied less to the working class: laboring women could be thick-waisted and manly, and the muscularity of a laboring man's body was tied more to animal qualities than to masculinity. The "poor white trash," marked by their lack of ambition, may have been for some ranked below the slaves, as they deliberately squandered their potential whiteness. Theirs was the lot of those who insulted materialism by "not wanting" without the protection of moral purity as an excuse. Their dirt or trash classified them: they had scant membership in the system at all.[15]

In emphasizing the white thing as a social agent, I do not seek to add to "race, class, and gender" the category of "things," but rather to locate the foundation of this triad in the material world and transpose its terms into more nineteenth-century terms. Many recent studies show a complex relationship among race, class, and gender organization. For example, Nakayama and Martin assert that "whiteness, like other categories, is 'leaky'; that is, race can only be seen in relation to other categories, such as class, gender, sexuality, and so on, that render any category problematic" (15). Monika M. Elbert assures us that "certainly it is absurd to consider gender as a category by itself—outside the attendant realms of race and class" (2). On the other hand, when they are broken down to their simplest material definitions, the defining social categories become names for one's relationship to things—names which, when folded into our own contemporary understandings of the triad of terms, serve to confuse relationships and groups. The terms of the triad were only just gaining meaning in the early nineteenth century—even "masculine" and "feminine" were being redefined, socially and materially—and their boundaries were slippery.[16] "Race" was used to mean any group of people, a nationality, a profession; "class" was denied even to exist because of Old World definitions that did not fit perfectly.[17] There was not a determinant triad: there were different relationships to the things that were becoming more plentiful and more demanding.

Building from this popular antebellum view of the way things built salient social categories, we can see the way authors and consumers reacted against and within their material boundaries. Continually refined, continually contested, the notions involving race, class, and gender challenge scholars who attempt to examine these notions in historical settings. By focusing on the material object as a constituent agent of these ideas, my work pinpoints visible moments of social construction—its physical setting, the limits of its reach, and who was implicated. For example, in whiteness studies, scholars distinguish racism from the racial acts performed by individuals and define various types of "whiteness" according to the many classes of white people that exist. A material culture view need not struggle with the "monolith" of whiteness—it is, at most, a piecemeal wall built from everyday things. Joe Kincheloe describes the field's " 'prime directive' " for most of the past decade to be the "effort to define and reinvent the amorphous concept" of whiteness. This effort is frustrated by many aspects of its amorphousness: the conflation of whiteness with white people or with white privilege; the generality of whiteness that does not account for individual agency (Wiegman, "Whiteness Studies"); the conception of whiteness as a unified force denying diversity (which is addressed variously in studies of class and whiteness, gender and whiteness, or ethnicities and whiteness: for example, David Roediger, Alexander Saxton, Eric Lott); the normalization and invisibility of whiteness (Toni Morrison; Ruth Frankenberg, *The Making and Unmaking of Whiteness*). Such an elaboration of the frustrations is crucial in defining "whiteness," I believe, and in clearing space for new questions and fruitful investigations. In the most definite delineation of whiteness, Ruth Frankenberg provides eight aspects, and nearly all attempt a physical expression of the idea: "Whiteness is a location . . . a 'standpoint' . . . a site of privilege . . . a site of elaboration . . . a product of history" ("Mirage" 76). On the other hand, when whiteness is approached as a material construct, it begins with such a concrete location, the thing; it demands everyday performances in its care and consumption; it depends upon visibility; its diversity comes from its many manipulators; it allows for individual use; and it has a definite shape.

Similarly, the field of gender studies has recently expressed frustration with the traditional monolithic view of nineteenth-century femininity.[18]

The question now being asked by gender scholars—"Were there separate spheres?"—attacks the binaric social fiction but relies upon an abstract notion that can always be complicated. Because nineteenth-century authors discussed and critiqued a popular belief in the "feminine sphere," we can ask in a material approach, "What was the actual shape of the woman's sphere as compared to its ideological designs?" and can locate it where white things were under the woman's influence. Viewing femininity as "built" by the accumulation and control of white things, I place this idea of the "sphere" in physical terms, and it becomes instead an indefinitely marked territory: extant and visible, but also shifting. My approach contributes to concepts of class by treating the thing as more than commodity—as a social being apart from as well as within the marketplace—and by recognizing one's skin as a thing to be valued and maintained. The archaeological approach is also particularly adept at identifying economic distinctions through artifacts, and it recovers a material past among the lower classes otherwise unrecorded.

The white thing, then, can become the handle for an abstract, ungraspable, and ideal concept. For nineteenth-century consumers and authors, the whiteness of the thing could become a part of a set, to be bought, cleaned, organized, displayed, and distributed. All of these social distinctions eventually, and primarily, devolved to race, as they considered whiteness or its lack in their formation. Race, as conceived in whiteness, was not so much a commodity as a collection of commodities and one's relationship to them[19]—so that who used them, how they used them, how it affected them, and in what specific objects the users chose to invest their anxieties become essential to our understanding of antebellum race. Race was a description that incorporated color, possessions, ambition, and potentiality. It was, in addition, a problem for everyone in antebellum America: whiteness was not yet normalized, and white people were continually conscious of their color and its dangers, privileges, and social implications. These questions of what and who and how necessarily pulled into whiteness considerations of class, gender, and purity. Whiteness could not be understood apart from those consuming it, the upper and middle classes; nor from the key managers of it, white women; nor from the associations that they would like to borrow from it, spiritual and biological purity. And it could not be conceived apart from its opposite—blackness.

My chapters are shaped according to an approach to the white things, as a series of steps that clarify "whiteness's" meaning. Chapter 1 elaborates on the appearances of white things as owned by the upper classes and planters and the contrast established through the darker things used by slaves. The archaeological data is culled from many sites and sources, treats a history of records concerning ceramics, houses, architecture, and gravestones, and ties these to statements made by their users and to their acknowledged racial implications. John Pendleton Kennedy, Frederick Douglass, and Harriet Jacobs approach the material economy differently, manipulating the message of white things in order to enforce, invert, or disrupt its cultural work.

The second chapter moves to the acquisition and use of white goods, how they became involved in ritual demonstrations of class status or upwardly mobile merit. This chapter includes specialization of tableware, specialization of white houses, the organization of white gravestones into rural cemeteries, and the work-discipline derived from standardized use. The tea ritual, the factory, and the frontier town become substantial settings where the things of class must be constantly negotiated, and the blackness of slavery intrudes or upholds the negotiations. James Fenimore Cooper, Susanna Maria Cummins, and Edgar Allan Poe propose alternately masculine, feminine, and antiquarian responses to the rituals and etiquette of industry; Herman Melville exploits the connections between them, complicating the factory and the dinner table with gendered and racial protests.

The third chapter looks specifically at femininity as a complicated enactment of whiteness which complements masculinity but more deeply affects the status of black and lower-class men and women. This chapter highlights the corset as representative of the black-female–white-feminine relationship, but discusses also white furnishings, architecture, and clothing fashion. Harriet Beecher Stowe, Susan Warner, and E.D.E.N. Southworth produced best-selling sentimental novels that make the material connection between white things, black people, and femininity; Nathaniel Hawthorne's *The Blithedale Romance* reveals the operation of these powerful white signifiers from the viewpoint of a troubled male.

Chapter 4 returns to an explicitly racial focus in its investigation of the care and maintenance of white things. The anxieties resulting from an antebellum equation linking spiritual purity, hygienic purity, and racial purity are manifested in discussions of racial passing, scars and tattoos, and filth. White skin becomes the significant white thing, the visible marker of these purities and the anxious ground upon which definitions of "black" and "white" take place. Stowe's *Dred* speaks for the tragic mulatto who cannot pass; Melville's *Moby Dick* exposes skin as the basic commodity in Ahab's quest; and Rebecca Harding Davis's *Life in the Iron Mills* establishes filth as a measure of race and class status. Finally, Edgar Allan Poe interrogates the physical composition of beauty, femininity, and whiteness as he disassembles the body in "Berenice."

These chapters investigate the problems and answers presented by one nineteenth-century assemblage, everyday white things, as utilized by those supportive of or antagonistic to their cultural work. In emphasizing both physical usefulness and visible color in things as they appear in households and literary settings, my study remains necessarily general: each set of artifacts, such as gravestones or ceramics, also warrants its own focused study. Things united by use, geography, or other appearance might undergo similar examination. Just as important as establishing a salient site of investigation, however, is an understanding of the central actors' relationship to the material things. The relationships that define "masculine," "feminine," "lower class" and "slave," as I have presented them, belong to an emergent capitalist, Anglo-American (white) viewpoint; and the dissenting voices propose alternate, inverted, or conflicting ways to relate—or even another set of things altogether. Certainly, my decision to locate my site in this industrialized whiteness leaves more areas suggested than addressed, including much of the vast population whose agency remains less visible in a capitalistic economy. In using the average consumer and the well-circulated author as my foundation, my work remains tied to the questions concerning these people and their self-conscious attempts to answer them. In focusing on these everyday concerns with a material lens, however, my work uncovers entire unarticulated conversations between author and reader, consumer and viewer—discussing issues too incendiary, ideological, or perhaps too intimate for open debate.

WHITEWASHING
America

CHAPTER ONE

THE POT CALLING THE KETTLE

White Goods and the Construction of Race in Antebellum America

In *I Know Why the Caged Bird Sings* (1969), Maya Angelou devotes an entire chapter to discussing a white woman's china. At ten years old, the autobiographical character, Marguerite, must learn, like all "Negro girls in small Southern towns," the "mid-Victorian values" of embroidery, elaborate table settings, organized meals, and the language of specialized ceramics (87). In order to do so, she must go to "the source of those habits": "a white woman's kitchen." This white woman, Mrs. Cullinan, keeps house with "inhuman" exactness: "This glass went here and only here. That cup had its place and it was an act of impudent rebellion to place it anywhere else. At twelve o'clock the table was set. At 12:15 Mrs. Cullinan sat down to dinner (whether her husband had arrived or not). At 12:16 Miss Glory brought out the food." Marguerite marvels at the proliferation of specialized dishes: there is "a salad plate, a bread plate and a dessert plate . . . goblets, sherbet glasses, ice-cream glasses, wine glasses, green glass coffee cups with matching saucers, and water glasses . . . [s]oup spoons, gravy boat, butter knives, salad forks and carving platter," which, taken together, "almost represented a new language" (88–89). The language of tableware belongs exclusively to the white ladies who gather each afternoon for cold drinks, but although the ceramics constitute a "white" language, they carry messages for the black servants of the household also. Marguerite and Miss Glory may serve with Mrs. Cullinan's dishes, but their own unspecialized drinking glasses are segregated to a separate shelf.

Marguerite soon discovers that Mr. Cullinan has fathered children with a black woman in town, but has left Mrs. Cullinan childless. Although this discovery is understated in Marguerite's story, the husband's interracial adultery informs the organization of Mrs. Cullinan's entire household. When Mrs. Cullinan organizes a minutely set table and enforces strict punctuality for dining, she claims a control over her husband which she clearly does not have outside the dining room. These manifold pieces of white china become surrogate children, through which Mrs. Cullinan might compete with the specters of nonwhite children introduced into the family by her husband's lack of discipline. She assembles her dishes into an army, ordering and maneuvering them as precisely as a general, hoping to drive out the blackness and all its manifestations—or at least confine it to a corner shelf. When Mrs. Cullinan tries to appropriate Marguerite also by calling her "Mary," Marguerite responds with the ultimate symbolic violence. Deliberately breaking the white woman's favorite dishes, Marguerite sends Mrs. Cullinan to the floor crying, " 'Oh Momma. Oh, dear Gawd. It's Momma's china from Virginia' " (92). But Mrs. Cullinan's comic overreaction becomes understandable in terms of the real battle—for here is a black servant girl, herald of an ineluctable invasion, systematically destroying Mrs. Cullinan's forces.

In the same way, the United States of the early nineteenth century fought to stanch the flow of blackness introduced by slavery, free blacks, and racial mixtures from invading the developing definition of "America." Everyday household goods were a means to self-definition and national definition, but they were also a desperate campaign against the blackening of that image and against the darkening conscience of a newly freed people practicing slavery. The "whitening of America," noted by archaeologist James Deetz, describes a consumer trend preferring increasingly white and refined goods from the Revolutionary War until the Civil War. In the whitening of dishes, house paint, and gravestones that Deetz identifies and the nineteenth-century whiteness of household interiors, sentimental clothing fashion, and literary heroines, antebellum consumers practiced a material exercise on a national level. These white things, I would argue, served a similar function to Mrs. Cullinan's plates: they recognized the dangers of black slavery by trying to overwhelm it and push it back—beyond the walls of the house, outside the surrounding lands, even beyond the grave. They acknowledged slavery's brutalizing effects by enforcing greater civilization and refinement. They rationalized its exploitation by stressing the difference between fine white china and coarse brown cups.

The "whitening" of America was in part a process of trying to establish definite boundaries between races: while washing the living spaces of white folks white, it continued to "color" whatever slave and servant spaces it could. Increasingly throughout the nineteenth century, white consumers knitted around themselves signifiers of whiteness, helping the nation attempt to segregate, deny, expel the blackness of slavery.

Touching all activities and all times of day, household objects explicitly linked slave labor with darkness and the master's wealth with whiteness. The white goods preferred by consumers were also the most expensive, refined, and specialized. White paint and architecturally accented houses boasted of a professional designer; a cornice could cost more than an entire room to install. The rough-hewn slate gravestones were replaced by smooth, mass-marketed white marble that had to be imported. Porcelain-quality ceramics appeared in specialized sets that required elaborate training for their proper use. The corresponding goods issued to slaves were marked for contrast—by dark color, coarse finish, chipped or broken or dilapidated condition, and unspecialized design. Slave areas were geographically designated where possible, as most slave houses were segregated to the rear of the plantations. More often, the segregation was visual: laws required slaves to wear coarse "negro cloth," ceramics issued to slaves were often dark or buff-colored, or chipped and unmatched hand-me-downs from the master's set, or perhaps the wooden troughs and tin plates described by Frederick Douglass and Booker T. Washington.[1]

Lydia Maria Child addresses a racial code that reveals the oppositional thinking becoming apparent by the nineteenth century: "as slavery inevitably makes its victims servile and vicious, and as none but negroes are allowed to be slaves, we, from our very childhood, associate everything that is degraded with the *mere color*" (*Appeal* 66, italics in text). Her emphasis on "mere color" also exposes the power that color, once unmoored from its original racial associations, attains. Nineteenth-century authors lifted racial readings from the "mere color" of everyday objects in order to draw added meaning from them. The children's abolition journal *The Slave's Friend* "tells young readers that 'the chestnut has a dark skin. . . . But its *kernel* is all white and sweet. The apple, though it looks so pretty, has many little black grains at the heart. . . . Now little boys and girls can't be abolitionists until they get rid of all these black grains in their hearts'" (qtd. in Samuels 160). A chestnut takes on racial applications, and an apple, drawing from these, also implies morality—without ever overturning a valuation based on color. A review of Hawthorne's *The Scarlet Letter*, written in 1851, complains of the immorality implied, but not mentioned, in the novel: "'the language of [Hawthorne], like patent blacking, "would not soil the whitest linen," and yet the composition itself, would suffice, if well laid on, to Ethiopize the snowiest conscience that ever sat like a swan upon that mirror of heaven, a Christian maiden's imagination'" (qtd. in Grossman 25). In a succession of similes, language becomes patent blacking, which gains personhood and becomes African: the blackness of these threatens the whiteness of linen, conscience, and a Christian maiden's imagination. In *Moby Dick*, Ishmael reads race into an everyday rope: comparing the traditional tar-covered hemp rope with the newly popular Manilla rope, he claims that "there is an aesthetics in all things" (238). Manilla rope "is much more handsome and becoming to the boat, than hemp. Hemp is a dusky, dark fellow, a sort of Indian; but Manilla is as a golden-haired Circassian to behold" (238). "Circassian" is another term for Caucasian, which includes a pun relating the woven rope to Circassian fabric. But the leap from seeing white rope as Caucasian or a dark chestnut as black to viewing the neighbor's white house as inherently racial seems tiny and inevitable.

Earlier in *Moby Dick*, Ishmael tries to undermine the negative associations of blackness with the subversive admission, "[A]s though a white man were anything more dignified than a whitewashed negro" (60). Ralph Waldo Emerson uncovers a similar prejudice in his apparently optimistic statement, "We may yet find a rose-water that will wash the negro white" (157). Although both philosophers attempt to minimize race by painting it as only skin deep, they reveal what pro-slavery writers also insisted: that blackness and whiteness were biologically inescapable and socially determining.[2] Both views suggest that the dark complexion itself is the source of slavery and racial prejudice, and that the plight of the "negro" may be countered by a cleansing treatment of whiteness. Blackness of the body merges into slavery, which as a condition describes tasks, privileges, social conditioning. In the racially charged atmosphere of antebellum America, a person could scarcely see white and not think of its opposite, which was not merely black, but black, Negro, slave.

Beneath the degradation of a mere color, Child laments the process of "racialization," in which "*slave* and *black* became synonyms" (Nakayama and Martin 16). Law and common practice worked to reinforce the connection between slavery and the color black, but the link also depended upon the coincidence of emerging industrialism and America's democratic experiment. In all the slave states except Delaware, Kenneth Stampp relates, "the presumption was that people with black skins were slaves unless they could prove they were free. Any strange Negro found in a southern community without 'freedom papers' was arrested as a fugitive" (194). Especially after the Fugitive Slave Act of 1850, "both legal and social presumptions equated being visibly colored with being a slave," and "the idea of race was inseparable from the idea of slavery" (Kawash 43, 42). Emerging industrialism fostered a visual culture, a social understanding of visual clues that could replace detailed biographical knowledge of people in an increasingly mobile society (Halttunen). The conflict between older and newer styles of status judgment formed itself into binary thinking—so that visual binaries took the form most clearly as black and white. Ownership of property, culminating in the property of one's own body, made up the outward show of status; slavery was cast as the ultimate lack of property or status.

"White" and "black" were signified by various types of property, however; they were material designations more than merely biological, so that users of the darkened goods were colored black, regardless of skin color. These objects worked to make race—and slavery—into a condition of color that seemed natural but not personal: white things, their ownership and proper management, constituted racial whiteness, and skin became simply another white thing. African American writers, abolitionists, and other social commentators might have attacked some of the racial assertions underlying the justifications of slavery—pointing to slaves' work discipline, manners, cleanliness, and even pale skin—but they also had to address the covert conversation carried on in the goods they saw and used every day. The very simple conflation offered by Child, of "everything that is degraded" with "*mere color*," remains simple, as increasing amounts of goods circulated and signified, reflected and reinforced the link between ownership of white things and privileged racial whiteness—and the assignment of, or defaulting to, darker things with slave conditions.

THE WHITENING OF AMERICA

The houses, dishes, and gravestones that Deetz finds becoming whiter after the Revolution did so in an archaeologically sudden amount of time. Houses underwent exterior and interior changes, becoming segmented

Orton Plantation, Wilmington, North Carolina, Exterior III. Photograph by Gottscho-Schleisner, Inc., 1945. White plantation house with columns. Library of Congress, Prints and Photographs Division, Gottscho-Schleisner Collection, LC-C602-CT-[043].

according to architects' designs and becoming white according to exterior fashions. Georgian architecture, describing a strict bilateral symmetry in a house's layout, spent much of the eighteenth century replacing Medieval housing styles and one- or two-room cabins.[3] This change created a greater universality in style among regions. Although regional differences existed—and these included dates when styles became popular as well as landscape layout and building materials used—similarities among Georgian houses "far exceeded the differences" (Deetz, Small Things 112). Before the nineteenth century, large houses were often painted white while the smaller ones were painted more "natural" colors.[4] But Georgian architecture by the late eighteenth century was characterized by whiteness: from the red, tan, green, or unpainted look of ethnically specific houses, popular choice moved to "nearly invariable whiteness" (Glassie, Folk Housing 156). Houses achieved this basic whiteness through evolution. Glassie traces a progression in house decoration strikingly similar to that of ceramic design once whiteness was achieved: "[i]n time the change [in house color] was from several basic colors (white, red, yellow) to one color with multicolored trim ... to one color with one trim color ... and finally to blank white."[5]

This style of whiteness was uniquely American. According to architectural historian Henry-Russell Hitchcock, "Romantic Classicism," which he uses to include the various "revival" styles such as Greek and Roman revival, arrived in the United States near the turn of the nineteenth century and remained until the Civil War, and these styles were characterized by symmetry and whiteness. The "almost universal use of Grecian forms in domestic building," he continues, was specifically American, because buildings derived not from European architects but rather from Americanized versions published in guidebooks (121). These various classical styles replaced, among the more progressive builders, the Georgian style. In Roman Classicism, the building imitates Roman temple form, with four column and plain white moldings (Blumenson 23). Greek revival follows Greek temple form, with columns and full entablature, and often the entire building is painted white (Blumenson 27).

Gothic revival houses, which became popular in the 1830s, were part of a counter-current Picturesque movement, emphasizing asymmetry, more elaborate and textured detail (Hitchcock 143). In the style of Gothic architecture, John Ruskin argues in 1851, "slavery is done away with altogether" (160). The standardization, division of labor, and repetitive manufacture that produces other revival styles implicate their consumers "in the slave trade," Ruskin argues: "and in a much more cruel one than that which we have so long been endeavoring to put down."[6] Ruskin not only comments upon an artistic response to a counter-cultural concern here, but also demonstrates how even building construction, however distant in time and place, is colored by considerations of slavery. Despite the presence of Gothic revival houses, nonetheless, the white house with green shutters was "almost a cliché for middling houses" by the mid-nineteenth century (Bushman 258).

At the same time, this whitening process was occurring with ceramics and the rules of dining. Before the middle of the eighteenth century, American households rarely ritualized meals. Usually, a table was set with only the essential plates, spoons, and drinking vessels, and "people typically ate with their hands and sat on benches, trunks, or the edges of beds" (Shackel 101). Meals were taken communally from wooden trenchers and pewter plates, or with unspecialized buff or red ceramics glazed in yellow or green. By the mid-eighteenth century, however, trenchers began to be replaced by more standardized, specialized dishes, and by whitish rather than natural-colored ceramics (Deetz, *Small Things*

47). European potters experimented in order to duplicate the fine white porcelain of China, which England finally mastered in 1792 (Majewski and O'Brien 24). By the 1780s, the popularity of English Staffordshire pearlware accomplished a "[n]ear complete whiteness of the ceramic assemblage."[7] Beginning with the nineteenth century, refinements in ceramic manufacture were paralleled by a movement towards even whiter dishes: pearlware eclipsed creamware; cream-colored ware improved upon yellow ware; and whiteware arrived between 1820 and 1830 as "a logical development along a continuum of refinements in paste and glaze." This popular whiteware, mostly used as tableware, was "almost pure white in color" but was almost always decorated (Majewski and O'Brien 22). Deetz explicitly states this progression from buff-colored ceramics in the 1750s, to an off-white dish with ivory-colored glaze, to a white body and bluish-white glaze, to a strictly white pottery with a colorless glaze in the 1830s (Deetz, *Small Things* 48). But whitening continued beyond the ceramic dish, and after 1850 the finer near-porcelain white ironstones "were either left plain or embellished with unpainted molded geometric, foliate, or floral motifs" (Majewski and O'Brien 23). A contemporary advisor prescribes a "'china of entire white'" as "'the most popular for everyday use,'" and the ceramic record confirms this practice (Wall, "Family Meals" 126).

Historian Alan Gowans notes the similarities between ceramic and architectural styles of the early nineteenth century, declaring that pastels set against white trims made "whole buildings, outside and in, resemble in effect contemporaneous Wedgwood china" (Gowans 168). Among architecture and gravestones, similarities evolved as well. A popular design on nineteenth-century gravestones was the classical column engraved as a border. Even more striking, larger markers of sculpted marble columns which appear broken at the top serve as a visual tale of a promising life prematurely ended. These designs emerge early in the century and continue to dot cemeteries at the Civil War. In both North and South, the widespread urn gravestones also refer to ceramic vessels; in the South, however, folk customs utilized actual ceramic markers baked into urn shapes (Brackner).

In the seventeenth century, a very few Boston gravestones were made from a "white, sandlike material," but in the eighteenth century stones were carved from dark-colored schists, slates, and sandstones (Deetz, "Material" 223). Contrary to popular belief, Harriet Merifield Forbes writes, much of the slate used was not imported; regional varieties and local stonecutters' skill lent irregularity to a graveyard's look (8). Even earlier, field stones from the surrounding country, roughly carved or not, were used to mark graves (Forbes 8). Soon after the American Revolution, however, grave markers began appearing in imported white marble, and churchyard graves became standardized and white.

Although the choice for white stones was simultaneous with the choice for white dishes, the marble that became popular in the early nineteenth century, "or at least some form of white stone, could have been used earlier" (Deetz, "Material" 223). These stones also showed change in shape and design. Halfway into the eighteenth century, the popular designs found on New England gravestones shifted from a death's head motif to a cherub, and by the close of the century to the willow-and-urn design (Dethlefsen and Deetz 504). The willow-and-urn motif "signals the end of the slate-gravestone tradition in New England" (Dethlefsen and Deetz 503). In addition, the rough blocks marking eighteenth-century graves gave way to a stone more smoothly finished, on both front and back (Deetz, "Material" 227). Great amounts of research have been done focusing on the changing styles of these stones in New England—although Southern and Western studies also enrich the record—but the whiteness of these markers throughout the early nineteenth century remains a given.[8]

The timing of whiteness's popularity in America is especially significant. In architecture, the white revival styles became popular in the 1790s. For ceramics, the technology for whitening also pre-existed its demand—it had been available since the 1560s—but consumer desire only grew at the turn of the nineteenth century (Yentsch, "Symbolic" 213). Pure white ceramics existed with Chinese porcelain in the seventeenth century, but, "significantly, [these] were never central to foodways" (Deetz, "Material" 223). In the North, gravestone styles shifted from local slates to imported marbles gradually, from the mid-eighteenth century until whiteness reached prominence by the 1820s. In the Southeast, however, the change was more dramatic: the year 1800 seems to be an invisible boundary, after which only a few rare dark stones appeared in the churchyards. The coincidental timing of these white goods points to a near obsession with whiteness in these decades: combined with an interest in impossibly white heroines among novelists with diverse political agendas, and with the mounting abolitionist movement, women's movements, and class riots, these white things represent an ideological army, expected to fight its battles on multiple fronts.

DIXIE CUPS

Color was the most overt indicator of ceramic vessels' functions and their users' status. Natural colors were most often applied to coarse storage or cooking vessels, while white was used for the finer display dishes. Ceramics were graded from the coarse earthenwares and stonewares, to the more refined earthenwares, to the dense, thin, and expensive porcelains. Although ware color in part depended on the clay available, color distinctions defined the type and use of vessels rather than the other way around. In other words, vessels used for food preparation, storage, and cooking were made predominantly nonwhite. In Philadelphia, for example, local potters produced inexpensive redwares for use in the kitchen, pantry, cellar and chamber, but "middling and upper middling Philadelphians owned little [of it], even to store prepared and preserved foods" (De Cunzo 69). Since wealthier urban households could afford to purchase fresh food, even storage became a lower-class activity. The "whitening" dishes were almost all refined earthenwares, meant for the table, and the porcelains were largely for dining or display (McKee, personal interview 1997). Coarse earthenwares and stonewares composed utilitarian storage and cooking vessels, and some pre-nineteenth-century serving and eating vessels (McKee, personal interview 1997). Despite available technology, "stoneware cooking or storage vessels were produced in the dark-toned tradition of earlier earthenwares long into the nineteenth century" (Yentsch, "Symbolic" 213). And the coarser local pottery almost never became tableware or tea sets (McKee, personal interview 1995).

Until nearly the Civil War, British manufacturers mastered the ceramic market, but the product imported to the United States was aimed specifically at Americans. By the 1790s, the British had circulated inexpensive creamware worldwide; in 1797, a traveler claims to have seen it throughout Europe, the West Indies, and America (Miller, "Marketing" 2–3). However, the whitish Staffordshire ceramics popular in the United States were manufactured with a sensitivity to this market. White ironstone dishes were made specifically for America and "not sold at all in Britain where they were made . . . presumably because there was no demand for them there" (De Cunzo 78). In fact, the United States was Staffordshire's largest customer "every year between the end of the War of 1812 and the eve of the Civil War," purchasing close to half of the manufacturer's exports. Staffordshire therefore accommodated some of its designs to American tastes—which included the whiteness of the dishes no less than their periodic designs of American heroes and events (Miller, "Marketing" 3).

The earliest examples of English ceramics made specifically for America began with Josiah Wedgwood and the Revolutionary War effort (Klamkin 3). Marian Klamkin offers a survey of patriotic china: Wedgwood's early products included intaglio seals declaring sympathy with the rebelling colonies with "the motif of a coiled rattlesnake and the legend 'Don't Tread on Me,'" first distributed in 1777. Afterwards, in the beginning of the nineteenth century, "yellow ware" in the shape of jugs, mugs, and punch bowls was manufactured and decorated in Liverpool for the American market (Klamkin 5–6). Most of the American-influenced pottery made in England before the Civil War consisted of inexpensive earthenware and was decorated with various American scenes or political messages. Presidential candidates from John Adams to Richard Nixon found their faces on plates and jugs of the poorest quality ceramics—the focus being the message rather than utility.

Aside from the busts and silhouettes of famous statesmen, images of architecture predominate in American designs. Plates celebrate the White House (with cows in the foreground), New York City Hall, Columbia College and Yale, Boston's Museum, State House, and Hospital—ranging even to the corner view of Mitchell and Freeman's China and Glass Warehouses in Boston. Even designs with non-architectural foci, such as a "Historic elm" in Massachusetts or the "Sternwheel steamboat" in Philadelphia include classical white architecture in the background (Klamkin 32, 31). American ceramics therefore trumpeted their coalition with architecture in the progress of whitening. America's participation in the world market of mass-produced plates accompanied a specifically American passion for Roman and Greek revival styles, telling of an evolution in the etiquette of dining and household use which necessarily left some people behind.

The Wedgwood company participated in American politics twice without acknowledging its involvement: with the "Don't Tread on Me" seals and with antislavery ceramics alone, Wedgwood did not place its mark on its products (Klamkin 6). As early as 1786, Josiah Wedgwood produced ceramic cameos that pictured the silhouette of a kneeling slave in chains. The uncharacteristic colors of black and white jasper were often accompanied with the motto, "'Am I not a Man and a Brother?'" This design was later copied by other ceramic manufacturers and set into "rings, shirt pins, buttons, brooches, and so forth" to be distributed to abolitionist Americans and British. Around 1837, a Staffordshire potter produced an elaborate antislavery plate whose design was then transferred to tea and dinner services. Printed in "a light purplish blue"—a color popular in Europe but less favored than the cobalt blue common to American dishes—images and pictures nearly blanket the white background. A gift to American abolitionists from the English Anti-Slavery Society, the original plates were to be sold at auction and proceeds donated to the Society of Abolitionists (Klamkin 102). Wedgwood also refrained from placing its mark on this design.

Wedgwood's ceramic participation in abolition made supporting the cause more visible, but its choice of settings also distinguished its purchasers. Painted on cameos for items such as rings and brooches, or printed on the dining sets of the highly refined, the image of the kneeling slave reinforced his contribution to whitened luxury even as he condemned it. Cameos did not become plain-looking pins, but rather were set in gold, surrounded by pearls to become an ornament, so that abolitionists could be seen as proprietors of their kneeling black "brothers" as much as their Southern opponents were. While the cameo's startling black-on-white reminded onlookers of a situation they may have preferred to ignore, it also reinforced the contrast between the wealthy white wearers and the objects of their energies.[9] This supplicating slave became, through ceramic mass-production, "the single most common visual representation of a black slave" (Savage 21). The abolitionist movement also produced black marble images of this slave as visual mementos, and the image found its way onto many products, from "books and broadsides to pincushions and pen wipers" (Savage 23). An even more sensational depiction of a fugitive slave cowering in a swamp, and hounded by a whip-wielding slave hunter and dogs, "became so popular as a symbol that dinner plates were made with the scene for a center motif; the handles of silverware were embossed with the story."[10] The troubling junction of an elegant meal and such a terrible image contributed to the racial politics of material things, I would argue, even as it denounced the abuses of slavery. The contrast between white comfort, sensually presented by the meal and the dining accessories, and black abuse, represented on dishes and silverware, enlisted the diners' sympathy but also emphasized their superiority—their wealth, refinement, self-mastery, and whiteness.

In producing ceramics, local American potters were successful with some "blue and gray" and yellow-with-brown-glazed stoneware, but Americans were largely unsuccessful with creamware; the British creamwares and other whitewares made up most of table and tea ware in the nineteenth century (Noel Hume 99–101). In the stonewares, the American pottery was also used for "storage, spittoons, harvest bottles, cream pans, and pitchers"—all marked for private, non-display functions (Noel Hume 101). Unrefined American-produced earthenware was "the match of [its] English cousins" (Noel Hume 99). Such coarse earthenware was also used for food preparation and storage rather than for display, and color ranged from red to green.

Shades of whiteness and fineness became almost a chart for household status: degrees off of white demonstrated the task's descending rank in the household. This distinction translated to the vessels' users as well: servants, slaves, and lower-class housewives cooked and "put up" food, while businessmen and families with servants and slaves held polite gatherings and ate from the dishes. Thus working vessels were marked as the out-of-style, less refined types, outlining the evolution of tableside civilization. In the white households of the South, much greater quantities of white ceramics have been found than in the North (Yentsch, "Symbolic" 221). Ceramics found on slave sites were distinct from those used by the neighboring planters; although slaves may have used discarded, unmatched dishes from the planter's household, they were more often issued dark, undecorated earthenwares. At slave sites in Cannon's Point plantation in Georgia, John Solomon Otto finds that these coarse earthenwares made up almost 70 percent of ceramic sherds found (105). The contrast between the planters' white dishes and the slaves' dark dishes highlights the suddenness of the material record's whitening. In the South, where slaves represent a conspicuous reminder of debt and danger, white plates were more abundant; on Southern plantations, where slaves greatly outnumbered their white masters, the material battle was even more pronounced.

This studied contrast to the dining ware of slaves reveals a conscious assignment of hierarchy to color, design, and specialization of ceramics. Otto suggests that slaves could obtain dishes in a number of ways: receiving a specially issued type from the planter, receiving chipped or damaged hand-me-downs from the planter's table, or purchasing their own dishes with money earned in their spare time (95). In the last case, the slave participates in the market and in the meanings that his or her dishes radiate. In the first two ways, however, the social meaning of ceramics lies in the master's power: "[t]he slaves' association with these ceramics is entirely material; no economic relation occurs between slaves and masters where these items are concerned, and the slaves do not enter the marketplace"

(Orser 100). The planter's savings when slaves obtained their own goods then had to be balanced against the risk of allowing them to assign their own meanings to these goods. For the majority of planters, meaning won out: most slaves used wooden plates and trenchers, discarded bowls and chipped plates, or specially issued dark ceramics.[11]

Use of white dishes and the manners needed to handle their specialized forks and plates indicated a degree of mastery usually withheld from slaves. In fact, the color of dishes illustrated the evolutionary difference between masters and slaves, as ritualized dining guarded against "a recognition that the process of eating might reduce all involved to an animal level of appetite and competition" (Kasson 139). Frederick Douglass acknowledges table manners to be part of white mastery, declaring that a slave child "is never chided for handling his little knife and fork improperly or awkwardly, for he uses none. He is never reprimanded for soiling the tablecloth, for he takes his meals on the clay floor.... He is never expected to act like a nice little gentleman, for he is only a rude little slave" (My Bondage 31). Freedom from the requirements of gentlemanly behavior, however, necessitates an association with the animal. Douglass later describes how at mealtime "the children were called, like so many pigs; and like so many pigs they would come" (85). Thus, when Frederick Douglass recalls eating from a wooden tray with an oyster shell, he reveals not only a material hierarchy ranging from "natural" slave dish to refined white tableware, but he also exposes the evolutionary justification embedded in ceramics: slaves eat in a decades-old tradition of wooden plates or earthenware, while the upper class dines on elaborately ordered white ceramics.

Speaking as an educated, successful, and mixed-race ex-slave—an embodiment of cultural contradictions—Douglass allows his readers to cling to the polarities that dishes enforce: gentleman or animal, master or servant, white or black. Indeed, these binaries inform the construction of whiteness that he would undermine. After conceding the civilized manners denied to slaves, Douglass asserts the superior etiquette practiced by them. He explains that slave children must show respect for elders, address them as "Uncle" and "Aunt," and acknowledge favors with a "*tank'ee*." Subtly, Douglass turns the exclusionary function of white etiquette against itself: "[s]o uniformly are good manners enforced among slaves," he claims, "that I can easily detect a 'bogus' fugitive by his manners" (My Bondage 48–49).

John Pendleton Kennedy explicitly links dining with civilization in his Virginian plantation novel, Swallow Barn (1832), as his narrator recalls an elaborate Southern dinner party that includes the area's gentlemen and their families. Among the bountiful meats, poultry, seafood, and pickles, the mistress somewhat disturbingly presents a ham "clothed in its own dark skin, which the imaginative mistress of the kitchen had embellished by carving into some fanciful figures" in a manner "worthy of imitation" (326). After describing in detail the layout of the table, the narrator gives equal attention to the slaves serving at the table: "A bevy of domestics, in every stage of training, attended upon the table, presenting a lively type of the progress of civilization, or the march of intellect; the veteran waitingman being well-contrasted with the rude half-monkey, half-boy, who seemed to have been for the first time admitted to the parlor" (326–327). Admission into the formal parts of the house directly corresponds to evolutionary development and intelligence for this pro-slavery writer—and this rule applies to the slaves as well as their masters. Of course, the "bevy" of servants stands separate in all respects from those dining: the slaves are described as part of the table setting, not as part of the company.

For the planters, participation in the dining room depended upon proper comportment within—the training in etiquette and manners that demonstrated proper use of refined goods. So strict did injunctions become against outbursts of any kind, that the narrator detects in a man's "rather obstreperous laugh" evidence of descending class status (328). From the gentleman's inappropriate laughter at the dinner table, the narrator finds him occupying "that questionable ground which a gentleman of loose habits and decaying reputation is pretty sure to arrive at in his descending career," which includes associating with lower-class men who make a "visible impression on his manners" (328). In this instance, the conviction that manners reflect high-class training is so powerful that a decline in class status must necessarily produce a lapse in manners.

As an overtly pro-slavery novel, *Swallow Barn* labors to present the rationalizations between planter and slave in a positive light. In a description of slave cabins, for example, their physical contrast to Frank Meriwether's sprawling mansion with its "thick brick walls" and courtyard "suggesting the idea of comfort in the ample space" the buildings fill, does not disqualify the cabins' own "picturesque" comfort (27, 28). The slave quarter consists of "hovels," some of which are "built after the fashion of the better sort of cottages" except that "age had stamped its heavy traces upon their exterior" (449). The roofs are mossy, the weatherboarding broken "into chinks" (449). The "more lowly" style of cabins, also the "most numerous," is "composed of the trunks of trees, still clothed with their bark," "with so little regard to neatness that the timbers ... jutted beyond each other": the hovels' dimensions are not more than "twelve feet square, and not above seven in height" (449). The cabins have a door and a window, and wood chimneys coated with mud. Despite their primitiveness, they form "an exceedingly picturesque landscape": "[t]he rudeness of their construction rather enhanced the attractiveness of the scene" (449). In all, the narrator summarizes, they could be compared in appearance to tea kettles (450).

Kennedy uses this setting to explain the happiness of the slaves, which renders such crowding "picturesque" rather than squalid. Although the narrator has claimed to have visited the plantation with Northern abolitionist preconceptions, observation of his cousin's management has changed his mind: "In short," he concludes about the slaves, "I think them the most good-natured, careless, light-hearted, and happily-constructed human beings I have ever seen. Having but few and simple wants, they seem to me to be provided with every comfort which falls within the ordinary compass of their wishes" (454, 455). With this posture, the narrator takes the slaves out of the range of the American economic system. They do not desire much; these desires are readily provided; they form a simple closed equation of not having and not wanting. Throughout the novel the narrator freely associates slaves with animals—in this same passage, they become "tarrapins luxuriating in the genial warmth," noisy "blackbirds," and "parasitical" (451, 454). In another nation, he admits, the black population might become respectable, but in the "Old Dominion" the slave system successfully shelters it from want.

GROUNDS FOR SEPARATION

One's house provided another evolutionary declaration, and the plantation landscape presented it to the field slaves, visitors, and passersby who were never admitted to view the master's china. In 1818, a Southern traveler notes that "'a journey from New Orleans to the mouth of the Sabine, exhibits man in every stage of his progress, from the palace to the hut'"—outlining that one's dwelling was always an exhibit advertising one's evolutionary distance from savages and slaves (qtd. in Bushman 383). In the seventeenth century, slave housing was similar to that provided for white indentured servants—often they slept in the master's house, or in any of the scattered sheds, or in large, "dormitory-style dwellings" (McKee, "Ideals" 197, 195). In the eighteenth century, slave quarters were removed to form a "village" of their own; one typical arrangement lined slave houses along the drive approaching the main house (McKee, "Ideals" 197; Lewis 38). These visible cabins served to demonstrate a planter's wealth, and would have been kept as ordered as possible; they usually belonged to the house slaves. J. W. Joseph also notes that field slave quarters in colonial times were more often located on the periphery of the plantation, away from the view of the master and freer from his control (58). Stored in unspecialized sheds, slaves received a treatment similar to other farming tools. In the far-off fields, the predominantly African slaves could be viewed as people, but ones with a closer connection to nature than to civilization—workers who were culturally as well as geographically distant from the European settlers.

At the end of the eighteenth century, the arrangement in general shifted from lining the forecourt of the main house to flanking the house on either side (Lewis 38). Common slave quarters for house slaves were smaller than the big house, which itself was usually smaller than a moderately sized Northern house. One room per slave family usually measured twelve or fifteen feet square. According to Olmsted, touring the South in the 1850s, slave cabins were usually "log-cabins, of varying degrees of comfort and commodiousness. At one end there is a great open fire-place, which is exterior to the wall of the house, being made of clay in an inclosure, about eight feet square and high, of logs. The chimney is sometimes of brick, but more commonly of lath or split sticks, laid up like log work and plastered with mud. . . . Several cabins are placed near together, and they are called 'the quarters'"(Olmsted 81–82). The most common type in the nineteenth century was a double cabin for two different families, with a central chimney serving both sides and a door on each half (Vlach, *Back* 22).

In the nineteenth century, slave cabins occupied the same space and category as other work sheds on the plantation: among the cabins were kitchens, stables, outbuildings, and overseers' houses. These separate outbuildings performed similar functions to the one large barn found on the Northern house lot. They served also, in their resemblance to slave cabins, to remind slaves of their place, among livestock and other household goods. North of the Mason-Dixon line, barn arrangement varied according to climate, but all conveyed a definition of work different from Southern barns. In New England, the layout was sometimes a courtyard arrangement, with house and barn parallel and sheds in between, forming a loose square. Sometimes house and barn each had separate clusters of sheds around them (Glassie, "Eighteenth" 415). Visually this arrangement allowed equal importance to the social building and the work building even though they were kept separate. In the South, the kitchen and various outbuildings were housed in small sheds ranging behind the planter's living quarters. This distancing of all work areas from the house proper rendered the main house a strictly formal white domain. Donald Linebaugh argues that the distance between the main house and such sheds as the kitchen, the dairy house, and the smoke house was a predominantly practical concern: stored food and processed milk carried with them strong odors, and the kitchen added excessive heat (3). Yet his argument fails to consider the implications of such practical concerns. The desire to segregate smells, to maintain a hygienic family gathering place, developed alongside the desire to segregate slave labor. In the not-too-distant past, Anglo-Saxon ancestors had been sharing their homes with the livestock.

Planters took pains to present these sheds and their functions in a certain way also. Some farms, for example, lined sheds up alongside the house, next to slave cabins. These would not only display the main house's grandeur better by contrast, they would present a united, productive front to those approaching by the front drive. Such flanking buildings would not proclaim their own presence, but rather would reinforce the status of the main house by stating their ability to provide for the farmer's needs. Often, however, the outbuildings were located behind the house, not intended for view by visitors (Joseph 59). In this way, white planters could connect the blackness of their slaves with the bruteness of manual labor, and send them both from their sight simultaneously.

Traditionally, overseer's houses were placed halfway between the main house and the slave cabins, clearly marking the rank and function of the inhabitant (Vlach, *Back* 136). Although mediating between the master and his slaves, however, the architecture of the overseer's house and the goods within it told different stories. Otto finds on Cannon's Point plantation that the overseer's house resembles the master's in "construction materials, permanency, square footage per occupant, and location"—thereby distinguishing the free whites on the plantation from the slaves (Joseph 60). As seen from material remains around the cabins, however, the overseer resided on closer terms economically with the slaves than with the master (Joseph 60). The discrepancy emphasizes the importance of visual ranking according to race: unless one entered the overseer's house or shared a meal with him, the overseer's relation to his employer would appear closer than his relationship to the slaves. The overseer's status on individual plantations varied, however. On some farms, the overseer's house was located among the slave cabins and distinguished only by its slightly larger size and position at the head of the street (Vlach, Back 136). How the overseer was housed thus depended on the emphasis that the planter placed on race in relation to class, or perhaps the race of the overseer: any visual links with the planter's house would be a claim for his whiteness and social superiority.

The layout and form of the house was therefore a racial statement similar to the assignment of dishes, and on Southern plantations the statement was made with greater emphasis. Frederick Douglass understands the meanings of the walls and dishes and, in shaping his narrative, uses these material messengers to reverse the binary and impose a slave's perspective upon his readers. His foremost argument against slavery is the ignorance it enforces. He begins his Narrative of the Life with a series of claims about the knowledge that has been withheld from him,[12] and then proceeds to withhold strategic knowledge from his readers throughout the narrative. As he imposes this perspective, he inverts the white readers' understanding of their environment—of white things. In his revision of the Narrative, My Bondage and My Freedom (1855), Douglass elaborates on the techniques and descriptions that have been successful in the earlier work. As he describes his plantation, for example, he begins with the buildings farthest from the great house:

> There was the little red house, up the road, occupied by Mr. Sevier, the overseer. A little nearer to my old master's, stood a very long, rough, low building, literally alive with slaves, of all ages, conditions and sizes. This was called "the Long Quarter." Perched upon a hill, across the Long Green, was a very tall, dilapidated, old brick building—the architectural dimensions of which proclaimed its erection for a different purpose—now occupied by slaves, in a similar manner to the Long Quarter. Besides these, there were numerous other slave houses and huts, scattered around in the neighborhood, every nook and corner of which was completely occupied. Old master's house, a long, brick building, plain, but substantial, stood in the center of the plantation life, and constituted one independent establishment on the premises of Col. Lloyd. (My Bondage 47)

The houses of Mr. Sevier and "Old Master" stand on either end of the slave housing, physically surrounding the hundreds of slaves for supervision and control. Mr. Sevier's house, small, red, and far away from the great house, marks him as a lesser overseer, while Old Master's is made of brick and at "the center of plantation life," indicating him as the chief clerk of Colonel Lloyd and of higher rank than Mr. Sevier.

While Old Master's dwelling may be between the slaves' and the plantation owners', and thus literally in the center of the plantation's work area, Douglass reveals a slave's perspective in designating it central. To the owner of the plantation, the great house would be central, balanced by the workyards in back and the formal entrance and lawns in front. The landscape according to upper-class viewers, Dell Upton argues, existed as a series of barriers, while the issue of control dominates a slave's vision ("Imagining" 74). For the wealthy white viewer, the early nineteenth-century landscape would have appeared as a network of white houses, with the terraced floral grounds as frames, and roads as a means from one to another. For this reason, Olmsted, as an upper-class Northern traveler, expresses exasperation when he receives directions from slaves or common folk. He quotes at length the directions received from a farmer, which include fallen-in cabins, fences, unidentifiable schoolhouses and hidden big houses. But of these Olmsted sees "hardly anything" except "a continuation of pine trees, big, little, and medium in size, and hogs, and a black, crooked, burnt sapling" (52). From a slave he repeatedly asks the distance to a certain house, but the slave can only estimate how long the journey will take (54). His frustration comes from a difference in perspective: the farmer's directions draw from a knowledge of the history of the area and of the endpoints of each small path. The slave's concerns are for the travelling time that he might control, rather than the measured land that he cannot. Olmsted only becomes confused when directed through ruined cabins and unused fields: these are the hidden and ignored elements of a planter's formal landscape. For Douglass, a slave who is absolutely ruled by Old Master, the plantation radiates from his overseer's house to the fields, hardly accounting for the formal grounds that would constitute Olmsted's landmarks.

Douglass recreates this viewpoint when he culminates his description with "the grandest building my eyes had then ever beheld, called, by everyone on the plantation, the 'Great House.'" He continues, however, reversing the perspective his audience would be accustomed to from reading travel literature such as Olmsted's. Illustrating the house from back to front, Douglass proceeds from its outbuildings, "all neatly painted," to the house itself, and finally to the formal carriage drive leading to the road. The great house was "a large, white, wooden building, with wings on three sides of it. In front, a large portico, extending the entire length of the building and supported by a long range of columns, gave to the whole establishment an air of solemn grandeur" (*My Bondage* 47). A model of Greek revival architecture, the great house simultaneously signifies mastery over the dilapidated slave cabins and upper-classness over the overseer's little red house. For Greek revival architecture, Gwendolyn Wright argues, popularity depended on its flexibility of meaning. In the east, its reference to ancient Greek democracies and the current Greek fight for independence praised "civic virtue and social reform," while in the West it represented "simple ways and democratic strength," and in the South, "the heritage of slavery and aristocratic leadership" (Wright 33). Possibly, a fascination with ancient Greece and its internal contradictions, combined with the whiteness and order of the architecture, seems more to indicate America's agonizing over its own best and worst ideas. Douglass reads the mansion's message both as it is intended and in the more cynical view of the exploited slave: it "was a treat to my young and gradually opening mind," he proclaims, "to behold this elaborate exhibition of wealth, power, and vanity" (*My Bondage* 47).

At the end of his description, Douglass arrives at the front entrance, which includes a "large gate, more than a quarter of a mile distant from" the house; the "road, or lane, from the gate to the great house, was richly paved with white pebbles from the beach" (*My Bondage* 47). Douglass thus concludes his description with the white road leading to the mansion as peripheral, if grand. Studying the Stocktons' late eighteenth-century site, Morven, in Princeton, New Jersey, archaeologist Anne Yentsch finds a user-oriented design to its paths also. According to Yentsch, the landscaping there similarly distinguished functions of the house, assigning rank to each activity according to the coloring of the walks. The area around the front door—the public entrance—and the entrance for visiting businessmen and clients were paved in a whitish limestone material and elevated from the rest of the yard. The entrance to the kitchen and the doorway leading to the well and icehouse, used by slaves and farm laborers, were paved in a "reddish brown fieldstone material" and depressed from the rest of the yard. Yentsch interprets these color-codings as denoting high (white) and low (brown) rankings, community-oriented versus family-oriented activities—but they can clearly also indicate the formal refinement belonging to the whites of the Big House as compared to the manual labor assigned to the slaves behind it ("Access" 258).

As the paths and work areas were color-coded according to the labor performed there, certain types of labor were also inextricably bound to race. Olmsted reports that "no white man would ever do certain kinds of work (such as taking care of cattle, or getting water or wood to be used in the house); and if you should ask a white man you had hired, to do such things, he would get mad and tell you he wasn't a nigger" (64). The entire plantation community understood the racial implications of the formal and work areas and the privilege or insult implied in the use of each.

In *Narrative of the Life*, Douglass uncovers the code of this white conversation in his discussion of Colonel Lloyd's "large and finely cultivated garden" (59). The "greatest attraction of the place," this garden is visited by people from far and near and abounds in "fruits of almost every description, from the hardy apple of the north to the delicate orange of the south" (59). Many urban and most rural households had gardens, but only the wealthiest arranged them into vast formal showcases for the house. More decorative than functional, landscaped gardens also carried an intentional message, and often intended to mislead. In the eighteenth century, these gardens were designed to enhance the visible impact of the house: its message of control and superiority was broadcast to the community. Typical of a Georgian garden was the same strict bilateral symmetry of the house. With outlined paths and molded flowerbeds and shrubbery, colonial gardens demonstrated a minute control over nature. These manicured grounds, providing a frame and a visual guide to the central white house, were meant to explain their owners' superiority, Leone argues, as a "natural" condition (Leone 250). Proper rules for constructing a garden resemble those for civilized dining or house construction; design guidebooks in the nineteenth century continued a tradition of order and mastery as asserted in eighteenth-century formal gardens. Measurements and precise math were necessary to create the right effect. Elaborate efforts accompanied the wealthy's display of scientific mastery, which by association, implied social and economic mastery as well.

Although visitors tour Colonel Lloyd's garden, his slaves are prohibited from entering and denied a view by its high surrounding walls. Douglass emphasizes the fruits of both the North and the South contained within this garden in order to implicate both regions in such a display of wealth, which nonetheless flaunts its exclusion of the black laborers. This garden is admired by the plantation's important visitors, but is also "not the least source of trouble" for the slaves (59). Since slaves are often tempted to steal fruit from it, the master paints his fence completely with tar, and whips any slaves caught with a trace of tar on their bodies. In this way, the slaves begin to realize "the impossibility of touching *tar* without being defiled" (59, italics in text). The master thus translates the monumental attraction of his garden into a statement of control and racial inferiority for his slaves. The slaves are made afraid of this transferable blackness, the tar, which becomes both boundary and threat—and their own blackness deflected back onto themselves. The inaccessibility promised by the garden's black walls reflects the exclusionary efforts of the plantation's white walls and dishes. But Douglass manipulates the reader according to these same principles. According to narrative tradition, we are entitled to a description of this pastoral paradise, but Douglass masters his slave's-eye view thoroughly, by leaving us also outside the walls.

GRAVE EXPRESSIONS

A large, black granite monument erected in the latter twentieth century stands in the churchyard of St. Peter's in Columbia, South Carolina, memorializing the slaves whose wooden gravemarkers were lost to a nineteenth-century fire. Since death records for the slaves were scarce, the church has merely devoted the now-blank grassy space at the back of the yard to these burials. Throughout the rest of the churchyard, tall and sculpted white marble gravestones eulogize deceased white parishioners. Although the black monument is reverential, the contrast cannot be overlooked: fire or not, the wooden slave markers were doomed to an early destruction, and their studied insignificance reminded onlookers that even dead, black and white had a status.

As the first years of the nineteenth century witnessed the shift to white marble that stressed this contrast, they also saw a change in the popular motif that white folks' gravestones displayed. Before 1750, Dethlefsen and Deetz report, the markers in New England cemeteries carry death's-heads designs "almost universally." After 1760, this motif traded popularity with the cherub design, although particularly in rural cemeteries, a transition design called "spirit faces" can be found. Less frequently—although more in the South—portraits of the deceased appear on the headstone. The change to white marble brought with it a change to the urn-and-willow design, which at the beginning of the nineteenth century became "absolutely universal" and "the hallmark of Victorian gravemarkers" (Dethlefsen and Deetz 508).

The dates marking the changes from death's head to willow-and-urn and slate to marble vary from region to region and in themselves are only estimates. Date of death on a tombstone does not indicate the exact date of

Line drawings of southern and northern death's head motifs (top) and cherub motifs (bottom).

engraving: sometimes years passed before families commissioned a tombstone for the deceased. At the same time, markers may have been engraved in advance of an order and waited years for a buyer, or one stone could have been carved to serve two family members though one still lived. However, Benes concludes that on the average in New England, stones were carved within two or four years of the individual's death (5). Studying the emblems on these stones, Dethlefsen and Deetz detect a "battleship" pattern of popularity dates: the range of years when cherubs predominate, for example, covers the twenty years from 1760 to 1780, with examples to be found less often in the years immediately before and after (505). In the Southeast, the shifts in style "lagged approximately twenty years behind the initial shift in New England" (Gorman and DiBlasi 89). The move from death's head to cherub occurred in Charleston cemeteries between 1750 and 1799 (Gorman and DiBlasi 89).

In Massachusetts, however, in cemeteries such as Burial Hill in Plymouth and Mount Auburn in Boston, the nineteenth-century shift to marble was more sporadic than that in Charleston. Burial Hill contains many dark slate tombstones with urn-and-willow carvings, even into the 1830s, and in fact has few decorated marble stones. In Charleston, the darker stones are nearly absent after the year 1799, and white marble becomes ubiquitous. Only a few nineteenth-century examples of black slate exist in the churchyards of Charleston: a willow-and-urn engraving for Solomon G. Low of Gloucester, Massachusetts, who died in 1822, and an 1809 tombstone with a skull and crossbones carved entirely in German.[13] Even these exceptions prove the rule. In Massachusetts, a slate willow-and-urn would not have been uncommon in 1822, and the

(Left) Willow motif on white marble, St. John's Lutheran, Charleston, South Carolina. Mrs. Lydia Ann Malt, died 1858. (Right) Willow-and-urn design on black slate gravestone, Burial Hill, Plymouth, Massachusetts. Stone belongs to Captain Rufus Robbins, died 1826. Photographs by Bridget Heneghan.

Charleston stone reminds its viewers that this was the dead man's native state. The elaborate script on the German stone, itself a rarity, renders a double difficulty in reading the inscription. This stone also mentions a foreign nativity: Germany.[14]

The reasons for such a definite break in gravestone color in the South may be explained by the scarcity of carvers. In Charleston, engravers would often stay for a few months to establish a practice, and then move back to New England and receive orders (Combs 6). The availability of raw material also played a role. Shipping costs, even for native stones, were often prohibitive: while marble quarries were found in Alabama in the early century, even Alabamans found local shipping costs to be comparable to importing from New England (Brackner 22). Possibly, if family members were required to ship a gravestone regardless, they chose the marble just coming into fashion.[15] The churchyards of Charleston also represented the wealthiest of slaveholding families, so that expensive marble stones at the beginning of the nineteenth century might be more monolithically present than in Northern churchyards.[16]

At the same time, Charlestonians bore color-related anxieties in 1800 that New Englanders had shed. By 1800, slavery had virtually disappeared from Northern states: Pennsylvania, Massachusetts, Connecticut, and Rhode Island legislated a gradual abolition beginning in the 1780s, and New York and New Jersey legislated effective abolition in 1799. By 1792 "there were antislavery societies in every state from Massachusetts to Virginia" (Franklin 93). Toussaint L'Ouverture, leader of the slave rebellion in Haiti, was "at the height of his power" in 1800 and other slave rebellions

Cemetery scene with white marble stones, obelisk, and willow tree, Mt. Auburn Cemetery, Boston, Massachusetts. Photograph by Bridget Heneghan.

surrounded the century mark (Franklin 101). On January 1, 1808, the African slave trade was outlawed federally. Southern slaveholders would have felt themselves attacked nationally and internationally and may have responded with an assertion of ideological purity in the form of white markers—monuments combining individual, civic, and religious declarations. After the Civil War, many nonwhite stones may be found in both North and South. As the official anxieties would have been liberated, preferences moved towards a greater variety of stones for gravemarkers.[17]

At the same time, rural cemeteries became popular in the cities of the North and South, providing landscaped gardens and shaded walks for burial grounds. Opened in Boston in 1831, Mount Auburn was the first American cemetery landscaped into a park-like setting. Mount Auburn directly addressed gravestone materials along with its rules for order and solemnity. Mount Auburn rules dictated that "carriages could not be driven faster than a walk, refreshments could not be brought in, no flowers could be picked and decorous behavior would be enforced at all times" (French 84). Whiteness, moral elevation, and good manners were explicitly linked by the gravestones: "Each family plot could be fenced, but only in metal or stone, not in wood. The grave markers would have to be of stone, except that slate, the traditional material for headstones in the old burial grounds was specifically disallowed. There were no specific restrictions on the style of gravestones, but approval by the trustees according to their canons of taste was implied" (French 80). Within the decade, several other cities imitated Mount Auburn's design.

Outside of the plantation plots of the upperclasses—which more closely followed these Northern cemetery styles—Southern whites developed a distinct, communal burial tradition. Beginning at about the turn of the nineteenth century, folk cemeteries share common traits derived from both European and African practices. While studies of Southern cemeteries are scarce because burials more often took place on isolated family plots, these rural graveyards are scattered throughout the Upland South, which extends south from Maryland and east from Texas (Jeane 109). The early model of folk cemetery is characterized by "hilltop location, scraped ground, mounded graves, east-west grave orientation, preferred species of vegetation, creative decoration, graveshelters, and evidence or practice of cults of piety" (Jeane 111). This style continued from the early nineteenth century until the Civil War. Since hills make poorer farmland, folk cemeteries are often located on hilltops, but the image produced by bare, mounded dirt, graveshelters, and special decorations contrasts sharply with the trend of winding garden paths or crowded churchyard cemeteries favored in the North. Theories clash concerning the origin of folk cemetery practices. D. Gregory Jeane argues that although "[b]lacks living in the same communities share some of the same cemetery traits," the folk cemetery "is a complex of cultural traits associated with white Anglo-Saxon communities" (120). He points to European examples of scraped graves, especially in Belgium and France, and finds analogues for graveshelters in the British "house-form tomb" and lych-gate (122). On the other hand, Vlach traces the use of shells, mounding, and broken pottery to African origins, and Terry Jordan argues that scraping the ground stemmed from African influence also (Vlach, *Back*; Jordan).

In folk cemeteries, all grass is scraped from the area surrounding graves, resulting eventually in "exposure of clay beds" and a hardened surface to the yard (Jeane 113). In addition, dirt is mounded above the grave, and these mounds are regularly re-formed after settling. Usually, the graves have no markers, although rarely they can be found with markers of wood or local stone. Even more rarely will these stones bear a name or date, "crudely inscribed," although wooden stakes might be carved into circles or diamonds. Jeane reports graves in Texas and Louisiana marked by stacked "clay turpentine cups." "What is decidedly missing" from all folk cemeteries, he adds, "is the frequent use of commercially produced gravestones of granite or marble" until after the Civil War (114). However, whitewashed stones can be found, and "[l]arge, white flint stones" used to mark or outline graves (Montell 112, 121). Shells can also commonly be found decorating graves, outlining several graves, lining a single plot, or covering the entire mound.

Graveshelters dotted the folk cemetery, and were constructed of wood, with "four corner-posts, often surrounded by picket fencing, supporting a shallow, gable-ended roof" (Jeane 115). For a society that often did not provide barns for its livestock, graveshelters seem a particularly zealous treatment of the dead. However, the gable-ended roof mimicked in miniature the I-house that signaled respectability; and the picket fence had become a middle-class mark of refinement by the middle of the nineteenth century (Bushman 160). The people establishing these gravesteads were among the lower classes, however, since plantation owners more often had their own family plots. Jeane reports that "no graveshelters have been observed in black graveyards" (115). In this view, rural folk designed their own version of white things, "making do" despite a shortness of means and materials. Perhaps denied a large white house in life, they might erect a tiny house for death. Turning from the prohibitively expensive marble, they might construct a monument from "conch, freshwater mollusks, and saltwater bivalves" (114). Lacking the resources to import white marble, Southern lower classes nonetheless marked their graves with whiteness.

Wandering in Savannah, Olmsted accidentally encounters a "graveyard for negroes" where some of the markers "were mere billets of wood, others were of brick and marble, and some were pieces of plank, cut in the ordinary form of tombstones" (174). While Olmsted transcribes the short misspelled messages of a few markers, he also recalls the elaborate inscriptions on a large brick tomb and a stone table. Both were placed for preachers by their church. In addition, Olmsted describes one white marble stone which records "the worth fidelity and virtue of Reynolda Watts." The marker, erected by her owner, gives credit to the owner for the virtues of the deceased: "Reared from infancy by an affectionate mistress and trained by her in the paths of virtue, She was strictly moral in her deportment, faithful and devoted in her duty and heart and soul a." The inscription abruptly ends because the rest of the stone is buried in sand. A few other stones, "similar in character to the above, [were] erected by whites to the memory of favourite servants," Olmsted observes, suggesting that the white marble stones were the contribution of masters rather than family members of the slaves (175). Also, if these markers were "similar in character" to the one cited, they seemed as much a memorial to the master's benevolent influence and the possibility of a perfect master-slave relationship, as to the slave herself.

When the narrator of Douglass's *My Bondage and My Freedom* reports his mother's death, he mourns the failure of any sentimental deathbed scene, since he is not told of either her death or her funeral. And though he mentions "the stately mansions of the dead"—the "vast tombs" of his master's white family that tell of its "antiquities ... as well as of [its] wealth" in his survey of the plantation, he reminds the reader that his mother's grave is, "as the grave of the dead at sea, unmarked, and without stone or stake" (48, 43). Again, he couches his complaints in terms that whites will understand, pointing to the denial of knowledge—of important deaths, or place of burial, or genealogical history—that gravestones mark.

Planters—even the reforming kind—had little to say about the burial of their slaves. A committee of Alabama planters resolved in 1846 that a slave should know that he or she will be "decently buried," and a Mississippi planter recommends that "an hour shall be set apart ... for his burial" (Breeden 289). The racial contrast implied by this disregard can be marked even in a contemporary abolitionist's observations. In the 1850s, "the Roving Editor" James Redpath toured the South in search of fodder for his abolitionist arguments. In the midst of his diatribes, however, he pauses to contemplate the cemetery of a town struck by yellow fever. His "tears [start] up unbidden," he writes, as he stands in a white cemetery and looks upon a grave marked only by "a shingle" (136). The tombstone's inscription is written in pencil; it "had nothing poetical, or solemn or sacred about it." Redpath reports to have "wept like a girl" at the thought of "[s]hingles for tombstones—no time for marble; for the chisel, a pencil—hastily used" (136). While sympathetic to the slaves, Redpath mourns the haste of this white burial; nonetheless, such a wooden marker would have been standard for a slave. Redpath inadvertently exposes the message delivered to slaves as he mourns this unusual arrangement for a white: the intent is not poetry, solemnity, or sacredness, but rather a nod towards protocol in the midst of more important business.

SLAVE QUARTERS, SLAVE EIGHTHS

In *Incidents in the Life of a Slave Girl*, Harriet Jacobs uses the full range of whitening goods in her assault on racialist middle-class pretensions.[18]

Like Douglass, she uses the tools of white householders to expose the evils of slavery in terms they can understand. She begins her message by identifying the markers of slavery and white superiority and then exaggerates them to unbearable proportions, until the claims themselves must be seen as ridiculous. Acknowledging that the status of black womanhood and "feminine" slave have no specific place in the material economy, Jacobs creates an alternate economy and then presents the excluding Anglo-American system from this outside perspective. Her claim for the text is greater than abolition, greater even than revising the stultifying Cult of Domesticity.[19] Her narrative exposes the cultural work of white things themselves as part of a cramped, closed economy, outside of which is teeming with people who can not only observe the participants, but also laugh at them.

In fact, ironic laughter occurs often in this story of a slave woman's trials—and she does not hide that it is directed at a white audience. Her narrative is full of material jokes, and the laughter marks the times she explains them. Jacobs provides her readers with a textual example, in fact, to illustrate this material mockery in written form: in what Jacobs styles a "Competition in Cunning," she attempts to free her children by sending letters to her master and her grandmother, supposedly from the North.[20] The content of these two letters, intended less to convey information than to mislead her master, makes two appeals. In the letter to Dr. Flint, she reminds him of her abused life in slavery. In the letter to her freed grandmother, she appeals to the mother-child bond and praises domesticity. The narrative's designs should be recognizable within these messages also; certainly, the scholarship has focused on Jacobs's project as addressing both the evils of slavery and the limitations of the Cult of Domesticity. But while both letters contain accurate statements, they are, in fact, taunts to those within the system. After Jacobs has sent these letters, she contrives to witness her master's reaction—in whispers through cracks in the walls, through open doors, or as reported by other servants. Dr. Flint's attempts in turn to deceive his slave become "as good as a comedy to [her]" (103). The comedy, she insists, is that those in power believe their own fictions and therefore fall prey to the fictions drawn by the outcasts.

That she sees through the pretensions does not make her competition less deadly serious, however. The conditions of her own and other characters' slavery are brutal and demoralizing, and her immediate project remains abolition and family freedom. Jacobs draws fully upon the conventions of white goods in exposing the evils of slavery and its physical signs. She detests the "linsey-woolsey" clothing that her mistress issues her, for example, because her grandmother provides her clothing, and the single rough dress provided by Mrs. Flint serves only as "one of the badges of slavery" (11). She invokes the sacredness of the cemetery when she claims that her master's sexual advances torment her even while kneeling at her mother's grave (28). And when a local reverend condescends to preach to slaves, he offers his kitchen as a meeting place. Traditionally a slave domain, this building becomes the proper place for slaves to hear his message of unquestioned obedience to masters. But he keeps them waiting while he remains in his "comfortable parlor," the traditional arena for upper- and middle-class socializing and display (69). Tired of waiting and aware of the architectural sermon silently delivered, the slaves leave to "enjoy a Methodist shout" (69).

A widespread prop in sentimental literature is the tea table, set with elaborate dishware and proclaiming white racial and upper-class superiority. In fiction, the tea table presents a feminized, sentimental vehicle for maintaining these messages. In her use of the white china of the tea table, Jacobs depicts how easily abused these powerful white things are—but ultimately she also has the last laugh. Jacobs's free black grandmother knows how to set a proper tea table, but one that overpowers racial differences in its appeal to sentiment. Often, Aunt Marthy shares tea with Miss Fanny, the old maiden who has freed her, and "[o]n such occasions the table was spread with a snow-white cloth, and the china cups and silver spoons were taken from the old-fashioned buffet" (88). Together the women would "work and chat, and sometimes, while talking over old times, their spectacles would get dim with tears" (89). In this scene, Jacobs images a novelistic ideal: the white owner and black ex-slave labor together rather than one for the other, and the women ultimately look the same through their tears.

But slave ownership perverts this sentimental success. When Mrs. Flint, who has been nursed by Aunt Marthy, becomes the owner of Jacobs and the sexual threat Jacobs represents, she no longer takes tea with Aunt Marthy (89). Mrs. Flint's duties as housekeeper involve the white china of the dining room: through this specialized dishware, she is responsible for training her family in time discipline and manners that the ritual of dining enforces. But her slaves see a different exercise at work. "If dinner was not served at the exact time" on communion Sundays, she would "station herself in the kitchen, and wait till it was dished, and then spit in all the kettles and pans that had been used for cooking" so that the cook would have nothing to eat (12). Mrs. Flint uses the virtue of time management as a means of torment. But even further, she affronts a basic rule of politeness by spitting, and offers this rude display as sustenance for her slaves. The gesture of spitting itself, which is often remarked on as a nasty habit among lower classes and men, reveals slaveholding's violence as Mrs. Flint unmakes her upper-class femininity to punish her slaves.

Dr. Flint likewise violates the code of the civilized and civilizing tea by transforming it into torture. While preparing to whip a slave, he orders the man to be tied to a joist in the work house, and "[i]n that situation he was to wait until the doctor had taken his tea" (13). Thus he posits his own gentility against the slave's depravity, and Jacobs draws on the symbolic power of tea even while she critiques its romanticized refinement. The slave, hanging in the work house while the master lounges in the dining room, is meant to realize the vast distance between their positions—especially since this is the slave who has quarreled with his wife for bearing Dr. Flint's child. Later, Dr. Flint extends this lesson in evolution when he forces his cook to eat the dog's food after the rabid dog rejects it. By building upon a knowledge of the civilizing influence of ceramics, therefore, Jacobs uses an ideology immediate to her middle-class readers, rather than relying on accounts of distant brutalities or the abstract problems of perpetual bondage. Seen from her outside perspective, however, these prized white things become repulsive.

After Jacobs finally finds her way North, she must herself struggle over the tea table. When she arrives at a hotel in Rockaway with the white child in her charge, the waiter requests that she stand behind the child's chair for dinner, and then take her own supper in the kitchen (176). Instead, she leaves the table, and refuses to comply with codes. In the end, she claims triumph: she traps the white waiters in their own racial system. The waiters are forced either to allow her to join the white dinner crowd, or to perform special services in bringing her dinner to her room. Eventually they "concluded to treat [her] well," so that this time, at least, she has the last laugh (177).

Since the narrator has demonstrated her understanding of the racial stakes of white architecture and ritual, she reveals her criticism when she signifies against them. In the first paragraph of the book, Jacobs describes her parents as "a light shade of brownish yellow" (5). Later, she challenges the enslavement of Africans based on race, asking, "And then who *are* Africans? Who can measure the amount of Anglo-Saxon blood coursing in the veins of American slaves?" (44). When she escapes, she challenges the practice indirectly, signifying upon her slavery by painting herself black. As she steals to her grandmother's house for her long confinement, she wears sailor's clothes and "blacken[s] [her] face with charcoal" (113). In this scene, a black woman, so often the imitated object of blackface plays, smears her own face with charcoal and tries to "'walk ricketty, like de sailors'"—which has its own humor even if afterwards Jacobs suffers the physical and emotional trials of the swamp (112). Like the white men performing in blackface minstrelsy, she must use artificial means to appear black, but her performance aims at escape from, rather than escape to, the imagined carefree life of slaves.

Jacobs similarly reveals her ridicule of white ideology when she arranges her house for patrollers. After Nat Turner's insurrection, Jacobs receives warning that "country bullies and poor whites" may search her home. She writes, "I knew nothing annoyed them so much as to see colored people living in comfort and respectability; so I made arrangements for them with especial care. I arranged every thing in my grandmother's house as neatly as possible. I put white quilts on the beds, and decorated some of the rooms with flowers" (63). Aware, she tells us, that she can annoy the poor whites, she decorates her house with the symbols of white femininity and respectability—symbols that exclude the soldiers as much as they do herself. She presents these invaders with the visual insult of a house neatly and carefully prepared, demonstrating discipline and economic success, decorated as if for guests, but owned and enjoyed by free blacks and slaves. Therefore, even while she taunts the violent patrollers, she creates a scene of refinement familiar to middle-class white readers; the home's invasion by ruffian males speaks more personally to them than even Jacobs's own helplessness before the men.

Finally, Jacobs draws upon the sentimentality of the graveyard scene when she decides to escape. She travels to the woodland "burying ground for slaves" in order to deliver her vow, that she will free herself and her children or die in the attempt: "For more than ten years I had frequented this spot, but never had it seemed so sacred as now. A black stump, at the head of my mother's grave, was all that remained of a tree my father had planted. His grave was marked by a small wooden board, bearing his name, the letters of which were nearly obliterated. I knelt down and kissed them, and poured forth a prayer to God for guidance and support in the perilous step I was about to take" (90–91). The scene recalls any number of embroidered, painted, or literary pictures popular in the mid-nineteenth century, of dutiful children kneeling at their parents' memorials, but Jacobs manipulates the props to create a different message. The markers are not white marble monuments, but rather a blackened stump and a decayed wooden board. They do not represent public memorials intended for display: her father's name barely remains, and her mother's marker only recalls a former tree. Her family, which owns a house downtown, could probably afford a monument, but they save their money for buying children into freedom and providing for enslaved relatives when their masters do not. Her father has marked the site of her mother's grave with a living tree rather than stone, emphasizing a value on natural beauty rather than artificial display. But even after the tree has died and blackened, the daughter kneels and kisses it. The voice she hears from these graves also counsels counter to the whitened message of feminine submission: Jacobs hears her father bid her "not to tarry till [she] reached freedom or the grave" (91). Jacobs invokes the preaching power of the gravestone for this message. As early American gravestones warned passersby to "Prepare for death and follow me," the father's marker also speaks. The wisdom of the grave beckons her not to mortality, however, but to the North.

When Jacobs effects her escape, she continues to use the messages she has been sent as a slave against themselves. When Dr. Flint offers to make her a "lady," equipped with a "small house ... in a secluded place," Jacobs rejects the position and the system that allows it (53). In fact, only when Dr. Flint's son at the plantation moves Jacobs from the servants' quarters to the great house does she resolve to run. She refuses to be a secluded "lady," but will not be allowed to be a servant only; the architecture finally offers her no position but escape. She then leaves not through a door but through a window—the parlor window. Escaping via the formal and social sanctum of the house, which seeks to deny her existence even as it tries to fetter her by its feminine ideology, she pierces its contradictions. In opening its window, she makes her existence felt through her absence and sacrifices Anglo ideology to the practical demands of a slave mother.

In her first hiding place, she re-inscribes her status as chattel, secreting herself in the upstairs storeroom of a sympathetic mistress, where things are put that are "out of use" (100). When inspection threatens, the slave cook Betty hurries her "across the yard, into the kitchen," where she stows Jacobs beneath "a plank in the floor" (103). The kitchen, Betty indicates, is her domain, and the architecture sustains her belief. When Jacobs is in Betty's kitchen, Betty considers her to be among " '*my tings*' " and therefore will fight for her (103, italics in text). In recommendations to improve slave housing, many planters suggest that elevating the floors and adding plank flooring would make a healthier, cleaner living space. Reform-minded slave-owners comment upon the "very natural . . . propensities" of slaves to accumulate trash about their quarters, and several suggest that elevated plank floors ensure that "air can circulate freely under them, and that no filth may collect under them" (Breeden 128, 134). One planter posits the benefits of flooring: "[w]hen thus elevated, if there should be any filth under them, the master or overseer, in passing, can see it and have it removed" (Breeden 120–121). Jacobs's hiding beneath the plank flooring only mocks the planters' supposition that better housing will prohibit slaves from keeping "filth" or contraband hidden beneath their floors.[21]

Her final hiding place Jacobs describes in detail, providing measurements and conditions: she stays in the garret of a small shed that serves as a storeroom, "nine feet long and seven wide," with the "highest part . . . three feet high," and with no light and no air (Jacobs 114). She provides measurements not much more cramped than the twelve feet square per family remarked upon by Olmsted and Kennedy. Her "dungeon" resembles the slave cabins that reformers criticize as being "always *too small and too low*," "[s]mall, low, tight and filthy," generating sickness with their "*bad air*" (Breeden 127, 120, italics in text). Explicitly, she compares her tight confinement to slavery itself, only preferring the physical discomfort to the spiritual one (Jacobs 114). As she describes her relief at boring an inch-wide hole in her crawlspace, where she can "enjoy the little whiff of air that floated in" and perhaps read or sew by its point of light, she positions her readers inside the low, cramped space that reformers only view from the outside. For example, a small planter claims that slaves " 'prefer darkness to light,' " but nonetheless recommends they be required to take some sun and be provided with a window in their cabins (Breeden 131). Another asserts that although blacks "bear crowding much better than white people" because "the negro does not consume as much oxygen as the white man," slaves should nevertheless not be overcrowded (Breeden 128). Within this hyperbolically cozy space, Jacobs combines the conventions of slavery and domesticity to illustrate the clash when they meet. A woman and a slave, she suffers an interiority within the attic room that becomes pathetic. She huddles next to her pinpoint of light to engage in the genteel pastimes of reading and sewing. Romanticization is impossible for such domesticity: Jacobs pursues her portrait of white femininity and slavery propaganda until the image is ridiculous.

Upholding this attic enclosure, Aunt Marthy's household has members both free and slave, with varying degrees of blackness and several different owners. The house itself flaunts the success of its inhabitants—an ex-slave owning a two-story house in North Carolina would have been rare. The descriptions Jacobs gives of her garret and its relationship to her grandmother's house correspond with a sketch that Jean Fagin Yellin provides of the house of Molly Horniblow, Jacobs's grandmother.[22] In Jacobs's descriptions, the garret belongs to a storage shed added onto the front end of Aunt Martha's house, overlooking the street. The storeroom, Jacobs notes, "opens upon a piazza," which also leads to the front door (Jacobs 114; Yellin 216). The long, deep house, with the entrance on the side of the house rather than facing the street, is similar to the house type appearing in Charleston, South Carolina—another Southern port city—at the same time. In Charleston, lack of space resulted in regulations allowing only a specific number of feet per lot to face the street; therefore, Charlestonians built narrow but deep houses. Their house lots were ordered front-to-back also: the front presented a formal architecture, while "functions of increasing dirtiness—descending from kitchen to privy—range[d] back along a workyard" (Zierden and Herman 205). Through the early nineteenth century, Martha A. Zierden and Bernard L. Herman find, Charlestonians increasingly enclosed their houses, building walls and shifting the entrance to the side of the house in a way that "not only blocked and channeled physical access . . . but also increasingly denied visual access" (207). In so doing, these citizens followed a trend which Upton believes was climaxed in Monticello: their houses remained a fixture on the landscape, but the inhabitants "could see and not be seen" (Upton, "Imagining" 84). Zierden and Herman believe this domestic enclosure was encouraged in Charleston by the perceived threat of slave insurrections (220).

Aunt Marthy's house, modeled after Molly Horniblow's, has its entrance on the side like these Charlestonian houses; however, the storage shed over which Jacobs hides contradicts the frontal formality that was common in Charleston. In Richmond, Virginia, on the other hand—where many African Americans worked skilled jobs—the typical home owned by free African Americans was a one-room wooden house with appended shed fronting the street, although some African Americans owned larger brick buildings (Kimball 125). What is striking about this layout is the prominent shed: whereas the trend in Anglo-American housing in the nineteenth century was to hide the outbuildings, camouflage them behind the big house or set them at the back of the city lot, Aunt Marthy's family positions her shed in plain view.[23] The ideal that suggests that proper ladies do not labor, at least in view of a visitor, does not affect her household: Aunt Martha makes her living as a baker, and she can be proud of an occupation that has brought her status and freedom for some of her family.

That the shed is not hidden affords Jacobs a narrative edge, as well: her garret looks onto the main street, so that she can observe city life even while hidden. From this position, she can "see without being seen," and observes her owner's comings and goings as well as several town scandals. Jacobs prepares the reader for this situation in an earlier chapter, "The Church and Slavery." She and her brother leave a sermon given by the Rev. Mr. Pike "highly amused," demonstrating again her desire to undercut sacred white precepts. His sermon, quoted at length, is a warning of God's perfect surveillance—a perfection aspired to by the slave owners who would walk down a slave street and detect from a distance any illegal filth beneath the cabins. Reverend Pike accuses, "Instead of serving your masters faithfully . . . you are idle and shirk your work. God sees you. You tell lies. God hears you" (Jacobs 69). He repeats his refrain, "God sees you," five times. Jacobs's amusement surely comes from the preacher's optimism—that slave owners have religious access to total control of their slaves and that the slaves take him seriously.

More accurately, the slaves, not their masters, have the better vantage from which to survey the complete lives of those who live with them. As Annalucia Accardo and Alessandro Portelli maintain, the Denmark Vesey rebellion of 1822 in Charleston, South Carolina, exposed what slaveowners needed to deny for their own peace of mind: the possibility of traitorous house slaves. Earlier and later rebellions likely stressed the same recognition, but participants in Vesey's rebellion were the same slaves whom masters trusted to protect their families when they were called out of town. One slave owner observed, " '[I]t is now well ascertained that most of the coachmen & favorite servants in the City knew of it [the rebellion] even if they had not participated in the intentions and plans proposed' " (77). Awake to such dangers within her own household, a planter's daughter remarks in her diary, " 'Every black man is a possible spy' " (79).

Jacobs claims to be haunted by her master's advances—"My master met me at every turn. . . . If I went out for a breath of fresh air . . . his footsteps dogged me. If I knelt by my mother's grave, his dark shadow fell on me even there" (28). Mrs. Flint also watches her, hovering over her in her sleep until Jacobs fears for her life. But Jacobs is also constantly aware of their presence, and when she retreats to her attic, *she* becomes the spying specter. The first person she sees from her loophole is Dr. Flint, and besides watching her children playing and neighboring slaves suffering in the street, she "peeped at" Dr. Flint on his way to recapture her as well (116). From the garret, she looks down upon the unaware actors, distanced by her inability to descend. Her surveillance is much closer to that described in Pike's sermon, because she remains invisible in her scrutiny. She even manages to be several places at once, when she mails letters from the North and hears them received while still in North Carolina. The world that for her white owners barely even registers visibly—the non-capitalist world of the gendered black woman, unsatisfied slaves, variously imprisoned bodies—can view the master's social fictions all the more clearly for being excluded from them.

At the same time, however, Jacobs never allows her joke to diverge far from practical, physical existence. Her torment as a slave, in the garret, and in the North is not only actual but corporeal. Her elevated garret perspective is also a "'dungeon,' a torture chamber, a prison, a grave," a symbol of "slavery's extreme entrapment" (Goddu 148). She can observe without detection, but she cannot be a transparent eyeball, because her body continues to be overrun with rats, infested with chiggers, spattered with turpentine, cramped with cold, and suffocated by heat.

The "Competition in Cunning" she stages with her letters is clearly won "by herself," but it is also an invitation to her readers to view their pretensions from the loophole of her social exclusion. The abuses of slavery, the limits of the Cult of Domesticity, the cultural products of her readers' environment of white things remain serious, as does her desire to establish an independent family household in the North. She *can* laugh, though, at the performances these white things impel upon her white neighbors. They are not funny, but they *are* a joke.

BLACKENING

The meaning attached to a concrete object made it not only ideologically powerful, but also liable to attack: the disenfranchised could use these goods to perform a subtle resistance. Slaves might safely display their rebellion through their own choice of dishes and housing. If slaves accepted the ideology of whiteness, the distinctions that white interiors and specialized, whitened dishes indicated, one would assume that, when possible, they would imitate these ware types and colors. However, Leland Ferguson argues that because South Carolina slaves crafted their own vessels in different forms than the planters' dishes, they enacted a material resistance ("Struggling with Pots"). "Colono Ware," which refers to "low-fired, handbuilt pottery found on colonial sites," was produced by Native Americans as well as African Americans, both of whom served on South Carolina plantations (Ferguson, *Uncommon* 19). At the same time that British manufacturers worked to create whiter plates, slaves produced their own vessels reflecting both Native American and West African traditions.[24] Colono Ware makes up 70 percent of all ceramics recovered in twenty-three South Carolinian slave quarters, and 48 percent of all ceramics recovered from rural sites. Since it comprises only 2.2 percent of urban ceramics recovered, it is likely that slaves wanted only the opportunity to create familiar vessels: urban slaves would have been more likely to be issued dishes (Ferguson, "Struggling" 31).

Other African traditions traced to American slaves show a twist to the assigned hierarchy of white dishes: rather than increasingly varied and specialized plates and cups, most Colono Ware vessels were large bowls, of the same size, and undifferentiated in design. Otto finds in nineteenth-century Georgia that even the handed-down vessels used by slaves were predominantly bowls (103). These vessels resemble those found in West Africa, where large starchy meals were served in communal bowls and eaten with the hands (Ferguson, "Struggling" 33). In making large earthenware bowls or using large serving bowls handed down from the planter—or even the wooden trencher described by Douglass—slaves retained African ties and actively resisted the developing ideology that privileged whiteness.

When slave houses remained on the periphery of the plantation and slaves built their own shelter, they could similarly signify against whiteness. Especially in the lowland swamps of Georgia and the Carolinas, these peripheral settlements showed greater African retentions: at Yaughan and Curriboo plantations were found "wall trench-mud walled and post-wattle and daub constructions" in slave villages, which reflect West African building techniques (Joseph 65). Vlach argues that even the modernized slave cabins of the 1840s and 1850s reflect African preferences, as they share the average twelve by twelve foot floor plan, gable-side door, and lack of windows (Vlach, *Back* 166). After the Revolution, masters exerted more control, drawing the cabins closer to the main

"Old Time Cabin." Photograph by Frances Benjamin Johnston, 1899 or 1900. The cabin is constructed of hewn logs with shingle roof and wooden chimney. In front, two African American men and an African American woman, rickety table and chair, and dark stoneware vessel. Library of Congress, Prints and Photographs Division, LC-USZ62-68312.

house and exercising more supervision. One ubiquitous story tells of a slave, born in Africa and taken to Georgia, who built himself a traditional African house in the 1840s or 1850s. A fellow slave recounts how the master tore it down because " 'he ain' want no African hut on he place' " (qtd. in McKee, "Ideals" 196). A slave woman in Mississippi, as reported by her daughter, resisted "whitening" by refusing a plank floor for her cabin, since " 'she was a African' " and was accustomed to dirt floors (qtd. in Vlach, Back 165). Vlach also cites several examples of slaves' resisting the imposed order of streets or row houses, when given the chance. A portion of Mount Vernon, "Muddy Hole Farm," had a black overseer, and there the cabins were "located . . . randomly among the trees at the edge of the cleared fields." Elsewhere on the plantation, in quarters supervised by white overseers, the cabins were "set in straight lines at regular intervals along the edge of a road." At a plantation in South Carolina, a slave village located far from the "central processing area" exhibits the standard row of slave housing, but the buildings "all were set at odd, irregular angles to one another" (Vlach, Back 14).

On the graves of blacks throughout the South, "broken crockery, broken glassware, broken pitchers, soap dishes, lamp chimneys, coffee cups, bits of stucco, and countless other items, generally from the kitchen, have been used" (Montell 120). Although Montell finds an African belief that breaking these ceramics released their spirits so they could accompany their owner to the next world, the choice of articles also points to an awareness of the message of white things. Soap dishes and coffee cups accompanied the dead to their final rest, perhaps serving them through the items' associations of wealth, or perhaps serving them in their final defeat by fracture. Censured as filthy, allocated to kitchen work, preached inferiority by pottery, nineteenth-century blacks may have killed greater spirits than those of the dishes when they placed their remains at the grave.

CHAPTER TWO

LIVING ON WHITE BREAD

Class Considerations and the Refinement of Whiteness

It was back in 1823, Quentin Compson says, that Thomas Sutpen was sent on the errand that changed his life. In William Faulkner's *Absalom, Absalom!* (1936), Sutpen marks for posterity the moment its history was made: he is sent to deliver a message at the plantation mansion, home of his father's employer. Although poor, Sutpen is unaware of poverty's importance as he passes the numerous status markers of the grounds, "following the road and turning into the gate and following the drive up past where still more niggers with nothing to do all day but plant flowers and trim grass were working, and so to the house, the portico, the front door" (229). As he stands at the front of "that smooth white house and that smooth white brass-decorated door" to be told by the black butler "never to come to that front door again but to go around to the back," his innocence of class and race hierarchy dissolves and his life becomes a means to avenge this insult (233, 232). Suddenly, the adolescent boy understands the resentment his sisters have against the better-housed plantation slaves, the urge his father has to strike the slaves and the futility of doing so, and he concludes that the only way to fight the wealthy plantation owner is with his own weapons: "land and niggers and a fine house" (238). The bitterness of his poverty strikes him as he returns from the errand, not having delivered the message, to look upon his own house in a new light. He views its "rough partly rotten log walls, the sagging roof whose missing shingles they did not replace but just set pans and buckets under the leaks, the lean-to room which they used for kitchen" and he thinks, with despairing laughter, "*Home. Home*" (236; 228, 235, italics in text).

In this 1936 novel, Faulkner provides a scene from the early nineteenth century; even more importantly, he provides the material clues that foretell the conclusion of Sutpen's vengeful ambition. Sutpen's project is doomed from the start because he fails to read the message built into the plantation house and grounds, so that when he imitates it he constructs only its shell without its signifying power. Sutpen is a member of the poorest class of whites in the South; approaching the front door of the plantation mansion, he trespasses on a view designed only for other wealthy planters. The front door stands as a final barrier to him but as an invitation to the proper visitor, whose gratified self-importance is proportional to the impressiveness of the grounds (Upton, "Imagining" 78). Sutpen notes, although he does not heed, the previous barriers: the first is the gate, which requires passage from the public access of the road. Sutpen then follows the drive "up past" the flowers and grass, but fails to comprehend the superiority suggested by its elevation. In the early nineteenth-century, formal drives were designed around careful landscaping, both of which demonstrated order and symmetry; often the view of the house from the road manipulated rules of perspective, so that the house appeared higher and larger. The house in *Absalom, Absalom!* stands a stark white, separating it from its natural surroundings and from the crude cabins that Sutpen's peers call "home." The final barrier between the house and door is a portico, marking the white house as most likely Roman classicist. Such a balanced, symmetrical style emphasized "public order and republican virtues," while insisting on the proper placement of all aspects of society—wealthy and poor, black and white, male and female, child and adult (Clifford Clark 43). When Sutpen is sent from there to the back of the house, to the undecorated working grounds used by slaves—he comes to glimpse the system that establishes and sustains the white plantation owner in his hammock. And when he returns to view his own one-doored house, he can then comprehend how that system denies him the planter's whiteness.

To understand his lower-classness, Sutpen must pass by the black gardeners and be rejected by a black butler because he has trespassed to the mansion's front door: though his rejection is based on class, it is couched in racial terms. Sutpen admires the white mansion, but he compares his own home to the neat slave cabins, and only then does he feel the depth of the insult. Class, race, and gender, at base, were constructed by one's relationship to material things in the early nineteenth century, and one's blackness or whiteness depended on access to white goods. Only upper- and middle-class white citizens were entitled to a racial "whiteness," therefore, since they could possess and maintain refined white things. Gender was displayed largely in one's attitude towards these things: "masculine" meant overtly ambitious and competitive, while the proper "feminine" attitude required one to pretend not to desire material things, but to value sentimental or spiritual or domestic comfort instead. Up to this point, Sutpen has been contentedly excluded from the capitalist economy of the South, neither having wealth nor wanting it. But his lack of desire marks him as poor white trash, beneath even the slaves who are provided finer housing and clothes. When Sutpen determines to acquire the significant things—in his mind, "land and niggers and a fine house"—he assumes an overwhelming desire for money and things, joins the marketplace, and creates an excessively masculine household— wild slaves and himself, mostly unclothed, engaging in hunting parties and then sleeping inside an unfurnished shell of a mansion.

Though a twentieth-century invention, Sutpen participates as an antebellum man in his material environment, without being fully aware of its import. As American consumers chose whiter and whiter products from the time of the American Revolution to the time of the Civil War, they created ways of marking and color-coding class as well as race. Those products that became whiter and that stand out in the archaeological record—dishes, house paint, and gravestones—were also becoming more specialized, demanding elaborate rules for their proper use. Homes that were painted white were also divided into several use-specific rooms, with a formal room designated for display—the parlor—becoming widespread. Gravestones became white at the same time their form became smoother, and the cemeteries lodging them gained a purposeful order and design. Whiteness implicated class distinctions, in that white paint and porcelain were among the more expensive options. Also, however, these white goods demanded a specifically upper- and middle-class mode of behavior: a new rigor in cleanliness for the body and household, the material and social tools for polite dining, the ability to succeed in a workplace that demanded time-discipline and specialization. To be "white" required these disciplines, and the poor or dissipated who rejected them forfeited whiteness and thus their white complexions, appearing in literature with faces that are "swarthy," "blotched," "red," or possibly "sallow." Those white-skinned people who could not afford refined white things settled instead for less expensive, out-of-fashion, or home-made items—creamware dishes, fieldstone gravemarkers, unpainted or dark-colored houses—unspecialized and nonwhite material markers. Their things and their use of things reflected back upon their skins to create racially liminal, off-white citizens.

In Melville's "Bartleby, the Scrivener," for example, the office workers illustrate the means to whiteness through work discipline, but also reveal its cost. The narrator, an elderly and "prudent" lawyer, suffers in his office from unpredictable, undisciplined workers. The first, Turkey, sports a "fine florid hue" after noon, at which time his behavior becomes characterized by a "strange, inflamed, flurried, flighty recklessness" (41). Indeed, his darkening complexion corresponds to his economic uselessness: "exactly when Turkey displayed his fullest beams from his red and radiant countenance, just then, too, at that critical moment, began the daily period when I considered his business capacities as seriously disturbed" (41). The second clerk, Nippers, is a "whiskered, sallow, and . . . rather piratical-looking young man" who suffers from "ambition and indigestion" and fidgets with "nervous testiness" and "unnecessary maledictions" in the first half of the day (43). Both workers are useful for only half the day, the narrator claims, and both by their personal habits threaten the respectability of his office. In contrast, the narrator praises Bartleby for being a "motionless young man," "pallidly neat, pitiably respectable," as he works "silently, palely, mechanically"—the narrator repeatedly pairs Bartleby's dependable discipline with his pallor (45, 46). The narrator values Bartleby's "steadiness, his freedom from all dissipation, his incessant industry," arguing that "his great stillness, his unalterableness of demeanor under all circumstances, made him a valuable acquisition" (53). Even his polite, incomprehensible " 'I would prefer not to' " seems a manifestation of proper bodily control and delayed gratification: in fact, his increasing reserve is merely an extension of industrial discipline as it gains a greater and greater hold on the employee.[1]

The terms defining class were also segregated according to gender, following a strict delineation of spheres, which, no matter how they were violated in individual instances, managed widespread mandates limiting professions and means of earning money according to gender. Women could not, for the most part, sell their labor and still remain "feminine." Women writers and some women performers provide one exception— provided they followed strict rules about subject matter in their writing, disavowing scholarly or economic ambition, or even wearing specific clothing styles for public appearances. In general, women's pursuit of class improvement involved domestic discipline as a form of training, of preparation for wealth, and the utmost display of the refined goods already possessed. For men, the formula for upward mobility was simpler and readily defined from Benjamin Franklin's *Autobiography* through Horatio Alger's rags-to-riches plots: discipline, work, integrity. The " 'horrors of idleness' " as "denounced from a thousand pulpits, and in publications both ecclesiastical and commercial" in the nineteenth century were a simple application for class mobility, but even leisure activities were gendered (Dimock 81). The connection between masculinity and labor was made clear: John Adams was eager " 'to prevent riches from producing luxury,' and to prevent luxury from producing 'effeminacy intoxication extravagance Vice and folly,' " and his caution remained the standard until the end of the nineteenth century.[2] Effeminacy, here—the first among the great evils imaginable—is clearly a lack of production, a failure of proper exertion and labor, a passive *having* and a lack of active ambition and acquisition.

Self-motivated work, the discipline demonstrated in factory work, and the ability to earn a living from it were so central to masculine class mobility that they were, at times, regulated against by slaveholders. Governor James Hammond spoke before the South Carolina Institute in 1850 claiming that " 'whenever a slave is made a mechanic, he is more than half freed.' " Many Southerners concurred, blaming the uprisings led by Nat Turner, Denmark Vesey, and Prosser on "industrial slavery," since these leaders were artisans (Shackel and Larsen 25–26). Although a letter in the *American Farmer* in 1827 sees industrial labor as a positive source of work-discipline " 'training the slave to habits of industry, in a business which will tend to prepare him for a state of freedom,' " Southern states enacted laws in the 1820s to the 1840s restricting free blacks from craftsman or factory occupations (Shackel and Larsen 24). Therefore, visible, regulated, self-motivated wage labor could distinguish not only the masculine worker, but also the white worker. Clearly, the distinction between waged and non-waged separated slave from citizen; for the most part, the visibility of the labor separated the masculine from the feminine.

The gendered nature of class was most powerfully asserted in the figure of the female factory worker, who embodied in the propaganda the contradictory distinctions of femininity and working-classness. Amal Amireh examines this figure as a manipulation by manufacturing interests: factories invited temporary female labor by promising an insulated, familial environment. Amireh argues that positing feminine workers as representatives of the factory system could protect industry, since to attack the system was also to attack a lady (10). Early industrial efforts recommended women working in the factory as a way to free men to work in the fields, and before the 1850s, women made up the majority of mill workers (4). With Lowell Mills as an exemplum, observers commented upon the women's "clean attire" and "healthy and cheerful faces" (7). Captain Basil Hall describes " 'the whole space between the factories and the village speckled over with girls, nicely dressed, and glittering with bright shawls and showy-colored gowns and gay bonnets, all streaming along to their business, with an air of lightness' " as the mill women walk to work. Anthony Trollope comments that " 'They are not sallow, nor dirty, nor ragged, nor rough' "; the idea that these women worked not from need but for adventure was also emphasized (qtd. in Amireh 6, 7).

The mill girls' femininity was spectacularly illustrated in a procession in 1833 celebrating the Lowell Mills, when nearly a mile of female workers paraded past Andrew Jackson: " '2,500 of them, each in an white muslin dress with a blue sash carrying a parasol over her bare head . . . he bowed to each couple as they came abreast of him until fatigue forced him to stop' " (qtd. in Amireh 1). The women's white dresses and parasols mark them as undoubtedly feminine, an upper-class designation as well as a denial of class as a consideration: the women are clearly not impoverished, but also not extravagantly dressed according to the latest fashion. The president's response to them is of a gentleman to a lady, although attempting 1,250 bows seems a hyperbolic attempt to establish gender. The effort and the display involved in "feminizing" female factory workers reveals the project as a merging of unrelated terms—feminine and worker—but also reveals the stakes involved. Outsiders' observations of mill women emphasize the women's contentedness, cleanliness, and appearance, so that industry could be seen as disconnected from the lower-classness of manual labor. However, observations generally stop outside the factory door: in many pro-factory representations, women are described going to work and leaving it, but not actually laboring, and mainly in this way could their "femininity" be retained. Furthermore, the women on parade mark their femininity by the simple white dress, thereby disavowing a desire for goods, so that their low wages and inability to gain wealth become not a mark of capitalist abuse, but rather a sign of their gender. In general, femininity participated in the marketplace not through visible labor, but as a preparation and training for economic success. "Feminine" women were called to display and enact an upper- or middle-class status through fashion and maintenance of refined goods, to enable class mobility by ordering a successful home and training family members in self-discipline and ambition. Outside of manufacturing propaganda, lower-class workers and manual laborers would have been viewed as neither "feminine" nor "masculine" but merely male and female.

Factory work was closely linked with slavery throughout the North and the South, connecting lower-classness to nonwhiteness through employers, material conditions, and labor. Shackel and Paynter find that 15 to 20 percent of slaves were employed by urban industry, about 5 percent worked in "industrial enterprises" by the 1850s, and about 80 percent of these slave workers were owned "directly by industrialists" (23). The connections between black slavery and wage slavery were well understood in Northern industrial towns; Charles Sumner denounced the alliance between the "Lords of the Lash" and the "Lords of the Loom" in the 1848 Whig Convention (O'Connor 45). The textile mills, upon whose leadership industrialism was developed in America, maintained multiple connections with the slavery concerns of the South. While cotton was bought from plantations, it was often also sold back to them after being processed in cotton mills, in the form of "negro-cloth"— "at least several mills producing negro cloth could be found in virtually every Northern state from New Hampshire to Pennsylvania and west to Ohio," including the model of industrial progress, the Lowell Mills of Massachusetts (Stachiw 36). Ronald Bailey traces the relationships between leading industrial manufacturers and slaveholders and finds marriage and family relationships between Northern factory owners—the Cabots, the Browns and Samuel Slater, the Lowells—and Southern planters; the Hazards of Rhode Island, also leading manufacturers, were involved in the slave trade before it was outlawed, and Rowland Hazard married the daughter of a planter at the end of the eighteenth century (Bailey 3–4; Stachiw 37). In 1860 a Massachusetts minister maintained that " 'Not one dollar in fifty passes through our hands that is not probably derived from this source [slavery]" (Stachiw 41).

The links between slavery and wage slavery traveled throughout the factory hierarchy. Comparisons of material conditions of factory workers and slaves helped both the "wage slavery" movement and slavery advocates, the latter arguing that black slaves enjoyed superior conditions and treatment compared to Northern factory workers. Use of the term "white slavery" was "fiercely rejected" by abolitionists, however, argues David Roediger; living and working conditions did not weigh as heavily as the freedom to earn a living or leave an employer, and such rhetoric weakened the straightforward legal evils of slavery (Roediger, "Race" 173). In a material sense, having fine goods was not as important as the ability to get them, and industrial workers agreed. During a shoe strike in 1860, a female worker said, " 'We know we are not a quarter as bad off as the slaves of the South,' " and William Craft stated that "he never met a poor person in Britain who 'did not resent it as an insult' when his or her circumstances and those of American slaves were compared" (Roediger, "Race" 177). Instead, white workers established as much ideological distance as possible between the two types of laborers: lower-class whites rejected the terms "servant" and "master" for referring to household laborers and master craftsmen, as these were too racially charged (Roediger, *Wages* 41, 50). Asked for her "master" in 1807, a New England maid responded that " 'none but *negers* are *sarvants*' " (Roediger, *Wages* 47). The relation between lower-class whites and slaves, couched in material terms, was a desire to gain things and a current lack of them. The distinction was in ability—white men could sell their time and get things, while slaves could not. The existence of a permanent class at the bottommost rungs of society made whites' temporary poverty more tolerable and enabled the working class to imagine that the important social distinctions were white and black rather than rich and poor.

Blackness, in this system, represents a lack of potential, a barrier from achievement and from upward mobility. Accordingly, blackness became a way of deflecting class tensions, of defining this mostly imaginary underclass, and of developing rules of civility that would produce disciplined workers among those who chose whiteness (Roediger, *Wages*).[3] Lower-class and undisciplined workers could not be "white"— they could not afford white things, nor use them properly, nor hide the physicality of their labor—and these lacks signified racially as nonwhite skin. Whiteness was expensive to gain and laborious to maintain, and downward class mobility signified also a racial danger. Blackness, revealed through black skin and dark-colored goods, was more than simply a stabilizer to the fluctuations caused by class mobilities or discrepancies; it was also a threat, the darkest place on a continuum of class, characterized by a series of negations—not able to have, not able to get, not able to use.

JUST IN FROM THE WHITE HOUSE

In 1818, a Southern traveler notes that " 'a journey from New Orleans to the mouth of the Sabine, exhibits man in every stage of his progress, from the palace to the hut' " (qtd. in Bushman 383). Although his emphasis is on the uncivilized state of the frontier, he reflexively equates civilization with palaces and barbarity with huts. This evolutionary outline was illustrated in the emerging popularity of standardized white houses and specialized architecture among the middle and upper classes, which contrasted with the vestigial log cabins and unpainted, one-room houses, or parts of houses, afforded by lower classes. Throughout the country, people with the means began "improving" their outdated architecture by creating parlors, front halls, and landscaping—and this organization was usually accompanied by an exterior white paint. Richard Bushman describes a house, owned by the Bixbys in Massachusetts, that underwent improvement in the late 1830s, when the oldest daughter reached marrying age. Their first project was to enclose the front hall, keeping the rest of the house hidden, and then to create a parlor from the former "best room." At the same time, the Bixbys removed unpainted clapboards and painted the house white; they also stopped scattering garbage throughout the yard and began collecting it into ordered, rectangular pits. Apparently, the Bixbys were among the last in the neighborhood to make these adaptations. In the central Massachusetts area, "virtually every house underwent changes much like those at the Bixbys" (Bushman 255). Among the improvements that David Goodale made to his 140-year-old house in 1841 was also the requisite coat of white paint. In addition to painting the house, he planted flower beds along the front drive, papered the downstairs rooms, and bought a sofa, an organ, and carpets (381). An "imposing house" constructed by William Brinton in Pennsylvania in 1704 also needed improvement by the nineteenth century. In 1820 it received a porch, and by the 1860s "the brick had been painted white, windows had been enlarged, shutters added, and a picket fence enclosed the foreyard" (261–262).

The trend that saw so many houses converted to white enjoyed dominance from the beginning until the middle of the nineteenth century. This popularity, which produced " 'assemblages of white boxes thrust as near as may be upon the street' " and made the white house with green shutters "almost a cliché for middling houses" carried changes in hygiene and etiquette in their wake (qtd. in Bushman 248, 258). When the Bixbys became concerned with social appearances, they did not merely coat the house's exterior. They removed the parent's bed and the dining ware from the "best room" to create a parlor. They collected household garbage into out-of-the-way trash pits instead of throwing it haphazardly into the yard. They created the initial barrier of a front hall, indicating that entrance into the family's life was excluded except for the select. With the addition of a few walls, the family's mode of life was changed; pathways through the house must be redirected, daily activities relocated, and disposal habits rethought. These changes called for more purposeful planning of activities, a more disciplined approach to household tasks, a more ordered organization of domestic time and space. They assigned a geographical space to people and events and helped accommodate the family to a social realignment that assigned a specific place to people as well. These improvements, not merely of house but of behavior and therefore social ambition, were indicated without by the whiteness of the walls.

These segmented, white houses appeared throughout New England, the Middle Atlantic, and the lower Chesapeake in regional but standardized forms. Architectural historian Fred Kniffen's interest extends from 1790 to 1850 and considers vernacular architecture only—mostly rural, middle- and lower-class houses.[4] His study, therefore, considers not the grand whitened mansions that dotted the landscape, but rather the imitative smaller houses that blanketed it. All classes of houses could be subject to the advice of architectural reformers, but the guidebooks agreed that one's class status demanded a specific style of home. And despite a lingering mythology of classlessness, qualifications for houses were explicit: "villas for the rich, cottages for the middle class, and farm houses for the laborers" (Clifford Clark 46). Middle-class respectability seeped into the architecture and emerged in the form of I-houses, a compromise between vernacular structures and Georgian architecture. Like the Georgian mansions of the eighteenth century, I-houses showed the bilateral symmetry with a central front door, usually one-room deep and two or more long, with a passage and stair fronting the entrance (Bushman 252). Viewed as a mark of "economic attainment" and of middle-class respectability, the I-house became a standard bearer of the clichèd white housefront throughout the country (Kniffen 16). Kniffen argues that although regional differences existed, all regions recognized the same version of respectability.[5]

James Fenimore Cooper marks the class-based distinction of whiteness in *The Pioneers* (1823), where he describes a frontier village caught between wilderness and civilization. Among the stretches of wilderness

MODEL COTTAGE.

Fig. 1.

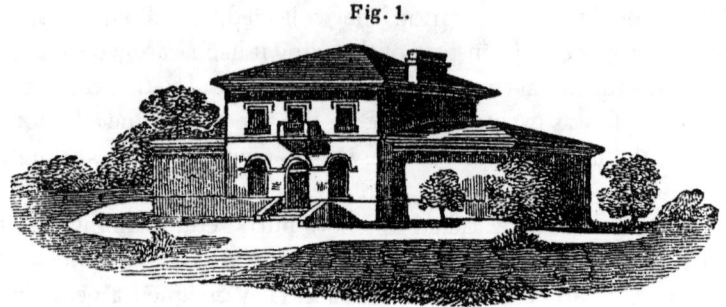

Godey's Magazine and Lady's Book, January 1850, pg. 411. Model cottage in Roman villa style. Designed for a middle-class household, it includes a central hall, symmetry, and white exterior.

in eastern New York can be seen occasional "spots of white"—clearings that reveal "the commencement of agriculture" which may grow into settlement (38). In town, some fifty buildings appear multi-colored from a distance—a few painted white on the front and rear, but more bearing "that expensive color on their fronts only, while their economical but ambitious owners had covered the remaining sides of the edifices, with a dingy red" (39). The front of houses receives the expensive whiteness before any other side; this color is intended for public viewing and public interpretation. Here Cooper iterates the ambition that can be marked by whiteness, even while combined with the cheaper red paint of a lower-class lack of means. In his fictional Templeton, the "better sort of buildings" are uniformly white, and fitted with green shutters (40).

Judge Templeton's mansion stands apart because of its awkward architecture less than its grandeur—its surrounding fruit trees and path leading from the gate to the front door. Templeton's house has a "composite order," made up of the ambitious misdirections of the town's architects and ultimately covered by an enormous painted roof. Scholars point to the house's architecture as an illustration of Cooper's vision of a unified society that can successfully combine many different ethnicities beneath the same superstructure.[6] Cooper's use of the term "composite," however, requires that the various elements co-exist separately. Using fictional architecture and dining ware, Cooper presents in *The Pioneers* a vision of an economically mobile society with potential to be ethnically united. The town, a reflection of the nation's possibilities, uses the material messages of white things to reinforce a strictly classed, raced, and gendered order: in Cooper's vision, black and white, lower and upper class, Native Americans and civilized Americans never do unify, but merely find their proper place together. Templeton's house demonstrates the Judge's ideal of unity—different traditions and viewpoints might be brought together under one roof. But Cooper does not believe in indiscriminate integration: the foundation of the house is separate from its structure. The harsher reality of Cooper's vision, illustrated and enforced by the novel's white things, allows co-existence for disparate groups only when all characters inhabit their proper place—in society, in the household, and at the dinner table.

In Judge Templeton's late eighteenth-century town, black slavery informs class distinctions only tangentially, but it colors the entire lower class. Non-slave servants to Templeton's household include Ben Pump, a former sailor whose fair complexion is "burnt to a fiery red"; Remarkable Pettibone, with a "saffron" face and yellow teeth, and "three or four subordinate menials, mostly black" (59–60). Judge Templeton's black slave is the first person to appear in the story, and he determines the course of the narrative both by his legal silence and by his exploitation by white men. Andrew Doolen writes of Cooper's treatment of this slave, Agamemnon, as an answer to contemporary discussions of the African colonization movement; the appearance of this slave and the free black man Freeborn demonstrate "an underlying current of racial violence that unsettles the formation of an ideal republic" (133). Neither black character has recourse to the law for protection, and therefore both become pawns in the struggle for social dominance between white men. Templeton society allows no agency for its black characters. Their blackness instead serves as an ideological threat to characters such as Natty Bumppo who refuse to participate in the capitalist economy.

Indeed, class-based whiteness will become a prerequisite for agency in the novel. Although the racially white servants insist on their distinction from the "black menials," they are aware of their economic and architectural nearness to them. Remarkable bristles when Benjamin suggests that Elizabeth Temple will be her new mistress— " 'don't make me out to be a nigger, Benjamin. She's no mistress of mine, and never will be' " (175). She then turns the racial insult back upon Benjamin, accusing him of belonging more to the kitchen than the "keeping-room of a house of one who is well to do in the world" (175). For his part, Benjamin allows that he might be a " 'black, beastly bear,' " but " 'dam'me if I'm a monkey' " (177). Nonetheless, the servants remain intermediate between the "niggers . . . stored snug below" in the basement and the mistress whom Remarkable has resentfully preceded to her mansion room to prepare it for the night (171). Natty Bumppo is a racial outsider—he lives in a cabin and a cave and battles against the free black man Freeborn for rights over a turkey at the turkey shoot. Like Freeborn, he depends upon others for his ability to gain things—he must take money from Elizabeth to shoot the turkey, and he depends upon a special dispensation from the Judge in order to hunt his woods. Natty's humiliation in the stocks becomes inevitable, though regrettable: since he has eluded a racial place in this civilizing town, he must be spectacularly assigned one.

Oliver Effingham is similarly excluded from social conversation—to the extent that Richard proposes he dine with the slaves in the cellar because he is suspected to have Indian blood—and he remains excluded until he demonstrates a mastery of white goods. Because his relationship to frontiersman Natty Bumppo, adopted father Chingachgook, and white grandfather Major Effingham all exert a claim on Judge Templeton's property, Jane Tompkins argues that his marriage to Elizabeth Temple "resolves . . . the competing claims of rival nations, families, and races" (108). However, I would argue that only the last, legal, white claim carries any weight in the novel. Cooper's depiction of a republican unity built upon many European nationalities is not the "composite order" represented by Judge Templeton's house: Effingham must demonstrate racial as well as class-based whiteness before this unifying marriage can take place. In the final scene of the novel, he reveals that he has razed his former cabin—once occupied by Oliver and Natty Bumppo—and in its place erected "a headstone of white marble" and a "rich monument, decorated with an urn, and ornamented with a chisel" (450). The larger monument is dedicated to Oliver's white grandfather, and includes a lengthy inscription that praises him as brave, religious, formerly wealthy, and Natty Bumppo's master. The second stone is briefly dedicated to Chingachgook, and it lists his several names. But as Oliver reads the inscription, Natty must correct Oliver's pronunciation of "Mohican," and the stone misspells Chingachgook (452). Oliver has become "white" by virtue of his parentage and inheritance of land and wealth; in this scene, he demonstrates his whiteness by a proper use of white things—the destruction of the uncivilized cabin and the dedication of a popular urn monument. In addition, he has begun forgetting a connection to his nonwhite parents, erasing even as he memorializes Chingachgook, and erecting a white monolith that excludes nonwhites from the "composite order."

"Serving the Dinner." Photograph by Frances Benjamin Johnston, 1899 or 1900. Table set at the Hampton Institute, Hampton, Virginia. Foreground shows a white tablecloth and white dishes, individual place settings. On the back cupboard are displayed pictured porcelain dishes. In the background, an African American woman in serving costume and a portrait of George Washington. Library of Congress, Prints and Photographs Division, LC-USZ62-117093.

The unity of the nation, in fact, depends upon its segregation, as Cooper demonstrates even in his description of a formal dinner including citizens of different European ethnicities. The Pioneers is set in 1793, although Cooper sets his fictional table accurately to reflect the current fashion in dining etiquette:

> The table-linen was of the most beautiful damask, and the plates and dishes of real china, an article of great luxury at this early period in American commerce. The knives and forks were of exquisitely polished steel, and were set in unclouded ivory . . . In the centre of the table, stood a pair of heavy silver castors, surrounded by four dishes [of various wild meats]. . . . Between these dishes and the turkeys, stood, on the one side, a prodigious chine of roasted bear's meat, and on the other a boiled leg of delicious mutton. Interspersed among this load of meats, was every species of vegetables that the season and country afforded. The four corners were garnished with plates of

> cake.... At each corner of the table, stood saucers, filled with ... 'sweet-meats.' At the side of each plate, which was placed bottom upwards,[7] with its knife and fork most accurately crossed above it, stood another, of smaller size, containing a motley-looking pie.... The object seemed to be profusion, and it was obtained entirely at the expense of order and elegance. (106–107)

The abundant and symmetrical food demonstrates the competence of this wealthy frontier household. The dishes of wild meat indicate both the wildness of the surroundings and the land's potential, but neither threatens the civilization and etiquette of the inhabitants. That Cooper describes every dish and diagrams its placement conveys the importance of such domestic skills to a proper household. The ivory-handled silverware, damask tablecloth, and china are the signifying white things that proclaim the household adept not only at providing food, but also at providing refinement. The properly placed dishes accord with contemporary (1830s) practice, the finest details of dinner-table management. Judge Templeton provides a "motley" feast to encourage his motley collection of guests, from various nationalities—but again, this order and refinement excludes the nonwhite servants and the black menials; and although the judge insists on including the dubiously raced Effingham, the reader does not see him seated. Indeed, this table setting is the ceramic parallel to Judge Templeton's composite house and the "motley" appearance of the town itself. Though Templeton would idealistically incorporate different European nationalities into his construction of a unified American republic, and though he would celebrate the ambition of the lower classes earning wealth and social status, the novel still segregates class and race along definite lines.

The dinner table is symmetrically arranged with everything in its place despite the alleged lack of "order and elegance." Even the "motley-looking" pies, artistically arranged at each plate, are "composed of triangular slices of apple, mince, pumpkin, craneberry [sic], and *custard, so arranged as to form an entire whole*" (108, italics in text). Profusion may even sacrifice order, but never segregation: the pies construct a unified whole despite their disparate parts, but the parts remain distinct. Indeed, part of the point may be that the pies would be much less palatable if blended together. Thus Judge Templeton's house remains more a joke than a serious symbol of American republicanism: the roof undergoes successive coats of paint in attempts to unify the aggregate elements beneath it—and each is as aesthetically startling as it is unsuccessful.

THE GREAT WALL OF CHINA

Cooper's use of table settings as well as architecture and house paint reveals his understanding of and endorsement of the classed messages delivered by ceramics in the early nineteenth century. In antebellum society, not only the price of wares, but the style and specialization indicated gradations in social status. In 1828, an etiquette book dictated that " 'a household should have a dinner service of china for company, a dinner service for ordinary use, and a third service for the kitchen' "—so that servants' and employers' dishes remained visually and physically segregated (qtd. in De Cunzo 60). By the second quarter of the nineteenth century, as pearlware and whiteware were developed, "creamware had lost its association with high-style vessel forms, was lower priced, frequently produced in more mundane forms (as common and unadorned chamber pots), and dominated the ceramic assemblages left by urban households of low to middle status" (Yentsch, "Engendering" 132). Therefore, by 1840, Miss Leslie's etiquette book recommends the outdated creamware for the kitchen workers (qtd. in De Cunzo 60). The yellowware of the lower-class dish corresponds to the lower-class complexion of Remarkable Pettibone, with her "saffron" face and yellow teeth.

As ceramics became more important to the meal, the decorations grew to overtake the entire body of the dish, highlighted by their white background. Class was yet communicated by the decorations, as more elaborate designs were found on the finer china. In the first stage—the late eighteenth century—dishes were plain, with molded decorations confined to the rims (Wall 147). From the turn of the century until the mid-nineteenth century, decorations on vessels increased. In the early nineteenth century, families used shell-edged vessels trimmed in blue or green. Finally, as focus shifted away from the food, decoration covered the entire vessel, most commonly with a willow pattern or Chinese landscape prints.[8] At that point, decoration served more to indicate class status (G. Miller, "Classification"). Cost of ceramics ranged from undecorated cream-colored ware, which was least expensive; to vessels with minimal decoration, such as shell-edged, banded, or stamped; to hand-painted floral decorations; to transfer-painted willow patterns or Chinese landscapes; and finally to porcelain as the most expensive (McBride and McBride 148–149). Over time and across class, ceramic price increased with its role in organizing a meal: Wall shows that families were willing to spend "ever-increasing amounts of money on the dishes that they used at family meals" (Wall, *Archaeology* 144). The whiter the dish and the more ornate its design, the more organized and specialized the meal, and the higher the exhibited class of the family.

As these ceramics soliloquized from the table, the table itself became a stage. A presentation of meals emphasizing dishware became part of the code of dining room propriety. While eighteenth-century diners concentrated on a mere abundance of food to show status, the turn-of-the-century focus became the "balanced and symmetrical arrangement" of food on the table (Wall, *Archaeology* 117–118). Nineteenth-century cookbooks and etiquette books often diagrammed the proper arrangement of the food on the table, stressing symmetry and order. Later, the focus shifted somewhat away from food: the table had a centerpiece, possibly a caster or salad, or even flowers. Food was still visible and set symmetrically around the table "on the diagonal or 'cross corners,'" as prescribed (Wall, *Archaeology* 119).

By the 1820s, family dinners as well as formal dinner parties were specialized, including at least two courses and more specific foods for each course. At this time, meals were also segregated for servants: whereas in the late eighteenth century, the servants ate with the family, by the mid-nineteenth century they ate separately and served only the less important courses.[9] Eventually, the meal was presented under covered dishes, so that the tableware was the focus of the table (Wall, *Archaeology* 148). At the height of the whitening trend, table settings assumed the appearance that the ceramics, rather than the servants, were providing food for the diners. In this way, the white china—which beamed at its economically successful family—could also ignore the darker hands that set it.

The etiquette built around salad forks and soup spoons exalted stricter body control and ideals of individuality. Each diner ate from a separate plate; his or her motions were more constricted so as not to intrude into the next diner's space. With individualized plates, such rules as not wiping one's mouth on the tablecloth, not reaching across another's plate, not returning chewed food to one's plate—in effect, keeping one's body and its functions to oneself—became popular. Diners further dissociated themselves from the animal act of eating by use of the fork, becoming widespread in the nineteenth century. Thus we understand why Cooper points out Natty Bumppo's use of a "broken fork," connecting him, but only tenuously, to civilization (*Last of the Mohicans* 51). Such rules had been elaborated and made more stringent since the Renaissance, according to Norbert Elias; Deetz finds that Renaissance ideas and practices only caught up to the American colonies in the last half of the eighteenth century (Elias, *The Civilizing Process*; Deetz, *Small Things*). Specialized tableware and industrialization landed in the country at the same time. Each helped to perpetuate the other, and each fostered an ideal of individual bodily control.

Racial whiteness required such specialization and self-discipline and became its own reward in the form of white, refined goods. Skill in handling sets of dishes and in managing subdivided houses and yards earned admittance into the closed class of "white" folks. For the upper class, this skill showcased a civilized refinement; but for the working classes, it also helped to accommodate them towards the special rigors of industrialized labor and the increasing distance it created between rich and poor. The availability of manufactured prestige dishes for the working class was both gift and curse: while resembling the privileged goods of the upper classes, dishes became a source for conditioning individual responsibility, strict control of movements, delayed gratification of desires, reverence for material things—all the qualities of a good capitalist worker. Among those included in industrialization's overview, however, these changing, whitening goods boasted and benefited the factory labor that helped to produce them. While mass production made ever-whiter dishes in their increasingly specialized sets more available to middle and lower classes, it also contributed to the creation of a permanent unskilled working class and demanded a specialization of labor separating the worker from his product. While the ebbing popularity of the term "master" among Northern whites signaled a denial of slavery or slavery conditions, it also marked the disappearance of that class of skilled "master" craftsmen of the century before. And while the term "hand" replaced the racially charged "servant," it also manifested the changing duties of an industrial worker, where the disembodied hands that operated specialized machinery were the valued part of the worker.

Assuming that "a person who left an assemblage of nothing but 10-in. plates ate—and thought—differently than someone who left an assemblage representing equal numbers of 6-, 7-, 8-, 9-, 10-, and 12-in. plates," Parker B. Potter sees in the spread of segmented ceramics a subtle and accepted coercion on the part of the ruling class (122). As lower classes acquired the less expensive dishes in sets—outdated creamware, for example, as recommended by Miss Leslie—they also began to imitate the regularized body control demanded by the dishes' proper use. The control demanded by the complicated rules of soup spoons and salad forks, in turn, helped accommodate a body to the specific and repetitive motions of factory work (Shackel, *Personal Discipline*; Leone, "Georgian Order"). The creamware plate that dominated the market at the end of the eighteenth century imitated expensive porcelain but was made affordable through mass production. Rather than convey the status it aspired to, however, "the mark that that plate bears most clearly is the mark of the regulated, standardized, segmented—and alienated—labor that went into its manufacture" (Potter 120).

The rise of industrialism required new manners in the workplace, as "masters" were replaced by morally distant "bosses," as alcohol came to be excluded from the workplace, and as workers were separated into stations rather than producing goods communally. As a steady presence in the home, the whitened plates helped to naturalize factory demands: "[a] worker taught at home to see standardization and segmentation as the way in which the world naturally works may have been more likely to see such organization in the workplace as appropriate" (Potter 121). Furthermore, the standardized behavior produced more predictable workers, decreasing the need for supervision. Such habits, designed to make a worker "punctual and self-disciplined," were "largely absorbed by 1830 and completely absorbed by 1860" (Leone 247).

These accommodations to self-control and repetitive, regularized movements were able to translate to the marketplace, therefore, as a work-discipline that promised economic success. For women excluded from most professions, factory labor offered a similar promise; but by mid-century, women were largely excluded from "direct participation in the industrial process" as well (Shackel and Larsen 22). Instead, the proper feminine participation in economic mobility centered within the household, as a site for training male workers and a place of preparation for the women. The feminine relationship to material things consisted in having them but appearing not to desire them, and an inability to earn them. Such a disavowal of material ambition was accomplished through the sanctification of household labor, which offered to transfer the woman's work to a spiritual realm. Jane Tompkins argues that domestic labor was presented to women as a spiritual exercise, "not a household task, but a religious ceremony" and "a strategy for survival" (169). By bestowing sacred significance on the drudgery of housekeeping, the housekeeper could work without seeming to labor. Spiritual or sentimental attachment in place of overt ambition rescued the "feminine" from a determined classed position in the marketplace; her role instead was as steward of her family's goods and ambitions.

Such an economic exercise inhered specifically in the tea ritual, partaking most acutely in display of fine white china and tabletop etiquette. When Jane Tompkins designs housework as a "religious ceremony," she focuses her comment on an introductory scene of tea-making in Susan Warner's TheWideWideWorld (1850). In the scene, Ellen Montgomery labors to make her mother's tea perfect, with bread sliced the proper thickness, and toasted to the proper shade of brown, as a way of coping with economic stress. On the other hand, Ann Douglas finds Ellen to be pampered and "[a]ristocratic," with skills that are "curiously ornamental rather than functional" (75). The two scholars' disagreement revolves around this simple ceremony. Douglas believes that Warner's privileging tea-making over shopping shows a sentimental divestment of women's role in the marketplace. Therefore, she concludes that sentimental novelists accepted the confinement of domesticity in exchange for a nostalgic and ultimately useless sanctity. Both scholars view tea-making as anti-materialist; I would argue that domestic discipline was itself seen as an economic activity. In my view, the proper tea ceremony is an elegantly furnished boot camp, set in an exclusively feminine environment, for basic training in domestic economics, bodily discipline and etiquette, social display, time management, and the unification of the family: in short, white middle-class womanhood. In fiction, the tea scene is an analog to the middle-class white woman's home life. It posits her life as a series of female family or social gatherings continually intruded upon and disrupted by men, and therefore requiring re-application of self-discipline, self-denial, and economic organization in order to keep the household intact. Her management of "tea" plays out such self-mastery, and therefore is a barometer of her feminine success. In American sentimental literature of the nineteenth century, the tea scene establishes a feminine world apart from, but responsive to, the economic struggles of the marketplace.

The ceramic settings and silver equipage of the tea-time ritual were instrumental in determining individuality, social rank, and etiquette in the early nineteenth century. The ritual was at once the most social and the most insulated of family events; "tea" became a concentrated version of the overall dining ritual. Offering tea was a mark of hospitality to visitors, while highly stylized social teas granted an opportunity to display manners and expensive settings. A tourist noted in 1795 that " 'the whole family is united at tea, to which friends, acquaintances, and even strangers are invited' " (qtd. in Roth 444). As a family affair, tea-making was seen as the "most feminine and domestic of all occupations."[10] It was a forum for imparting the regularized discipline imbedded in the proper handling of ceramic sets, and for reinforcing a feminine domestic economy. In 1781, Abbé Robin remarked that " 'there is not a single person to be found, who does not drink [tea] out of china cups and saucers' " (qtd. in Roth 451). Yentsch explains that the tea ceremony gained popularity in the late seventeenth century as a "prestigious masculine beverage," but "became a focal point in women's lives by ca. 1740" ("Symbolic" 224, 223). The "ritual use of food involved men as individuals," Yentsch argues, "and women as mothers, wives, and daughters, but not as individuals in their own right." By the turn of the nineteenth century, tea "did become feminized," although it continued to carry its other inherited meanings (224).

Drawing upon the ceramic message of sanctified labor and physical purity, tea scenes teach a feminine economics that can smooth over class distinctions and conquer poverty. The scene of Ellen's tea making in *The Wide Wide World* falls purposefully before her unsuccessful shopping excursion and immediately after Ellen learns that her father's failed lawsuit will force her to part with her mother. The juxtaposition is important. The bread-winner cannot provide for his family; the dependent females respond with a tea ceremony whose every movement and measurement is carefully disciplined. Indeed, as Tompkins argues, Ellen's tea is a way of coping; Ellen asserts her affection for her mother and her devotion to higher duties when she prepares the tea and toast. Tea-making is also, however, a preliminary exercise in self-control for Ellen. Later she and her mother will shop with money supplied by a grandmother's pawned ring. Such a sacrifice enables Mrs. Montgomery to buy the luxuries "which she thought important to [Ellen's] comfort and improvement" (29). The women in the household practice independently the work-discipline that should produce a successful capitalist, and they provide the luxury and comfort that should inspire the worker towards spiritual and economic improvement. On the night that Ellen discovers her father's economic failure, however, she fails to complete the tea ceremony: the kettle boils for over an hour, and she drops the toast into the ashes (14–15). The young Ellen cannot respond properly yet to the patriarch's failed discipline, though she tries. Her mother, however, demonstrates feminine economy by providing money and luxury despite the shortness of means.

In Caroline Kirkland's *A New Home, Who'll Follow?* (1839), the narrator measures class status—for lack of sufficient material clues on the frontier in Michigan—by the quality of the tea ceremony. Her progression westward takes her away from the benefits of class and segregation. She describes the first cabin she sleeps in during her voyage as "a log-house of diminutive size, with corresponding appurtenances" (8). Her hostess boasts of the house's "private like" sleeping area, which consists of a six-foot wide room fully occupied by three beds, and an attic loft strewn with beds and partitioned by "[s]undry old quilts . . . fastened by forks to the rafters" (9). At this house, the women place their comb on the same shelf as the spoons and scatter "loose hairs on the floor with a coolness that [makes her] shudder" when she thinks of her dinner (14). Despite these insults to etiquette, the women spread a large dinner, serve the laboring men of the household, and later set the table for a strictly feminine tea. Though wary before, the narrator looks forward to this "more lady-like meal" (15). The settings are placed before the laboring men during dinner; but they become lady-like when segregated into a tea for women. In a novel describing the trials of frontier life, the narrator sobs only once: when she misses this tea.

Class does not necessarily coincide with refinement and wealth, however, if feminine discipline is lacking. At a rare house occupied by an educated and upper-class woman, Mrs. Clavers immediately detects "that the hand of refined taste had been there" (74). Here, a "smooth-shaven lawn," "beds of flowers of every hue," and "white-washed log-walls" mark the house as distinguished, making the society-schooled narrator immediately blush over her own "inky stockings" (74). The family's insistence on class markers has alienated neighbors, however, and these are the only folk available to bolster their upper-class image by laboring for them. Without servants, the undisciplined aristocrats cannot manage their house. The floors are an unwashed yellow, even though "a great box filled with sand stood near the hearth" as cleanser; dirty dogs lie nearby, and a man composed of "[p]ride and passion," "reckless self-indulgence," and dirty fingernails glowers in a rocking-chair (75). In spite of the house's vestigial luxuries, Mrs. Clavers observes a lack of household efficiency and a consequent decline in manners. Neither wife nor husband practices the work-discipline preached, and thus "Mrs. B——" swoons at a slight alarm and "Mr. B——" is recklessly self-indulgent, so that neither is economically productive. At the end of their visit, the narrator encapsulates her anecdote by gravely remarking, "We were not invited to remain to tea" (76).

Maria Susanna Cummins's *The Lamplighter* (1854) followed *The Wide Wide World* as a mid-century bestseller, but even more than a female spiritual bildungsroman, the former is an account of feminine training in how to become upwardly mobile. For Gerty, tea-making becomes part of the process in feminine success, training and demonstration of an evolving domestic discipline that will move her from her early squalor to an ultimate middle-class home. Gerty begins the novel as the orphan charge of Nan Grant, who feels the child to be "a dead weight upon her hands" and scolds, beats, and starves the girl regularly (8). Because she lives uncared-for in a "dark, and unwholesome-looking house," "scantily clad" as well as "uncombed and unbecoming," Gerty has not learned to suppress her anger or control her violent fits (5). Gerty is "unbecoming" in several ways: she has no economic potential because she has not been taught to have, want, or use refined goods. Through a succession of tutors, Gerty must learn to participate in the marketplace enough to care for things, to use them properly, to desire wealth, and finally, to disavow that desire. Only then can she enjoy or even obtain a feminine position within a household, or be a maker of a home. Cummins presents this education as a literal enlightenment, as a clearing away of darker negative things and an organization of the remainder in order to create the space, or potential, for social success.

The novel begins by explaining Gerty's deprivation, which includes not only love and care, but also light and space: the first line is, "It was growing dark in the city" (5). In Gerty's neighborhood, the darkness comes unnaturally early; in the "narrow streets and dark lanes" where the "poor are crowded together," even the snow that makes "everything look bright and clean in the pleasant open squares, near which the fine houses were built" loses "all its purity" (5). Gerty lives in a "low-roofed, dark, and unwholesome-looking house," and Nan Grant often locks her in the "dark garret (Gerty hated and feared the dark)" (8). Cummins quickly equates the darkness and closeness of the novel with moral disorder, asking for "man or angel to light up the darkness within" and rendering Trueman Flint, the lamplighter, such an angel as he begins Gerty's process of enlightenment (9). But the light is also classed: the darkness belongs to lower-class houses and habits.

Part of her darkness comes from idleness. Nan Grant does not send her to school or give her any chores except for fetching milk, and Gerty "had nothing to do at all, and had never known the satisfaction of *helping* anybody"; she "was always idle" (14, italics in text). Before she can learn economic usefulness, however, she must learn proper feminine usefulness—Nan Grant is a poor role model who takes in boarders, supports a lazy full-grown son, and looks upon Gerty as a useless commodity. Gerty's first lesson, therefore, is in sentiment: when True gives her a kitten, she must learn how to love and protect it. Gerty has wished for a pair of shoes, but fulfillment of a practical need would not help to prepare her for life in the same way: her need for feminine sentiment overrides her mere physical needs.

After True takes Gerty to live in his small apartment with him, Gerty receives her second lesson in feminine economy. This lesson combines cleanliness, tea-making, and filial devotion. Mrs. Sullivan, the gentle neighbor, decides to subject True's messy apartment "to female intrusion" by straightening it (32). Helping Mrs. Sullivan clean and organize the rooms gives Gerty her first taste of "*that* happiness—perhaps the highest earth affords—of feeling that she had been instrumental in giving joy to another" (36, italics in text). Thus happiness arrives with discipline and self-denial. Drawing on her homemaking instincts, Mrs. Sullivan arranges the room so as to make "a parlour of it" and thereby conjure refinement from the tiny working-class space (37). Whereas True has cluttered up his apartment "to such an extent that one almost needed a pilot to conduct him safely through" it, Mrs. Sullivan, a model of feminine success within the limits of poverty, with a "dress almost quaker-like in its extreme simplicity, and freedom from the least speck or stain," manages to "clear up and put to right" the room so efficiently that True believes half his furniture has been removed (33). For Mrs. Sullivan, "cleanliness and order" are "the cause of virtue and happiness, so completely did she identify outward neatness and purity with inward peace" (33). Gerty participates in the renovation in order to learn such organization—the clearing away of clutter that precedes economic success. True has gained through this feminine industry more than half the space of his apartments, and a subdivided bedroom and parlor—a material gain wrought in the cause of spiritual improvement.

For the next step in the operation, Mrs. Sullivan gives Gerty "careful instructions" on how to "set the table and toast the bread for supper" (37). The teacups and saucers have been placed, for this purpose, in "regular rows" along the lower shelf, so Gerty can reach them (37). After this ceremony, Gerty resolves to conquer her temper and appeal to God as a continuation of her love for True. When Gerty has demonstrated that she can use the ceramics properly, taking care of the things themselves and also managing the tea-time ritual for True's comfort and training, she receives her own white thing: "one of those white plaster images, so familiar to every one, representing the little Samuel in an attitude of devotion" (39). It is, perhaps, Gerty's diploma marking the extent of

True's tutelage: it is significant that he obtains this present from a "furren" boy, who offers him a choice of black or white statues as thanks when True has helped him collect them (40). Although True is kind to the foreign boy, the stranger remains excluded from the group because of his odd manners and unintelligible language. His foreignness highlights Gerty's own whiteness, and the white statue marks her social potential. Willie warns her to "'take care and not break it,'" transferring the early lesson in caring for a kitten to an inanimate object and linking economic use of a thing with the thing's pious message (41).

When Gerty has learned to use things properly, she still must be taught ambition: she can improve economically only when she begins to desire better circumstances than True has provided her. Willie, her future husband, arouses such desire when he takes her "window-shopping," looking in the windows of fine houses and imagining themselves within. One night she and Willie follow True as he lights lamps, and Willie shows her an elegant family tea through a mansion window:

> Rich carpets, deeply-tinted curtains, pictures in gilded frames, and huge mirrors, reflecting the whole on every side, gave Gerty her first impressions of luxurious life. There was an air of comfort combined with all this elegance, which made it still more fascinating to the child of poverty and want. A table was bountifully spread for tea; the cloth of snow-white damask, the shining plate, above all, the home-like hissing tea-kettle, had a most inviting look. A gentleman in gay slippers was in an easy-chair by the fire; a lady in a gay cap was superintending a servant-girl's arrangements at the tea-table, and the children of the household, smiling and happy, were crowded together on a window-seat. (57)

The window scene outlines social evolution for Gerty: the luxury marks the range from Nan Grant's squalor, through Mrs. Sullivan's efficient coziness, to a pinnacle of comfort involving snow-white damask and shining silver. The light and the whiteness of the place attract her: she renounces her former poverty with the exclamation, "'I hate old, dark, black places,'" and her ambition ever after will be to escape the blackness or rearrange it to make space for refinement. Everyone inside the fine house is "smiling and happy." In contrast to Gerty's odd face, the eldest girl necessarily has "fair hair . . . in long ringlets over a neck as white as snow," blue eyes, and "a cherub face" (57–58). Gerty's ability to possess white things has been marked by an encounter with, a tribute from, and the exclusion of a distinctly foreign person. Her ability to desire is marked by an abnegation of the dark and the black. The fine house's comfort also excludes manual labor: the father rests in an easy chair while Gerty's guardian lights lanterns on the street. More importantly, the mistress supervises a servant rather than sets the tea herself. Furthermore, as a social tea and its elaborate etiquette presume a discerning audience, the rich children are comfortable on display. When True lights a nearby lamp and Gerty becomes visible to them, however, she cannot stand the scrutiny and runs away. Nevertheless, her career of increasing discipline is fixed as she breathes to Willie, " '[A]n't it splendid?' " (58).

In this scene, Gerty learns how to desire fine things; but in order to become femininely successful, she must also learn how to disavow that desire. Her social education is completed in a trial with the housekeeper, which concludes in "the first instance of complete self-control in Gerty, and the last we shall have occasion to dwell upon": scarcely 150 pages into a 500-page novel, Gerty's economic education is complete. Mrs. Ellis, the main housekeeper at Gerty's new home (she has become the ward of Emily after True's death), resents Gerty's intrusion, and one afternoon takes revenge by throwing away all of Gerty's sentimental treasures. These things include the figure of Samuel, True's clay pipes, his lantern and hat, some toys and books, and "a few other trifles" (141). When Gerty learns that Mrs. Ellis has spitefully burned them, she hides herself before crying, and though she repeatedly begins to exact revenge or to tell Emily of the housekeeper's offense, Gerty ultimately does not mention the incident. Her success has come from her learned ability to treasure things, and her ability also to attach less importance to them than to her own self-control. Only after this triumph can she be ready to exchange her initial "low-roofed, dark, and unwholesome-looking house." While her final home is not a mansion, she begins her own family with Willie in a "well-lit, warm and pleasantly-furnished parlour" in their "own home" (507).

THE NICK OF TIME

The discipline produced by creamware dish sets also manufactured them; a large part of using white things properly involved using them at the proper time and employing them with the most efficient use of time. Dinnertime work-discipline was paired with time-discipline, and etiquette books emphasized a strict use of time as well as of forks and napkins. Lydia Maria Child begins her 1830 *The Frugal Housewife*, for "People of

Moderate Fortune," advising, "The true economy of housekeeping is simply the art of gathering up all the fragments, so that nothing be lost. I mean fragments of *time*, as well as of *materials*" (3, italics in text). As important as "a few shillings saved," she insists, is for all to be "kept out of idleness" (3). Similarly, Catharine Beecher includes in her 1841 *Treatise on Domestic Economy* a chapter on table manners, which rehearses prohibitions against reaching, eating noisily, and using the tablecloth for a napkin. In another chapter, "On Habits of System and Order," she explains the most necessary skills to a housekeeper, the "right *apportionment of time to different pursuits*" (145, italics in text). The use of italics by both authors shows an insistence on this aspect of organization: time-discipline must be emphasized as a novel virtue in industrial America. Moreover, "*systematic and regular*" use of time is demanded of the successful housekeeper as well as the successful business manager (151, italics in text). Beecher suggests allotting a day for each activity, if not certain hours of the day, according to the ranking of the activity; and "mere gratification of the appetite is to be placed *last* in our estimate" (146).

Special awareness of time appears in the gravestones at the same time. As opposed to the birth and death dates popular later, early nineteenth-century gravestones often carry a death date along with the deceased's exact age, in years, months, and days. Such a precise figuring of the loved one's lifetime recalls the role age plays in Frederick Douglass's critique of slavery. He begins *Narrative of the Life* establishing the access to time as part of "an inflexible barrier of meaning" (Gates 87). His first paragraph is a series of unknowns—he knows *where* he was born, but is ignorant of dates. Henry Louis Gates, Jr., glosses this ignorance as an oppositional definition: "The knowledge the slave has of his circumstances he must deduce from the *earth*; a quantity such as time, our understanding of which is *cultural* and not *natural*, derives from a nonmaterial source, let us say the *heavens*: 'The white children [Douglass writes] could tell their ages. I could not'" (87, italics in text). Slaves become those who cannot tell time, and therefore their grouping with horses and cattle could be rationalized as natural.

If the mastery of calendar time marks differences between slaves and masters, the mastery of expensive and more esoteric measurement marked differences between finer gradations of class. In the first half of the eighteenth century, Mark P. Leone argues, the upper class used "clocks, scientific instruments, and musical instruments ... to show that newly aggregated wealth was legitimate because its possessors understood natural law through direct observation, which justified both hierarchy and individualism" (240). Those who mastered time, measurement, and mechanics through these difficult-to-obtain goods thereby justified their mastery of lower classes. Cooper reflects this class justification in *The Pioneers*, when the Judge furnishes his hall with "a heavy, old-fashioned, brass-faced clock," a "Fahrenheit's thermometer," and a barometer, which is "consulted, every half-hour, with prodigious exactitude" (61–62). Here, the Judge publicly displays his control over time and the elements and a regulated behavior towards these instruments, which explains his means to both city and frontier wealth.

Wage labor and industrial production contributed to the equation of time and money, but it valued everybody's time exactly and rendered time itself the main commodity. The attendance to time by factory workers was more than a claim for power and freedom; it was a careful accounting and use of their main economic asset. As argued by E. P. Thompson in his important article, "Time, Work Discipline, and Industrial Capitalism," the widespread use of watches in the nineteenth century helped to internalize a minutely structured sense of time and produced the work-discipline crucial to industrial labor. While not a white thing itself, time discipline regulated the use of white things—in fact inhered in them specifically. A complete set of china would be rotated according to time of day; guidebooks explained and diagrammed specific placement of dishes for breakfast, lunch, dinner, supper, tea time—even brunch. Women's clothing, ideally figured as white, was also styled according to time of day, as well as location and occasion.

In "Devil in the Belfry," Edgar Allan Poe imagines time as a product divorced from its uses, as a thing that can be kept, spent, and wasted according to contemporary notions.[11] His description of the town's seven clocks—"[I]ts faces are large and white, and its hands heavy and black"—is not accidental (739). The factory that exploited the clock depended upon these distinctions between white faces and black hands. Ralph Waldo Emerson laments industry's division of labor by parodying its use of a "hand," describing people as embodied body parts, "so many walking monsters—a good finger, a neck, a stomach, an elbow, but never a man" (64). In Poe's "A Predicament," the hand of a clock literally beheads the heroine, rendering her a disembodied head and a headless body. The body has the final voice as Signora Psyche Zenobia decides to die, because the body cannot retain possession of its things: "[d]ogless, niggerless, headless," nothing remains for her (353). Fanny Fern points to the time-discipline of mill girls as an obstacle to their enjoying nearby refinements, declaring that "[t]hey might as well be machines, for any interest or curiosity they show, save always to know *what o'clock it is*" (qtd. in Tichi 159). It is time that creates these hands, time that they sell, and time that keeps them in the underclasses. In claiming such time by constantly watching the clock, workers also lay claim to their own servitude, granting power to the clock for both their work and their freedom from work.

Poe's villagers in "The Devil in the Belfry" are appropriately round-faced, as they are the ones who read the clock; the devil, dark-skinned and clad all in black, resembles a hand—either of the clock or of the factory. Moreover, the devil evokes "righteous indignation" because of his neglect of "such a thing as *keeping time in his steps*" (740; italics in text). The village, set in an imaginary Dutch borough, is the picture of factory efficiency. Landscaped in the image of a clock, sixty houses sit in a circle and point towards the central green: like Boott Mills, they face the central concern of the town—in this case, the clock tower. The houses themselves "are so precisely alike, that one can in no manner be distinguished from another" (737). Each house has its own small garden, growing strictly cabbages. Standardization reigns even in reproductive matters: to each house belong three boys, "each two feet in height" (738). As in the Boott Cotton Mills, class distinctions are perfectly discernible in this society—the highest class of gentlemen has the longest coat-tails and the most chins.

All citizens carry watches. Even the household pets sport timepieces, unwillingly, tied to their tales. Keeping time is the sole occupation of the villagers—they neither use it nor spend it well, but rather monitor it and hoard it. The stasis of the village is the result of such a strict time consciousness, a factory-work ethos with its perfect standardization and regularized behavior. Poe's critique is directed not at industry but at both the lower-class and the upper-class workers: one's *keeping* time is evidence of one's slavery to time. The villagers are perfectly obedient to their main clock, which demands not only hourly obeisance, but also attempts to Americanize them, as it calls out the time for each hour: "'One!' said the clock. 'Von!' echoed every little old gentleman in every leather-bottomed chair in Vondervotteimittiss" (741).

The devil who disrupts such organization has a "countenance . . . of a dark snuff-color, and he had a long hooked nose, pea eyes, a wide mouth, and an excellent set of teeth" (740). He wears "a tight-fitting swallow-tailed black coat . . . black kerseymore knee-breeches, black stockings, and stumpy-looking pumps, with huge bunches of black satin ribbon for bows" (740). He carries a fiddle—instrument of slaves and poor whites—grins, and capers about, resisting "such a thing as *keeping time* in his steps" (740). Chaos erupts as this "very diminutive foreign-looking man" enters town, beats the timekeeper of the tower, and makes the clock strike "thirteen." His face and his grin are "sinister," as he threatens to and succeeds in destroying the perfectly regulated community. Poe's intentions in handing the devil victory are unclear: the narrator calls "all lovers of correct time" to rise against his disruptions, but the villagers themselves have been contented slaves of time. In fact, their response to the clock's strike "Thirteen!" reveals their utter reliance on the clock: men, women, and boys react with horror thinking that they have lost an entire hour.

The villagers and the devil, as they together form a sort of clock face, represent the threat of stagnation and the threat of violence, respectively. With his snuff-colored face and black suit of clothes, the devil remains indeterminately raced: he is dark like a clock hand, or like an African American slave, or like a lower-class worker. Alternately, he is an ambiguous embodiment of all these, resembling a blackface minstrel who introduces chaos into the staid order of the working community. The devil, like a minstrel, represents the wildness that has been abandoned for factory discipline and siphoned onto an imaginary slave, who may be possessed by the donning of a black mask. As such, his violence mimics the riots staged in Philadelphia, Poe's home during part of the 1830s and 1840s. "The Devil in the Belfry" was published in Philadelphia in 1839, and that town was the locus of marked interracial tension during Poe's stays. One of the worst riots in Philadelphia occurred in May 1838 and targeted the second Anti-Slavery Convention of American Women, but destroyed a black church, a black orphanage, and the hall holding the convention (Lemire 177). In 1834, a race riot occurred between working-class whites and the "interracial clientele" of a tavern (Roediger, *Wages* 103). A few miles down the road in Columbia, Pennsylvania, another race riot prompted workers to decide on "the complete removal of Blacks." Between 1829 and 1841 in Philadelphia, at least nine other race riots occurred. At the same time, blackface was a popular pastime in the town, and in the 1830s it was the "'most common disguise' in the festival maskings" at Christmas (Roediger, *Wages* 103; 105). Often these disguises were used in attacks on blacks as well, as in the 1834 and 1840 riots associated with Christmas celebrations. Roediger observes, however, that mobs of blackfaced working-class men "often went to elite places of entertainment and sometimes attacked municipal watchmen—to mock the respectable, middle class, orderly and wealthy" (106).

The standardized, oppressive order of Poe's fictional town brings most readers to welcome such variety as a fiddle-wielding foreigner, and the violence he does the belfry watchman seems spirited exercise rather than malice. The rioting workers of Philadelphia saw a connection between attacking municipal watchmen, impersonating blacks, and attacking blacks. Poe paints his devil as indeterminately raced, although Poe has him playing the Irish songs " 'Judy O'Flannagan and Paddy O'Rafferty,'" emphasizing the Irish folk music which comprised much of minstrelsy's songs and the Irish immigrant majority among minstrelsy audiences and actors (742). The devil is not a black man, but rather imaginary blackness embodied: the blackness that threatens workers who might be tempted to abandon the time-discipline regulating a factory. Also, he represents the personified blackness that threatens contentedly working whites who oppress the lower classes and slaves. For this reason, the villagers are painted as German: their victimization can remain humorous because they are not Americans, even though the reader cannot tell who exactly represents the greatest threat. Poe seems equally unsympathetic to the villagers' initial contentment and their final despair, as the resurfacing blackness destroys their master, clock time, but also reveals their purposelessness without it. The riotous undiscipline of the black foreigner intrudes upon the order of the village. But that order has only been produced by the expulsion of the "devil" elements of society and the consequent erasure of any lingering traces, so that Vondervotteimittis seems to have been the same since time immemorial. The village only becomes interesting when the unpredictable black hand joins the round white faces of the clock-watchers—but interesting is also painful.

THE WHITENESS OF THE WAIL

Propaganda and design for nineteenth-century factories celebrated the order and discipline of a factory-manufactured life. When the Boott Cotton Mills in Lowell, Massachusetts, opened in 1835, its landscape and housing were designed to afford all the benefits of a middle-class country home, while controlling " 'the total living environment for labor' " (Mrozowski and Beaudry 193). The structure of boardinghouses and overseers' houses provided a model of moral supervision and "corporate paternalism" for the mill girls (195). The carefully planned town provided "row upon row" of housing for operatives, but also gardens for the nicer yards that passing workers could enjoy (194). Landscape designers placed trees and grass throughout the grounds to "temper the urban landscape" (196). Individual boardinghouses had backyard lawns, weak imitations of higher-class gardens, where the young women could perform everyday housekeeping chores. Advertisements and landscape paintings displayed large white buildings bordered by immaculate streets and grassy courts, whose focal point "was not the church or the town square but the industrial complex that was the reason for [their] existence."[12] Overall, Boott Mills tried to duplicate for its workers all the refining benefits of a middle-class home: besides these garden promenades, they offered free or discounted lectures, library use, and mandatory Sunday school. It was not the fault of the corporate planners if the mill girls, as some complained, could not take advantage of these refinements because of exhaustion and lack of time (Tichi 170–174).

In a late-century reminiscence of her factory-working childhood, Harriet Hanson Robinson outlines the classes of laborers. The highest class, the agents "lived in large houses . . . surrounded by beautiful gardens" and a "sometimes open gate in the high fence" (14). The second class, the overseers, lived in "the end-tenements of the blocks, the short connected rows of houses in which the operatives were boarded," much as Southern overseers lived at the head of rows of slave cabins (14). The third class, operatives, were the lowest class in the factory, "men" or "girls" who performed the most repetitive, mechanical tasks. But Robinson also briefly mentions a fourth class, not included in the factory scheme because they labored with the "spade and the shovel" outside its machinery. Likewise, their housing resided outside the deliberate order of the factory setting; they lived not in rows but "clustered around a small stone Catholic Church," in "hundreds of little shanties" among "disorder and riot" (15). It is this Otherness of class, a ranking outside of the unofficially acknowledged three-class system, that forces the poorest of manual laborers to relate to and distinguish themselves from slaves. This other class is also constituted of characteristics shared with slaves, although sometimes imaginary: a tolerance of disorder, dark and overcrowded shanties, earthen floors, and overriding uncleanness.

The original, ordered plan of the mills soon began to decay, however. Fanny Fern lists among "what ails the working-girls" their lack of ritualized meals—neither the proper food nor time to eat it, but rather a breakfast "hastily swallowed." Their shared room is "close and unventilated, with no accommodations for personal cleanliness," and their garments include "a soiled petticoat," "a greasy dress," and some pathetic attempt at feminine ornament. Predictably, they labor endlessly in a "large, black-looking building" (qtd. in Tichi 158–159). Mrozowski and Beaudry find evidence that boardinghouse yards were heavily used and quickly went to weeds, although the higher-class homes sustained their lawns. For the upper-class houses, situated next to the operative's buildings, earth was imported to elevate the yards, and the houses themselves were positioned above white "cut granite blocks" (202). Factory expansion also overtook much of the space set aside as courtyards and greens. At the same time, the town planners sought to expel the class of day-laborers and canal-diggers involved in construction of the mills: no housing was provided for those. As described by Robinson, this "fourth class" of citizens remained architecturally unacknowledged.

In "Paradise of Bachelors and Tartarus of Maids," Herman Melville explicitly investigates the relationship between the dinner table and the factory. By pairing the two stories, of a heavenly dinner party and a hellish factory, he connects class and gender in disorienting ways.[13] Part of the cause for this confusion, it seems to me, is that Melville is hardly concerned with the characters in the diptych at all, but largely interested in their things—and the story's gender and class are both constructed from these.[14] That which is deemed "feminine," an anti-materialistic preparation for participation in the marketplace, is frozen, literally, in Tartarus: perpetual potential is in fact poverty. The stories are not a critique of wage slavery, but rather an examination of the way white things shape class and gender, how they exclude but account for black slavery. What is finally built is a completely colored and unintegrated setting, where the identities created remain constant, and only the white things are mobile—cotton, cloth, and paper circulate throughout the economy.

In part, Melville dislocates the sexes, creating a distant locale for effete dining gentlemen and visibly laboring women, in order to highlight the emptiness of an etiquette-driven Paradise and the harshness of the efficiently industrialized Tartarus—although etiquette and efficiency were the height of fashion. Casting pale female virgins as victims in "Tartarus of Maids" becomes more mythically touching than documenting overworked men; imaging their whiteness as checked by the dark overseer stirs subterranean racial fears which alone render the factory's efficiency frightening. Furthermore, Melville draws the connection between the factory work and seven course meals: both participate in the commodification of race, both suffer and profit from the suppressed blackness of slavery, and both perpetuate the power of white things without being fully aware of their ramifications.

Melville begins the diptych by dwelling on the difference between pre-industrial, Medieval London—full of stalwart knights and their manly battles—and the industrial city dinned by hurrying tradesmen and superficial lawyers. Nonetheless, the narrator faithfully relates the details of the dinner, house, and company, in the style of a gossipy letter to a friend. Melville pocks his narrative with question marks, exclamation points, and self-contradictions—such as when he rejoices over the company, exclaiming, "It was, indeed, a sort of Senate of the Bachelors.... Nay, it was, by representation, a Grand Parliament of the best Bachelors in universal London" (206). The narrator's constant gushing and backtracking alert the reader to his wispiness, and contrast him to both the manly Medieval knights and the silent sickly maids of Tartarus. In this fashion, the narrator dubiously declares the private dinner a modern-day ritual as noble as the Crusades. The qualities that make for polite dining become valorized: more evolved than the haughty and gruff ancient knights, modern Templar lawyers have "warm hearts and warmer welcomes, full minds and fuller cellars, ... good advice and glorious dinners," and are "finer fellow[s]" for it (205, 204). In this way, Melville contrasts the manly traits of bygone knights with the "masculine" manners of the bachelors, distinguished not by conquests but by possessions.

Invited to dine "at a private table," the narrator escapes from the mud and trade of the workplace to a "refuge" with "a park to it, and flower-beds, and a riverside"—a setting that, if gendered, might be seen as feminine.[15] As he climbs "well up toward heaven," the narrator enthusiastically describes the marks of refinement surrounding him: his own gloved hand pinching a card, the old and snug furniture, the low ceiling of the room. These details betray not only that the narrator is of a lower class and therefore easily impressed—he is a salesman, of the middling class—but also that domestic details would be expected when one relates a fine dining experience. The subsequent details are even more emphatic in their precision: he names every course. His description here contrasts the ancient construction of manhood—involving battles and armament—with the modern "masculinity," which requires simply the celebration and proper use of material things.

The ritual begins when "[i]n good time nine men sat down to nine covers" (206). Such segmentation of place settings initiates the discipline of dining, and we understand that this "good" time—measured by "wine-chronometer"—regulates the courses (208). The bachelors' meal closely follows current etiquette manuals' prescriptions for the most elaborate and structured dinners:

> These courses mounted in scale and importance from the relatively simple, light, and uncooked to the richer and more lavishly prepared.... It began, typically, with raw oysters and champagne. Then waiters offered a choice of a white or brown soup and poured sherry. Then fish with Chablis. Next an entrée.... Then a slice of roast (with claret and champagne). After that, perhaps some Roman punch ... [and] game such as canvasback duck (Madeira and port); salad; cheese; pastry or pudding; ices and sweet dishes. Then liqueurs. Then fruit ... accompanied by sherry or claret. And then waiters passed nuts, raisins, sugar plums, and dried ginger.... Gentlemen sometimes remained by themselves at table ... with their wine and cigars, liqueurs and cognac. (Kasson 134, italics in text)

Compared to this description, Melville's narrator lists a nearly textbook meal: ox-tail soup with claret, turbot with sherry, roast beef, then mutton, turkey, and chicken pie with ale, game-fowl with red wine, tarts and puddings, cheese and crackers with port, and followed by snuff rather than cigars.

Such protocol and its corresponding demands to order would have been familiar to Melville through contact with his own domestic affairs while working at home (Kelley, "'I'm Housewife Here'"). In 1854, Melville gave his wife Mrs. Pullan's *The Modern Housewife's Receipt Book: A Guide to All Matters Connected with Household Economy*, which provides advice for everyday and elaborate meals as well as overall ordering of the household. The gift suggests both a mutual concern over domestic affairs between Melville and his wife and Melville's awareness of a need for household direction. Laurie Robertson-Lorant argues that later that year Melville drew from this cookbook to compose "Poor Man's Pudding and Rich Man's Crumbs" (342). In "Paradise of Bachelors," the meal's deviations from protocol serve to connect it visually to the factory's setting— the early soup and most of the wines are red, like Blood River, and the fish is "snow-white, flaky, and just gelatinous enough," recalled by the snowy factory's vats of "albuminous" white paper pulp (207, 218). But the list itself establishes Melville's company as among the finest and most knowledgeable of prevailing etiquette.

Beyond the meal, the bachelors also show themselves familiar with more encompassing rules of etiquette and thereby demonstrate their worthiness of such riches and abundance. While their conversation at table may appear to signal their effete but bland distancing from real life, the anecdotes merely conform to polite dictates. Systematically, the narrator relates the conversational contributions of Bachelors One through Eight—his own story might be the Ninth. Each gentleman obeys the mannerly maxim "not simply to fall silent but to engage in conversation while eating, keeping the table talk light and steering away from 'heated discussions' and 'heavy or abstruse topics.'"[16] An etiquette book of the time gives a sample conversation in which diners tiptoe around even the most vaguely personal comments (J. F. Kasson, "Ritual" 137). For the men to discuss anything less patently dull than Flemish architecture or "Saracenic scenery" would be low class.

Finally, the narrator comments on the rules of bodily control that accompanied the rise of segmented and ritualized dining. Among the multitude of toasts, the bachelors continually "expressed their sincerest wishes for the entire well-being and lasting hygiene of the gentleman on the right and on the left" (207). Hygiene evolved alongside table manners until the nineteenth century, when both became not only the mark of good breeding, but also a necessity in a democratic society. Melville mocks this obsession with manners in the seriousness of the bachelors' toasts to hygiene, and in his repetitious praise of polite behavior. Throughout the dinner, the narrator claims, "nothing loud, nothing unmannerly, nothing turbulent" occurs (208). "Decorum" must be the final impression left on the narrating salesman: the "remarkable decorum of the nine bachelors—a decorum not to be affected by any quantity of wine—a decorum unassailable by any degree of mirthfulness—this was again set in a forcible light to me, by now observing that, though they took snuff very freely, yet not a man so far violated the proprieties . . . as to indulge in a sneeze" (209–210). Thus, in the details that assure us that this dinner is elite yet boring, Melville establishes a ritual of precision, segmentation, and etiquette that will produce the same habits in the factory.

The story begins to implicate such ritual dining with white goods and racial whiteness as the narrator, enjoying the evening's luxury, can only find expression in the song, "Carry me back to old Virginny!" Recent scholars who mention this line discuss the pun on "virgin," which calls into question the bachelors' sexual practices: Karcher adds that the narrator recalls a slave system in the American South that promotes an upper-class male sexual exploitation of lower-class females.[17] Wiegman believes that this reference to Southern slavery presents "class and race hierarchies as repressed aspects of the male bond" ("Melville's Geography" 740). Although both recognize the confluence of gender and race construction, the song should also be situated historically. Melville's narrator recalls the slave system from the comfort of his dinner table, but he also recalls the American tradition of minstrelsy. Caroline Moseley has located the song as a minstrel piece, since "Paradise" predates the more familiar Virginia state song.[18] On the other hand, Edwin P. Christy's minstrel version appeared in various forms throughout the 1840s. It was published in *The Ethiopian Glee Book* (1848), was advertised with "Oh! Susannah" in 1848, and provided the melody for an abolitionist song in 1856. Therefore, Melville could have expected his audience to be familiar with the song and its sentiments, and its choice as the narrator's luxuriating exclamation provides an unelaborated comment on industrial discipline and blackness.

"Old Virginny" begins, in the voice of a slave, longing for the work of earlier days: "The floating Scow of Old Virginny / I work'd in from day to day, / A fishing 'mongst de oyster beds, / To me it was but play." Work in a slave state, as opposed to the singer's current Northern situation, was "but play" because of its pre-industrial freedoms—freedoms indebted to the fluid schedule of fishing compared to the regimentation of wage labor. The third stanza connects "Virginny" to animals and a friendly Nature, asking that "when I'm dead and gone / Place this old banjo by my side; / Let the possum and coon to my funeral go, / For dey was always my pride." The only other stanza recommends a different course than Melville's bachelors have taken, one that images happy domestication and economic discipline: "If I was only young again, / I'd lead a different life; / I'd save my money, and buy a farm / And take Dinah for my wife" (Moseley 14).

Melville's readers may not have been familiar with the entire text of the song, but in that it is characteristic of minstrel songs, it reflects on the racializing of the diptych. The two stories problematize the trend of industrialization, etiquette, class and race construction; blackface complements their concerns in popular form. At the same time, the portrait of blackness that minstrel plays produced enabled and necessitated the increased whiteness in material goods. The imaginary slave of blackface, in particular, defined "whiteness" in the same terms as white dishes did—as wealthy, well-mannered, disciplined, and domesticated—but he also kept conspicuous the actual slave, who would allow more comfort if he remained hidden. The dining ware then works to unite the bachelors and to flood the place with whiteness so that the slave's dark form fades into the background.

As with the tableware, the main purpose of Tartarus's factory is to produce whiteness. By populating the mill with "girls" and drawing clear gestational imagery, Melville locates the labor of "whitening" with women. The birthing analogy of the paper-making machine has become a scholarly commonplace; the vats of pulp resemble semen, the nine minutes suggest nine months of pregnancy, the ex-nurse waits for the "moist, warm sheets" to be "delivered" into her hands, and the process ends with a sound "as of some cord"—an umbilical cord—"being snapped."[19] Here, Melville associates economic with biological production. The one does not necessarily substitute for the other, however. Literally, the women do not merely produce marketable items—if they did, then "Tartarus" could be read solely as a lament over the mill girls' oppression. Instead, it is the whiteness of the items, their standardized inevitability, and their social circulation that terrify.

A process of whitening begins even before the narrator reaches the factory. A bastion of civilization, the building stands as "a large whitewashed building, relieved, like some great white sepulchre, against the sullen background of mountain-side firs" (211). To get there, the narrator first passes the "black-mossed" ruins of an old saw-mill, which hearkens to "primitive times" when pines and hemlocks covered the region (211). The saw-mill contrasts with the paper mill: the former represents the bygone, pre-industrial organization of labor and appears layered in blackness next to the factory's enormous white face. Nature repeats the hierarchy of color: blackness coats the doomed and primitive, just as dark dishes and blackface signaled slavery and lower-classness.

As the narrator travels towards the factory, white things replace the natural, the animal and the wilderness, with disciplined, repressed civilization. First, the narrator describes the forests surrounding him: the frozen trees feel the "all-stiffening influence" of the cold, which penetrates to the "vertical trunk," until "many colossal tough-grained maples [snap] in twain like pipestems, cumbering the unfeeling earth" (212). In order to elucidate this imagery, the narrator continues that his horse is startled by one of these fallen trunks, which lies across the path "darkly undulatory as an anaconda" (212). From the beginning of his passage, therefore, the narrator begins to remark on fallen phallic images—as nature and manhood alike are overcome by the force of the surrounding white. The Black Notch yields to a "white-wooded" summit filled with "white vapors." His horse, Black, becomes "[f]laked all over with frozen sweat," and "white as a milky ram" (212). Indeed, the black male horse becomes whitened and feminized—through his layer of milkiness—while yet remaining male underneath.

The process continues, and becomes even more linked with femininity, as the narrator enters the factory square. He begins his journey wrapped in "buffalo and wolf robes," a fur tippet, and "huge seal-skin mittens"—all notably from wild animals (212, 222). As the narrator enters the mill, he removes the animal furs that associate him with the surrounding wilderness, and the animal images of the forest come to be replaced by the "iron animal" of the factory. As he sheds his animal coverings, he reveals further evidence of whitening. The frost has produced on his cheeks " '[t]wo white spots like the whites of [his] eyes' " (216). Besides the narrator, only two males inhabit the building, and both are distinguished from the unnumbered pale women by their coloring. Old Bach is repeatedly "the dark-complexioned man," and Cupid a "red-cheeked" boy (216). The women, on the other hand, are marked by unalloyed pallor: their whiteness becomes disturbing when described as "hueless," "blank," "pallid," and "sheet-white." The narrator's white cheeks therefore undercut his masculinity, although only in spots. But the whitening which associates him with the women remains indelible, as even when he leaves, his cheeks look " 'whitish yet' " (222). The paper mill therefore conscripts both feminine and masculine power for industrial production, banishing the natural elements of pre-industrial life, and in the process domesticating citizens into a flaccid femaleness.

Melville's narrator suggests that the women act as slaves to the machine, which rightly should be the "slave of humanity" (215). We understand, then, that the women work to produce whiteness, but in the process subjugate themselves to the means. In disseminating the ideas and behavior that will build disciplined, upper-class, and refined families, women first delimit their own spheres to a colorless home. In addition, the girls are induced to labor by the men—one dark, and one red. More than an economic incentive, these "colored" men become the cultural necessity for whiteness: they haunt the feminine workplace just as slaves and servants inhabit the wealthy white woman's home. Through an intense attention to the Cult of Domesticity, white Americans could rationalize or evade the ethical problems posed by African American slavery and Native American genocide; through an emphasis on white female chastity they could divert any imaginary threats of miscegenation. The dark men therefore become the ideological drivers of this gang of pale-producing women.

The factory women produce whiteness with all its cultural implications. Beyond the showers of white paper, vats of white pulp, and baskets of white rags, the factory is responsible for consummate work-discipline. The women work "'twelve hours to the day, day after day, through the three hundred and sixty-five days, excepting Sundays, Thanksgiving, and Fast-days'" (222). Importantly, the specifically American holiday of Thanksgiving is honored, since the business is interested in producing specifically American workers. The machine conforms to "unvarying punctuality and precision" (220). It processes the paper methodically, "inch by inch," constantly refining the pulp (219). The time-discipline that frightens the narrator—the cycle of production lasting exactly nine minutes—finalizes the connection between factory work and table manners. In "Paradise," "nine gentlemen [sit] down to nine covers," drink from "nine silver flagons," and tell nine affable anecdotes (including the narrator's) ("Paradise" 206–208). In "Tartarus," this ritual is translated into nine-minute precision for the intervals of production.

Nonetheless, this process must also be seen to parallel birth. The inevitability of production translates to the inevitability of reproduction. Therefore, part of Tartarus consists of its parturition, just as part of Paradise depends on its childlessness. The factory women are certainly producing offspring—the narrator draws the connection himself between "the human mind at birth" and "a sheet of blank paper" (221). And beyond producing white paper and "whitened" children, the women broadcast them. The narrator thinks upon the "strange uses to which those thousand sheets would be put": "sermons, lawyers' briefs, physicians' prescriptions, love-letters, marriage certificates, bills of divorce, registers of births, death-warrants, and so on, without end" (220). The mill women oversee all aspects of domestic life and the most noble and lucrative callings. Thereby, they commodify whiteness, creating a standardized product that promises access to economic and social success—while they remain forever in the factory.

But these women are not house mistresses, wives, and mothers. They are all maids. The narrator involuntarily bows in "pained homage to their pale virginity" (222). As if he were again singing "Carry me back to old Virginny," the narrator reacts with chivalry to the chastity of the women—a chastity imposed, he acknowledges sadly, by the system that asks them for whiteness. Little Eva, not her mother, is the ideal feminine figure, and mythical chastity levels all proper women to virginity. That they are " '[a]ll maids' " fills the narrator with a "strange emotion," but their work has been effective: rather than stay and try to mend his cheeks, which remain white, he departs because " 'time presses' " him (222). That these are the narrator's last words is telling—leaving a warehouse full of eligible maids, he finds himself pressed instead by time. His devotion to work and time-discipline "presses" him just as the machinery inside presses paper, and he is equally a product.

Paper functions as an ideal example of portable whiteness for Melville: it is unthreateningly present and habitually used everywhere, and it is clear that the narrator has never before really *thought* about paper. As with the plates at the bachelors' dinner, the narrator believes paper to be unsignifying, blankly waiting for a message to bring it into existence; he does, however, read its meanings, from the faces of tradesmen "hurrying by, with ledger-lines ruled along their brows," and from the face of the factory "girl," "ruled and wrinkled" as she plies a mechanical harp to draft lines on the paper. In addition, the benign envelopes for which the narrator needs this paper feed the slave institution in the South, as he sends seeds through Missouri and the Carolinas as well as "all the Eastern and Northern States" ("Paradise" 211). In this way, Melville reminds his reader of the tensions embedded in the act of reading and writing. Those who thought seriously about slavery and the wage slavery of industrialization were troubled by their own dependence on slave-produced cotton paper for their very abolitionist arguments, and Melville implicates the one holding his story in these oppressive systems as well. Granting the illusion of power by its potential to be moved, removed, and marked, these white things actually function to sustain slavery and to create new types of slavery in the factories and homes.

Cooper's *The Pioneers* negotiates class, race, and gender by carefully placing each thing and person in its hierarchical space, with consideration of color-codings valued from white, to off-white, to black. Melville attempts to separate class from gender, and both from race, but finds that the items constructing these categories circulate among them, tying them together inextricably. The feminine convention of the tea ritual simplifies this seeming confusion by treating class as an activity rather than a status or place. The sentimental heroine such as Gerty in *The Lamplighter* must constantly perform the highest class that her means allow her, and in performing, inspire her family towards it, but not aspire to wealth or status herself. The "feminine" experience of class is therefore different from the "masculine," at least in the upper and middle classes. The masculine achieves his class status; here, upper-, middle-, and lower-classness are measurable in tangible goods. The feminine experiences class not as a position, but as a challenge—it is not measurable except in the moment of its performance and transmission, therefore requiring ritual and discipline for its display. Since class was also a racial designation, with "black" defining the greatest distance from wealth and privilege, the "feminine" experienced racial whiteness as a performance as well: she must visibly distance herself from the laboring black body and continually expunge blackness from her household. In the emergent capitalism of the early nineteenth century, upper-classness required a gendered partnership—the accumulation of refined goods, coupled with carefully regulated instances of proper use.

CHAPTER THREE

UNMENTIONABLE THINGS UNMENTIONED

Constructing Femininity with White Things

When Scarlett O'Hara determines to conquer the heart of Ashley Wilkes in Margaret Mitchell's *Gone with the Wind* (1936), she understands that it will take the perfect dress and a tiny waist. Therefore, she cannot conquer alone; she calls in Mammy, who urges her to wear the proper style of dress and lectures her about ladylike behavior. Mammy, in fact, shows herself to understand the rules shaping femininity even as she violates all of them. She shuffles into Scarlett's room with a tray of food in her "large black hands"; she is a "huge old woman" and a "shining black, pure African"—but she cautions Scarlett against "'gittin freckled affer all de buttermilk Ah been puttin' on you all dis winter'" (25, 80). Most memorable, of course, is when Mammy laces up Scarlett's corset, cinching her tiny waist to seventeen inches to fit her green muslin dress. Scarlett readies herself, "bracing herself and catching firm hold against of one of the bedposts. Mammy pulled and jerked vigorously and, as the tiny circumference of whalebone-girdled waist grew smaller, a proud, fond look came into her eyes" (81).

This shrinking corset manages to romanticize within its fabric the many underpinnings of nineteenth-century femininity, pairing and reconciling the conflicts upon which this femininity depends. First, the lady's presentation must be constructed. It is built from among understood fashion rules and choices of dress; it is created within the confines of a private, feminine architecture, the lady's bedroom; it is the product of a collusion of women. Secondly, it depends upon invisible "vigorous" labor: Mammy struggles and tugs while Scarlett struggles to stay put. Finally, Mammy must participate in this construction. Scarlett's invincible femininity contrasts at every point with Mammy's mere femalehood. Scarlett is proud of her impossibly small waist—and as America approached the Civil War, corsets grew smaller and fashionable women laced themselves more and more tightly; in contrast, Mammy "lumbers" and "shuffles" her "huge" body and arrives everywhere huffing. Mammy has a shining black African face, but Scarlett bleaches her skin with buttermilk to erase any freckles. Mammy's dress is simple, although she might adorn herself with garish colors or a turban according to a slave's taste; Scarlett debates among several dresses, considering the occasion, the time of day, her own personality, and the company she will be keeping.

Mammy's pride in viewing Scarlett's fashioned femininity reveals the romanticism of the scene: she not only knows that what "a young miss could do and what she could not do were as different as black and white," she enforces the difference, and loves her mistress for illustrating it (79). Mammy understands and agrees that a "feminine sphere" exists, has definite boundaries, and must exclude her, despite her mastery of its rules.[1] In this scene, the two women's bodies become part of a portable geography, and the mistress's fashionable clothes create a visual segregation even within the same room. The things that became whiter in the early nineteenth century—dishes, house paint, and gravestones, as well as interior walls and furniture, women's clothing, and the sentimental heroine's skin—did not only become more ordered and refined. They also came to center around the "woman's sphere": the house grew to be gendered as feminine as men left to work outside the home, and the cemetery assumed a feminine aspect with its angelic engravings. The way these white things were used, and by whom, constructed an antebellum understanding of "femininity." The class implied by white things also underlays this understanding: one had to be able to afford refined white goods in order to manage them properly, so mainly upper- and middle-class women could be deemed feminine. In addition, the things' whiteness, which sentimental fiction developed as an ideal, included white skin, so that black women were always excluded from a feminine designation.

In antebellum America, "feminine" participated in a set of binaries—feminine and masculine, as well as feminine and female. "Female" designated the corporeal woman, the body made concrete through manual labor or physical marking—blackness, deformity, slovenliness. Sarah Josepha Hale, editor of *Godey's Lady's Book*, decries the use of the term "female" because it insists on the body: "'When used to discriminate between the sexes,'" she argues, "'the word *female* is an adjective; but many writers employ the word as a noun, which, when applied to women, is improper, and sounds unpleasantly, as referring to an animal. . . . It is inelegant as well as absurd'" (qtd. in Berlant 272). She refers, in part, to the problem of physicality for women: she enters a conventional struggle where "women and blacks could never shed their bodies to become incorporeal 'men,'" and therefore gain access to the rights and privileges of fully fledged citizens (Sánchez-Eppler, *Touching Liberty* 3). "Female" signifies a physical form, and therefore ungenders the feminine: according to Hale, the proper woman can best be referred to by adjective, eliding the noun that marks her as a person, place, and thing.

"Feminine," I would argue, can be better imagined as the proper relationship to material things; the feminine "sphere" can be marked by the range of a woman's command over these things. Feminine depended upon a seeming contradiction, variously expressed throughout the nineteenth century: the claiming of valuable things joined with a disavowal of their importance. "Masculine" might be read as an opposite, because in it, the desire for goods was not disavowed but rather emphasized: competitiveness and marketplace aggression marked masculinity. The female fell short of femininity in both ways: a working-class woman or slave could not claim expensive things, nor could she unclaim the things she possessed— she had to use them as tools, instruments, in order to earn her living. Lori Merish posits the proper feminine response to things as "sentimental materialism"—its own internal contradiction—which allows women to value products, but only through "loving proprietorship," not "instrumentalism" (*Sentimental Materialism* 153). Instrumentalism, the use of a thing as a tool, either for physical work or for social climbing, is unfeminine because it fails to disavow possession. Yet class remained, theoretically, a suspended judgment in relation to gender. A poor woman might demonstrate her femininity by showing the proper relationship to the few things she had; a wealthy woman might exclude herself by valuing her things for their expense or display, or by valuing money over sentimentalized things.

The feminine sphere was therefore a concrete conception: the delimited area where a woman could both claim things and claim not to need them. This relationship was materially expressed largely through white things. Claiming things in the material world, in everyday life, took the form for women of visually allying themselves with their household goods. Through clothing styles, women could match the white things in their houses—the dishes, the furniture, the interior décor—and in the cemetery. Clothing fashion, following a constantly varying design, traveled throughout the feminine sphere tying all things together visually. This same fashion disavowed her claim by so manipulating her body as to suggest a disembodiment and link her to a spiritual world where refined goods could not possibly be an economic benefit to her. The corset rendered her body as thin and unsubstantial as possible; her clothing matched the furniture and allowed her body to blend in with its surroundings; her modestly downcast eyes directed the gaze elsewhere. At the same time, the popular depiction of women in literature and the graveyard remained, in spite of fashion, a simple white dress. The sentimental heroine's ubiquitous white dress was nod to both a classically ordered society and the Quaker's spirituality, and was cast as the ideally feminine clothing. In addition, the white dress was a blank slate, a denial of fashion's materialism, as well as a disavowal of the "things" it referred to—including the woman's own body. Popular cemetery trends in the early nineteenth century worked along with other white things, to separate the body from the spirit, but to render the spirit physically accessible and at the same time feminine. Indeed, "femininity" as established by one's relationship to things is not a bodily identity at all, but a claim by the mistress that her body is a disconnected, tightly controlled white thing among the other refined white things in the household. Her corset and clothing speak not of ownership of this body, but merely of management of it—just as the mistress manages her white china and household furniture.

Through this visual disembodiment she also rescued herself from being another white thing, merely one of the collection of refined household goods owned by the male householder, since she could be separate from her own body and from her body's physicalizing labor. The things were her domain even if not her possessions; she herself was not part of that domain—as she was "in the world but not of it"—and therefore not possessible. Femininity as an articulated identity was an expansion of the bodily identity—a woman's things were a part of her; her household was a "second body." The feminine woman therefore ruled a realm more farflung than the effusive and uncontrolled, perspiring and uncorseted, corporeal limits of the working female. Thus imaged, however, femininity could be exercised only within a carefully controlled environment, and in this way was entrapping and constrictive—only as mobile as the woman's household or another specially designed setting. Such a built identity was necessarily a source of anxiety: a woman's best-loved things might be lost or appropriated and therefore compromise her femininity; at the same time, a male was always in danger of becoming feminine should he use or value these things in a feminine way. Mammy's participation in *Gone with the Wind* is therefore a crucial twentieth-century review of romanticized femininity. Mammy voluntarily, even lovingly, refrains from encroaching upon Scarlett's sphere, and therefore saves Scarlett from the female power negotiations constantly enacted in actual antebellum households.

The sympathy imagined between white and black women, based on sex, was reproduced in a feminized version of the Wedgwood abolition china, figuring a black female silhouette kneeling and crying, "Am I not a woman and a sister?" Such sisterhood was imagined in both directions: women's rights activists adopted an argument of "sex slavery": according to Karen Sanchez-Eppler, the abolitionist-feminist could "'emphasize the similarities in the condition of women and slaves'" although the "alliance attempted . . . is never particularly easy or equitable" ("Bodily Bonds" 414, 409). Unlike the efforts of industrial reformers, whose use of "wage slavery" was contested both by ex-slave abolitionists and by slavery apologists, the women's rights movement's connecting slavery to wifehood was not protested—both institutions depended upon the power of "patriarchy" (Roediger, "Race" 182). The connections between women and slaves, but not between industrial workers and slaves, rested in the physical fact of freedom: though factory workers might be materially poorer than well-treated slaves, they could leave their position without physical threat. Wives, like slaves, legally owned no property and could not travel alone. Mary Chestnut from South Carolina felt the connection strongly enough to claim, "'There is no slave, after all, like a wife'" (qtd. in Donaldson and Jones 3).

Sojourner Truth echoes the ceramic plea for sisterhood in her often-anthologized "Ar'n't I a Woman?" But her question is disingenuous, as she displays her body, her muscles, and her ability to labor, as proof that women do not need excessive protection. She allies the "niggers of de South and de women at de Norf" against white men and solicits applause among abolitionist-feminists (to use Sánchez-Eppler's term). But though she disputes the white construction of femininity by saying, "Dat man ober dar say dat women needs to be helped into carriages, and lifted over ditches, and to have de best place eberywhar. Nobody eber helps me into carriages, or ober mud-puddles, or gives me any best place," she ultimately cannot claim company with the "women at de Norf." In the article reporting her speech in 1851, Frances Gage concludes her praise by stating of Truth, "She had taken us up in her great strong arms and carried us safely over the slough of difficulty, turning the whole tide in our favor."[2] Gage re-establishes the privilege of feminine weakness and merely transfers the labor from men's arms to those of a black woman. Similarly, though Hale emphatically denounces the use of the noun "female" as animalistic, she reveals that exemption from this term does not apply to the working class. Boasting that her *Godey's Lady's Book* supports many women for its production, she claims, "Not to reckon the host of female writers, who are promptly *paid*, there are besides more than one hundred *females*, who depend for their daily bread on the money they receive for colouring the plates of fashion, stitching, doing up the work, and so on" (Dec. 1842, qtd. in Piepmeier 193, italics in original). The writers, perhaps, enjoy the advantage of the adjective, but the manual laborers cannot claim as much.

Gillian Brown traces the way "both labor and women are divested of their corporeality" through a "[d]isengagement from the body that labors," since "to be a working body is virtually to be a slave." Figuring women's work as spiritual exercise, writers such as Catharine Beecher render the body performing it ethereal; further, the body could be dissociated from the individual self (Gillian Brown 63–64). The equation, fully borne out in fashion but articulated through the progression of gravestones, was that manual labor required a body, a laboring body was a slave, and slaves were black; whiteness therefore required the absence of visible labor and, to be safe, the absence of a visible body. The feminine sphere was the narrow space where such fictions, with the help of servants and specialized architecture, could possibly be performed.

The possibility of becoming a "pure spirit," the necessity of its being white, and the importance of its femininity was established within the cemetery among the gravestones. In the nineteenth century, the cemetery became a feminine domain.[3] In an early study of New England gravestones, Dethlefsen and Deetz note that the inscriptions on eighteenth-century stones "indicate a heavy paternal bias," since stones for women and children name ties such as "wife of" and "child of" while stones for adult men simply state their names. This bias weakens, however, at the turn of the century, as seen by the use of a "Mr." or "Mrs.," or the deceased's name alone. From 1840 until 1900, they argue, "some slight maternal bias is present," shown by the stones' naming the wife first or using

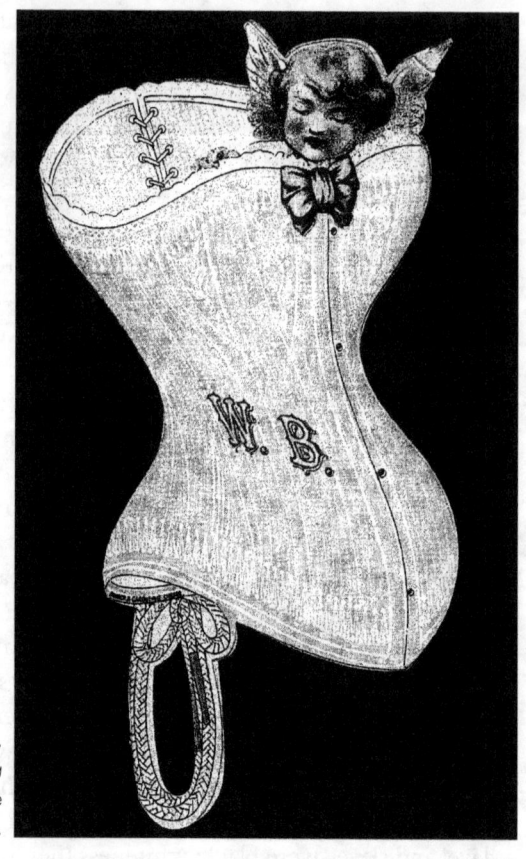

Trade card for the W. B. Corset. Disembodied corset, topped by a cherub design, linking the feminine with the cemetery.

larger letters for the wife's name (509). Those who could not read could also believe the cemetery to be a new part of the feminine realm, however; a cult of piety imaged the cemetery as an extension of the home, and the markers themselves displayed designs explicitly linked with femininity. When Justice Joseph Story dedicated Mount Auburn cemetery in 1831, he announced his wish "'to provide a home there with our friends, and to be blest by a communion with them'" (Combs 190). The theme of heaven as the site of the protected or re-united household occurs throughout the nineteenth century in consolation literature and on epitaphs, and the cemetery is the physical entranceway to heaven. Reverend Theodore Cuyler offers to bereaved parents the hope that "'as this link is formed with the heavenly world, may you be gathered there at last, an unbroken household'" (Combs 189). Heaven became the site of the ultimately idealized household. In this way, women came to take charge of issues surrounding the cemetery and death, as these were extensions of their rightful place, the home.

As the use of darker slate in the eighteenth century waned and was replaced by use of white marble around the turn of the nineteenth century, the popular motifs displayed on gravestones changed as well. Death's-head designs appeared early—before 1750—to be replaced after 1760 by a cherub design. As stones began to be purchased in white marble, the popular design became "urn-and-willow" in the early nineteenth century (Dethlefsen and Deetz 508). The changes in gravestone iconography were also accompanied by an altered apprehension of the connection between body and spirit, or body and self, as seen on gravestone inscriptions. A popular example from the earliest slate stones contains the sentiment, "Remember me as you pass by":

> *Behold and see as you pass by*
> *As you are now, so once was I;*
> *As I am now, so you will be—*
> *Prepare for Death and follow me.* (Neal 27, italics in text)

Indicating the deceased on these stones took the form of statements such as, " 'Here lies . . . ' " or " 'Here lies buried . . .' " (Deetz, *Small Things* 71). These phrases meet with the death's-head design in emphasizing the physical reality of death and perhaps a reluctance to expect anything better than decomposition. When motifs merged into cherubs, with fleshier faces and happier expressions, the inscriptions turned to " 'Here lies the body of . . .' " or " 'what was mortal of . . .' " (71). Deetz suggests that the addition of these few words signals a new emphasis on resurrection. The gravestone marks the burial not of the person, but of the body alone—the soul has traveled elsewhere. The power of the deceased's speech then wanes, and epitaphs discontinue their direct addresses to the viewer. In an example of a cherub stone, the epitaph addresses the viewer but refers to the dead in the third person:

> Here cease thy tears, suppress thy fruitless mourn
> his soul—the immortal part—has upward flown
> > On wings he soars his rapid way
> > to yon bright regions of eternal day (72)

The detachment of the spirit from the body is here a matter of display, presuming an audience. The cherub design, generally found on dark slates, nonetheless is a fleshed and happier version of the leering skull design it replaces. At the same time, the cherub face has no body, and somewhat feminine features.

As gravestone design shifted to the urn-and-willow, inscriptions began to exclude the viewer altogether. On the white stones of the nineteenth century, the deceased were usually memorialized with "Sacred to the Memory of . . ." Deetz reads in this change a depersonalization of the marker and a "secularization of religion," since the deceased is more often praised for worldly accomplishments on these stones (72). Indeed, these depersonalized messages appear as the stones shift to white, and one of the most popular motifs is the image of an urn memorial over which a female figure mourns, or sometimes a grieving woman and children. Although this picture calls to mind a widow grieving over her lost husband, in Charleston, South Carolina, churchyards even the gravestones for adult women generally depicted mourning females.[4] These images of grieving women, while they acknowledge a viewer, never address one: they become a white portrait of a woman dissociated from the world, even as they publicly display her. Where a body-spirit division on earlier stones allowed for a feminine disembodiment, the later "depersonalized" feminine portraits replaced her body with a detached white thing, and then affected not to notice an outside gaze. The same femininity is expressed repeatedly in *Godey's Lady's Book*: the drawings of fashion models are standardized, white-skinned blonde ladies with eyes downcast (Halttunen). The downcast eyes disavow attention, even as the images display fashion. Gravestone motifs performed the same work: to detach the body from the spirit and embody the spirit instead in refined white goods and images.

Women used clothing fashion likewise to ally themselves with their household furnishings, architecture, and dishes, thereby designating all as part of the feminine domain and marking themselves with the whiteness of their things. As the nineteenth century began, popular styles in dishes and women's dress paralleled architectural house paint trends. In the first years of the nineteenth century, women commonly dressed in "classically draped white gowns . . . drawn in at a high 'empire' waist" which "displayed plain surfaces and clean, vertical lines, with a minimum of distracting ornamentation" (Halttunen 73–74). At the same time, undecorated creamware adorned the fashionable, higher-class tables. Meanwhile, Roman classicist houses, popular from 1790 to 1830, showed the verticality of plain white columns and moldings.[5]

By the early 1820s, just when paneled, colorfully rimmed dishes appeared, "classical dress had been fully transformed into romantic dress" (De Cunzo 90). The romantic gown "was a profusion of flounces, flowers, ruching, thick piping, and colored ribbons, and was further ornamented with plenty of jewelry" (Halttunen 74). It "disguised the body with tight lacing, padding, and whalebone supports, and called attention largely to the costume itself" (Halttunen 75). The paneled ceramics echoed the paneled dress of fashionable women: the shift of focus from the flesh to its containers took place on both the table and its mistress. These decades also gave rise to Gothic revival houses, with all their ornamental trim. Glassie further documents the white homes with many-colored trim appearing at this time in folk housing, which was far less responsive to architectural trends.

By the time Glassie notes houses becoming monochromatically white, ceramic manufacturers had produced a completely white ironstone and female fashion had shifted to a sentimental gown, ideally rendered in white. In 1836, clothing styles changed abruptly to a "sentimental form [which] was long and willowy, with narrow, sloping shoulders and a slender, lengthening waist" (Halttunen 75). A shift to a "willowy" fashion in clothing coincides with the appearance of willow patterns on tableware, and to the predominance of the "willow-and-urn" design appearing on the nearly universally white marble gravestones. The inside of the house, argues Beverly Gordon, corresponded to the woman's clothing as well—aesthetically and technologically. At mid-century, the furniture of the women's rooms such as the parlor was draped in "richly textured cloth" in lambrequins or valances (Gordon 296). The "scalloped edgings and fringes of these valances" she continues, "also echoed the undulating edges of the trim on fashionable women's dresses." Furthermore, construction of women's dress mirrored the construction of home decoration: at mid-century, the crinoline of hoop skirts was shaped by the use of "lightweight steel hoops as structural support," which was "paralleled in furniture design by the use of steel springs as an internal support in the upholstery"—a technology available for furniture by 1830, but not popular until it was also used in clothing in the late 1850s (Gordon 296, 297).

As the house was viewed as feminine, rooms were defined by gender within the house as well. Specifically masculine rooms included the study or library and any number of smoking rooms, billiard rooms, and "odd rooms" depending on the extravagance of the house (Spain 117). The study, as a wholly masculine domain, was where the gendered topics of business and politics could be freely discussed (Spain 123). Some cottage design books suggested that the study have a separate entrance so that "gentlemen with a 'professional occupation or literary taste' could come and go without disturbing the family." The dining room and parlor were designed for co-recreational contact, although the parlor was deemed feminine (Spain 123). But beyond the parlor, the feminine rooms were kept private—the upstairs nursery and the kitchen in the basement or the back of the house were not intended for visitors' view. The bedroom, also a strictly feminine and strictly private room, was usually isolated to the back of the house or the upstairs. Victorian houseplans often did not even label the bedrooms out of "a sense of modesty" (Snyder 16).

Furthermore, furniture was designed in the early decades to address its user as much as its use. Michael J. Ettema argues that from the 1840s to the 1870s, when refined furniture partook of codes of conspicuous consumption but before it came to be designed for "art" or "aesthetics," furniture design "was primarily categorized by social situations of use" (193). The rigidity and complexity of furniture design was determined by the degree of formality associated with a room and its occupants: the "hall was the most formal, followed by the reception room, drawing room, dining room, library, sitting room, bedroom, kitchen, and finally, servants' rooms." Each room required "its appropriate ceremonies, postures, gestures, and topics of conversation" (193). The furnishings of each informed the visitor of his or her degree of welcome and of the formality required, and each room enforced this formality by the structure of its furnishings. For example, the hall chairs were generally straight-backed and unpadded, with a plank seat "because it would not be damaged by contact with wet or soiled outer garments; because it contributed to the stern, somewhat intimidating grandeur of the hall; and possibly because it was uncomfortable" (Ames 32). Degree of formality and depth of admittance into the house spoke of the visitor's class as well: Clarence Cook writes that because only socially inferior visitors are kept waiting in the hall, " 'messenger boys, book-agents, the census-man and the bereaved lady who offers us soap, . . . considerations of comfort may be allowed to yield to picturesqueness' " (Ames 34).

The distinctions between "formal" and "informal" merged with the gendered divisions of "private" and "hidden." Servant quarters, the kitchen, and work areas were generally in the back of the house beyond numerous formal barriers. In upper- and middle-class houses, labor and blackness were cast beyond these boundaries, hidden and denied to public view. The privilege of such privacy declared upper-class status and refinement and belonged to the construction of white femininity. Stansell finds that working-class women "observed no distinction between public and private" as their work "spread out to the hallways of their tenements, to adjoining apartments and to the streets below" (41). Similarly, Lori Merish finds the narrator's bursting unannounced into Uncle Tom's cabin for a readerly tour to be an indication of his slave status, even within the picturesque walls that Stowe has provided him ("Sentimental Consumption"). Within the same novel, Stowe idealizes the dissociation of visible labor from femininity in her portrait of a Northern household, which fully expunges the blackness of slavery but not its implications. "There are no servants," but the housekeeper still sits in the "family 'keeping-room,'" "sewing every afternoon among her daughters, as if nothing ever had been done, or were to be done,—she and her girls, in some long-forgotten fore part of the day, 'did up the work,' and for the rest of the time, probably, at all hours when you would see them, it is 'done up'" (*Uncle Tom's* 150, italics in text). Stowe even invokes in this ideal the audience, or visitor to the house, claiming that we would never see the mistresses do work: the place of the proper lady, as far as we ever know, is always the parlor and never the kitchen or cellar.

IN THEIR ALABASTER CHAMBERS

The physical explanation of this "femininity," based upon having but not desiring, having done but not doing—because other bodies, nonwhite bodies, publicly do the work—is illustrated in two scenes, interestingly cut from the published novel, of Susan Warner's best-seller *The Wide, Wide World* (1850). Although the scholarship debates Ellen's role in the marketplace—whether she ultimately renders herself an "ornament" or actually participates in the marketplace in a sentimental or literal sense—few scholars have noted that her participation in, and shrinking from, the world is clearly marked in racial as well as class terms. Insofar as the novel privileges "female subjectivity" and outlines a strictly feminine struggle and means of coping with it, it also describes an escape from waged labor that characterizes the black servants, the brown farmhands, and nonwhite mercenaries in the story. This escape entails, for Ellen, not only a sentimental self-control and an enclosed domesticity, but also an upper-class refinement and a dismissal of blackness. In the novel's final chapter, resurrected in the 1987 published version, Ellen Montgomery marries her patriarchal brother-figure, John, and moves into an interior room that he has painstakingly prepared for her. Guiding her through a room full of statues and paintings, John explains to Ellen the intellectual and spiritual import of each item. The "luxury of the mind" that these things represent nonetheless also speaks of material wealth—fine works of art, antique frames, and items from across Europe. Within her "delightfully private" room, which offers access only through John's room, lies also a beautiful escritoire with "costly antique garniture." Within one of its drawers lies another "concealed drawer," and within this lies ample "gold and silver pieces and bank bills." Ellen shrinks from this stark vision of wealth—" 'Money!' said Ellen, 'what am I to do with it?' "—just as she is horrified to tears when an old gentleman gives her money as a Christmas present (582). But the money, as well hidden as her desire for it, supports the morally charged room. The escritoire, necessarily, has not been purchased but rather inherited, from John's "father's mother and grandmother and great-grandmother," thoroughly establishing a tradition of femininely managed and disavowed materiality. This ultimately elaborated vision of femininity constitutes the happy ending—perhaps understood well enough that Warner could excise it from her published draft. It demonstrates the proper relationship to money—which is to remain hidden, denied, and disavowed, as well as possessed—and also the proper relation to things—explained as moral teachers and sentimental treasures rather than utilitarian devices.

As the novel demonstrates, the improper attitude about money can also deny white women access to the whiteness of material femininity. Aunt Fortune's industry provides her with white walls and dishes, but her house cannot *appear* white because she openly values money and because she does not invest her industry in producing refinement, only utilitarian objects. Although the aunt's name provides a pun as "Miss Fortune," it also links her to a mercenary domesticity as she runs her farm and performs her own manual labor in order to maximize her profits. Aunt Fortune's insistence on performing the rough chores of the house, her failure to provide for refined articles such as silver spoons, wash basins, or clothed furniture, marks her as less than white despite her industry and money. She is nearly "masculine" in her acquisitiveness, and nearly "female" in her manual laboring. Accordingly, when Ellen approaches her house for the first time, though she "strained her eyes, [she] could make out nothing, —not even a glimpse of white" (98). Miss Fortune's house does indeed show a few marks of improvement: the "cheerful-looking" kitchen walls are white. But in Ellen's initial view, even these white things "were yellow in the light of the flame" (99). Her room, likewise, though "perfectly neat and clean," is carpetless, with walls "not very smooth nor particularly white" and unpainted doors faded to "a light-brown colour" (102). Attempting to look on "the bright side of things," Ellen enjoys the novelty of "brown bread," even though she must breakfast with a primitive two-pronged fork, with Mr. Van Brunt the field hand, and without a silver spoon (106).

On the first day of her stay, Ellen rushes to "find something pleasanter" than the "very brown outhouses" with "very rough walls" and "brown beams and rafters" strewn with rubbish and all manner of "what not" (106–107). In her excursion, however, she muddies her stockings. The reader can sympathize with Ellen despite her obvious class pretensions when Aunt Fortune dyes all of Ellen's stockings from white to "a fine slate colour"—a clear message that Ellen must struggle alone for the femininity that allows disembodied escape from labor (113). Uncomfortable and dissatisfied, Ellen "seemed in her imagination to see all her white things turning brown" (113). This literal browning signals Ellen's lifelong trial: Ellen must spend the rest of the novel learning the discipline, self-denial, and piety that she enjoyed with her mother, when all her things were white.

Alice and John Humphrey's house offers hope for redemption, both in spiritual and classed terms. Alice's is a "large white house" though not lately painted; within, Alice's bedroom floor is painted white and covered in the center by a carpet, the curtains are white dimity, the "toilet-table" is "covered with snow-white muslin" (161, 163). In the upper kitchen, Alice dons a white apron and upon a white table rests a "white moulding-board" where she prepares for baking "nice little white things" (168). Alice does not, however, work in the lower kitchen, where the servant does the rough work, and she pities Ellen for her lack of washbasin and other feminine furniture. The redundant whiteness of the household reinforces one of the last lessons delivered by Ellen's mother as well. Before her final departure, Mrs. Montgomery directs Ellen to a Bible passage: " 'And one of the elders answered, stating unto me, What are these which are arrayed in white robes? and whence came they? . . . And he said unto me, These are they which came out of great tribulation, and have washed their robes, and made them white in the blood of the

Lamb'" (28). Later, John interprets for Ellen a white camellia as "the emblem of a sinless pure spirit, —looking up in fearless spotlessness. Do you remember what was said to the old Church of Sardis?— 'Thou hast a few names that have not defiled their garments; and they shall walk with me in white, for they are worthy'" (324–325). White garments, always worn by Ellen whenever her clothing is commented upon, mark the femininity her mother represents: an escape from the dirt that colors her stockings at Aunt Fortune's, a moral spotlessness that happens to adhere to refined households, and the freedom of being a "pure spirit"— detached from mercenary or bodily concerns.

Ellen ultimately accomplishes an ideal whiteness through a futuristic forgetting, a focus on heaven that can whitewash her things on earth and allow her to transcend the corruption of the market. Lori Merish points to the popular idea, "regularly repeated in architectural pattern books and home decorating texts, that domestic possessions constitute a 'second body'" as evidence of the importance of things in reflecting bodily identity, especially in discussions of race (231). The bodily statement made by things differs according to user, however: for slaves, their specially issued dark things reflect the darkness of skin that determines their slavery, working as a "second body" that over-corporealizes them. For feminine women, white things are instead a replacement for a body; the whiteness of her household reflects her spirituality or bodilessness. Ellen Montgomery's feminine project likewise achieves whiteness through a process of expunging blackness—racial as well as spiritual.

The second elided scene that helps explain "femininity" was unearthed by Susan L. Roberson; it appeared in Warner's original draft but was cut in order to shorten the published version. As Roberson reports, the scene occurs in an early chapter after the "old gentleman" has finished helping Ellen purchase her clothes and material. In this scene, Ellen stands on the street eating the figs the gentleman has bought her, when she sees a little black girl in a "dress miserably thin and poor," "large & clouted" shoes with "great holes through which her feet could be seen peeping out," and no bonnet or cap. Because Ellen "could not help drawing a comparison between her own condition & that of her less favoured fellow creature," she offers the girl, Rebecca, her figs. Later, Rebecca appears at Ellen's hotel apartment to return Ellen's lost purse, Mrs. Montgomery lectures her about honesty, and Ellen and her mother resolve to visit the girl later with gifts afforded by the money she has returned. When Ellen sees the girl on the streets, Rebecca is foraging for coals discarded in household coal buckets, and her blackness is emphasized by the coal ash covering her hand. But when Ellen returns home and tells her mother about the old gentleman's kindness and her adventures in shopping, she does not mention the incident with the "little coal carrier," so that her later appearance is a surprise (Roberson 19–20).

That Warner has written this passage and then "expunged" it, Roberson argues, shows not only "Warner trying to come to terms, if only briefly, with relations between the races and the role of white Americans in alleviating the distress of poor, subjugated black Americans," but also the "porousness of space" separating class and race.[6] But Ellen "expunges" this encounter before Warner does: Ellen's relation with the black girl is forgotten in her account of the day's shopping. When the Montgomerys later visit Rebecca, they find her living in a cellar marked by a sign reading "Washing done by Mary Ann Richardson." Here, they meet her mother, a "stout black woman," whose laundering has brought the marketplace as well as "a variety of unsweet and unsavoury odours" into the home. Rebecca sits "[f]lat on the floor" for lack of furniture. Ellen has sacrificed a new winter bonnet in order to present Rebecca with a "brown stuff" frock and "stout shoes" (24–25). This scene explains even better the flight from blackness that white garments signify throughout the novel. In the expurgated section, Ellen sacrifices a new travelling bonnet, which she can afford because the old gentleman has bought her a new winter bonnet himself, in order to buy Rebecca's dress and shoes. This sacrifice is marked by the old-fashioned white bonnet she must wear instead when she travels to Aunt Fortune's later—a scene unexplained in the published novel. The white bonnet therefore represents her earliest gestures of self-sacrifice, for which she suffers mockery by her fashionable fellow travelers. Though her mother has had to pawn her grandmother's ring to buy clothes, Ellen can still look upon Rebecca's "round uncovered head" and think of her own "new blue silk hood" and feel "some token" is due to mark her own happier condition (19). Although Ellen is herself the object of charity, she distinguishes herself from the black girl by her feminine rather than manual labor: she sews, while Rebecca digs in coal buckets.

Ellen's avoidance of blackness and brown-ness manifests itself directly in simple naming that occurs throughout the published novel as well: just as she shrinks from slate-colored stockings, she would rhetorically erase all evidence of stains. When she and Nancy Vawse begin naming the rivers and streams around them, Nancy suggests for one, "Black Falls," because "the water's all dark and black" (Warner 122). Ellen exclaims, "Black . . . why!—I don't like that" and submits with "Well . . . let it be Black, then; but I don't like it" (122). When trying to decide a name for her new horse, she rejects naming him after his color, because " 'Brown' was not pretty" (378). Alice's early geography lessons hint that Ellen's erasure is racial as well as color-coded. Ellen prefers not to try naming countries, she says, because " 'I can't remember those queer countries in Asia and South America half so well as Europe and North America' " (172). Besides shrinking from the "queer countries" whose inhabitants are predominantly nonwhite, she forgets even to shrink from Africa, a continent certainly notable enough and closely linked to Southern and Northern markets and populations.[7] Africa, as with the African American characters, is necessarily excluded, but Ellen's ideal white femininity attempts further to weaken the threat of blackness, lower-classness, and manual labor by erasing the exclusions.

WAIST NOT, WANT NOT

The architecture of a house, the form of the furniture, and the decoration and construction of clothing set out to distance the white woman from her enabling labor and servants. Though the women's movement might have commiserated with slaves, most white women in the upper classes would not have felt themselves aligned with the household help and would have emphasized the distinctions. To this end, a more popular "slavery" for middle- and upper-class white women was fashion. *Godey's Lady's Book*, although devoted to promoting new dress fashions in an intellectual manner, redounds that " 'Fashion is the voluntary slavery which leads us to think, act, and dress according to the judgment of fools' " (qtd. in Halttunen 67). While the early nineteenth century saw the popularity of men's conduct books such as William A. Alcott's *Young Man's Guide* (1833), which "discussed at great length the importance of dress," fashion became the specific domain of women during these years (Halttunen 40; Merish, *Sentimental Materialism* 235). Whereas from the beginning of the century men's fashion adopted a "plain, dark, uniform three-piece suit" that remained relatively constant over the decades, women's fashions changed frequently and featured bright, ornate decorations, requiring from women a constant vigilance and service to remain in style (Merish, *Sentimental Materialism* 235). The fashion rules expounded in two volumes of men's advice books—which were repeatedly reprinted over the decades before the Civil War—required instead weekly and monthly updates for women's dress, especially in periodicals such as *Godey's Lady's Book*.

Women were associated with clothing from the early stages of its production to the final product: those women who worked in factories largely worked in textile mills, and weaving "homespun" was traditionally a female occupation outside of industry. Sewing and embroidery were viewed as a determinant female skill. Readers of popular literature could expect a woman at leisure nonetheless to be working on needlework at any time of the day, and genteel women in straightened circumstances could still sew for others as a socially acceptable means of earning a living. The connection between sewing and femininity was "'deemed to be natural'" by the nineteenth century: "'Women embroidered because they were naturally feminine and were feminine because they naturally embroidered'" (qtd. in Yentsch and Beaudry 229). White middle- and upper-class women's clothing was the most mobile means to display a household's wealth and refinement. A contemporary author remarks, "'Fashion says that the chief use of woman is to exhibit dry goods fantastically arranged on her person" (qtd. in Nelson 21). Besides displaying current fashion, and social status based on the elaboration of ornament and expense of the fabric, a woman's dress also proclaimed the time of day, the activity she was engaged in, and her proper location—"the ballroom gown, lawn party dress, riding habit, walking dress, or morning wrapper" demonstrated her mastery of the etiquette of fashion as precisely as her sets of dishes did (Mattingly 7).

Despite the specificity and variety of fashions sported by women, however, the idealized portrait of the American woman remained simple: in literature, in monuments, and on stage, the ideal woman after the Revolution always wore white. Between 1783 and 1815, Americans developed the self-representative figure of Columbia, a "bareheaded, or helmeted," woman "wearing a simple white dress surrounded with the attributes of freedom" (Cunningham 182). The "classical" style in the first decade of the nineteenth century mimicked this simple whiteness, as women's fashion imitated not the dress of ancient Greeks but the "appearance of classical statuary" (Halttunen 73). Eventually this simple whiteness became ornamented, and "frills began to appear" by 1803, complicated further by "[f]lounces, vandyked borders, gores, puffed and frilled hems" until replaced around 1822 by "romantic" fashion (Halttunen 74).

Nonetheless, the ideal of the simple white dress remained pre-eminent, as represented by Stowe's Little Eva in *Uncle Tom's Cabin* (1854). The most famous feminine symbol of the century, Little Eva is "[a]lways dressed in white," never "contracting spot or stain," with "long golden-brown hair that floated like a cloud" around her head, a "deep spiritual gravity" in her "violet blue eyes," and always a "half smile on her rosy mouth" (230–231). The Veiled Lady of Hawthorne's *Blithedale Romance* (1852), whom the narrator Coverdale confesses to love at the end, also appears as an untouchable, spiritual mist: her figure "came gliding upon the platform, enveloped in a long veil of silvery whiteness," and she remains unaffected by all attempts to shake her otherworldly composure (185). The literature likewise makes a clear connection between a woman's white dress and her spirituality. Indeed, *Godey's Lady's Book*, as it advises young ladies on the "True Principles of Dress" in 1845, reminds its readers that if they "recall the works of any good author, his description of his heroine (that mirror of perfection) will be a rigid adherence in the same rule: as, for example: 'Her dress was of simple white muslin, flowing in graceful folds even to her feet'" (326). The magazine offers to "multiply examples" of this standard, but wishes instead that ladies "look for themselves, and find cause to prove the truth of this assertion." Thus the periodical invested in fashion variation and complexity appeals to literature for the ideal conception of female dress—white and flowing—even as it contradicts it on surrounding pages.

As textile manufacture made material more available to lower classes and female factory workers gained possible means to buy these goods, control over clothing and access to fashion became a space for contesting class and race constructions. *Godey's Lady's Book* admonishes women to dress according to class; like flowers, they should seek the "accordance of the dress of the blossom with the plant beside which it dwells." Beneath the prepositions, *Godey's* cautions its readers against spending a disproportionate amount on clothing or becoming "overpowered by too much vanity" and attempting to "outshine [their] companions in color and material beyond their grasp" (vol. 28: 326). Just as with dishes and housing design, clothing was a "barrier which had to be surmounted by those entering the more privileged bourgeois circles and as a standard which could be applied to the claims of those seeking admission from below" (Halttunen 62). Competitive dressing, or overt imitation of the fashion standards designating a higher class, would have been a violation of the feminine disavowal of instrumental things. More gravely, inordinate interest in fashion could be viewed as a moral issue for working-class women—a temptation to prostitution as both a means and an occasion to wear fine clothes (Valverde). The Society for the Relief of Poor Widows claimed in 1822 that " 'the greatest proportion of the Misery, and Poverty which actually exists among the lower classes in this City, arises principally from the two following causes—viz.—Intemperance among the men, and the Love of dress among the Women' " (qtd. in Stansell 164, 44n). At mid-century, a magazine editor called for the return of the tradition of servant girls who would wear the clothes of a menial, " 'which differed in make and material diametrically from the "robe" or "gown," worn by the lady mistress' " (qtd. in Stansell 165).

Fashion depended upon visible contrasts in its assertion of femininity; the transferability of such material identity meant that class and racial distinctions in clothing were carefully guarded by the upper classes. Slaves and free black women also recognized clothing as an important ingredient to femininity, sometimes rejecting the slave-issue clothing and imitating the white mistress. Former slave Maggie Black recalls for interviewers "her own efforts to imitate [white women's] wide skirts by using vines for hoops" (Weiner 14). Another slave woman remembers, " 'We wore hoop skirts on Sunday jest like the white folks. I never did like them things; if you didn't sit down this-a-way, that old hoop skirt would shoot up like this. I never had no use for them things' " (Weiner 114–115). This unidentified slave shows the elements of a battle between white and slave women, but also the intricate construction of femininity based on white goods.

An imitation of fashion should be read as a claim to ladyhood, as ladyhood was depicted through clothing. The sameness of dress constitutes only one part of femininity, however, as the unidentified slave testifies. Though she wears hoop dresses on Sundays, she never does, in fact, have a "use" for them: they cannot signify femininity unless accompanied by the feminine furniture and household, as well as white skin. If she sits the wrong way, the slave claims, her skirt "shoots up," rendering her ridiculous rather than genteel; white women in the big house had specially designed chairs to accommodate their enormous skirts and rescue them from such disasters, as well as training in the proper way to manage their bodies as they sat and stood. Chairs designed specifically for ladies had bracket arms or no arms, in order to accommodate the hoop skirt (Robertson 81). Slave furniture, on the other hand, remained unspecialized at best: for example, in *Uncle Tom's Cabin*, slaves arrive at

Uncle Tom's to sing hymns, bringing their own seats—barrels with boards laid across them, and overturned "tubs and pails"—as even Aunt Chloe's "rickety chairs are moved away" (30). The unidentified slave woman, if allowed to sit in the planter's house, would be afforded only the uncomfortable lower-class chairs—where she could hardly "use" her hoop skirt at all.

On the plantation, the mistress was generally in charge of preparing clothes for the slaves, at least cutting the cloth for others to stitch, to ensure that fitting was correct and distribution fair (Weiner 43). Slave clothing was typically made of "negro cloth" or simply handed-down clothing from the white householders, following a pattern similar to ceramic distribution. Clothing for slaves was recognized legally as powerfully constructive of identity: laws in many Southern states forbade slaves to wear clothing resembling that of their masters. Slave laws in Charleston, South Carolina, in 1822 decreed that " 'Negroes should be permitted to dress only in coarse stuffs such as coarse woolens or worsted stuffs for winter—and coarse cotton stuffs for summer . . . every distinction should be created between the whites and the negroes, calculated to make the latter feel the superiority of the former' " (qtd. in Stachiw 35). The free use of finer clothing, the law claims, had given slaves " 'ideas not consistent with their condition and made them "insolent to whites" ' " (qtd. in Merish, *Sentimental Materialism* 238). While house slaves in particular might receive handed-down clothes—as one former slave recalls, " '[M]aster's children and his wife would have white cotton suits made, and after they got tired of them they would give them to us' "—and thereby acquire the white clothing of the ruling class, some states "denied slaves the right to wear clothing that appropriated the status of free whites, even when those clothes were deemed no longer adequate for white masters" (qtd. in Starke 70; Mattingly 11).

Most slaves, however, as field hands, received an allotment of clothing once or more during the year—shirts and pants of wool and cotton, and shoes, with distinctions made only for summer and winter. Women would have received dresses, although one former slave recalls that slave women would "cut up men's pants to make 'pantalets' " (Starke 70). An insistence on coarseness in the material, as well as a broad disregard for specialized clothing based on activity or time of day—even, for women, a disregard of gendered clothing—trumpeted the differences between white and black on the plantation. Even as Frederick Law Olmsted surveys a gang of mixed-sex slave workers, he recoils from black women who appear so distant from feminine fashion. In his example, slave women work alongside the men, repairing a road with their skirts tucked up, wearing heavy shoes and men's caps or handkerchiefs. Taught no feminine refinement by their unladylike clothes and occupation, the women in particular suit their animal-like housing. Olmsted describes them as "[c]lumsy, awkward, gross, elephantine in all their movements; pouting, grinning, and leering at us; sly, sensual, and shameless in their demeanour: I never before had witnessed, I thought, anything more revolting" (162). Olmsted traces these women's degraded capacity to their clothing as a natural course and nearly concludes that their character suits them to their situation, since they seem fat enough and unconscious of their misery.

Not coincidentally, these women belong to a degraded plantation, and their housing reflects and enforces their brutalized character. In the Carolinas, where most houses for whites were made of logs "hewn but little," with the spaces between the logs "not 'chinked,' or filled up in any way; nor . . . lined on the inside," the slave cabins were respectively more humble. Here, the cabins were the smallest he has seen—twelve feet square, "built of logs, with no windows—no opening at all, except the doorway, with a chimney of sticks and mud. . . . I should have conjectured that it had been built for a powder-house, or perhaps an icehouse—never for an animal to sleep in" (161). His final choice of words then seems ironic: far from producing "anything . . . revolting," the plantation hovels attempt to convince not only the slaves but a sympathetic outsider of the propriety of the institution.

In Olmsted's estimation, the femininity marked by dress lays claim to social status and class as well. Lori Merish asserts that "[b]lack women's appropriation of fashion commodities can be read as an effort to dislodge the black female body symbolically from slavery's processes of ungendering and inscribe that body as 'feminine,' thus claiming the privileges of gender in nineteenth-century civil society" (Merish, *Sentimental Materialism* 236). Another slave asserts equality on the grounds of clothing—Lila Nichols from North Carolina describes her mistress's attempts to whip another female slave, " '[A]n' de 'oman sez ter her, "No sir, Missus, I ain't 'lowin' nobody what war de same kind of skirt I does ter whup me" ' " (qtd. in Weiner 122). As Nichols attests, this is a conversation among women: the rebellious female slave refuses to be whipped—subjected bodily and physically marked—by someone in the " 'same kind of skirt.' " Her claims are two-fold. If her mistress indeed wears a skirt of the same material, her slave claims a class equality that weakens the mistress's dominance. If she intends to imply that they both wear skirts, the slave is claiming sisterhood—a shared gender—that also challenges the dominance of one over the other. Either way, the slave understands the material makings of gender and claims "femininity" as a class, gender, and ultimately racial construct through this article of clothing.

As this female attests, clothing could be a transferable signifier of class and femininity; in response, "white middle-class women typically complained of the 'inordinate development of negro women's love for dress'" (Mattingly 11). As the Industrial Revolution made corsets more universally available, the complaint extended to lower-class women as well (Steele 36). While upper-class women "liked to think of themselves as distinctively different from the laboring classes," and "[c]aricatures not infrequently contrasted the ample torsos of working-class women with the diminutive corsets worn by bourgeois ladies," working-class women of the United States wore corsets as well, even in factory work. Slave women and free blacks might also wear corsets, especially the house slaves (Steele 49). Nonetheless, corsets, especially tightly laced as they became in the mid-nineteenth century, combined with dress fashion to render the fashionable lady incapable of heavy labor. The sentimental style popular after 1836 consisted of a small top and tight sleeves, "making it virtually impossible for the wearer to raise her arms above a right angle to her body" (Halttunen 75). In addition, the petticoat, designed to add fullness to the skirt, was worn "five or six at a time, [and] impeded a woman by adding to her frame an additional weight of as much as fifteen pounds" (Nelson 23). Thorstein Veblen's *The Theory of the Leisure Class* (1899) claims that the corset seemed designed for its "elaborate insistence on the idleness, if not the physical infirmity of the wearer"—or at least "to impress upon the beholder the fact (often indeed a fiction) that the wearer does not and can not habitually engage in useful work" (182, 179). The corset could be a visual denial of work, therefore, but it was also a visual denial of the body. Cartoons compared the corseted figure with examples of female beauty depicted in ancient art, ostensibly arguing that the corseted woman was less beautiful because unnatural. But such cartoons also illustrate the feminine woman as unbodily, by the contrast her shape has to an actual female body. The contrast was rendered even more spectacular, then, when cartoons and literary descriptions drew working-class and slave women as thick or corpulent. Thus the corset colludes with household architecture in implying that the lady does not work; indeed it requires the laboring force that it defines itself against for the leisure it proclaims.

Corsets were nearly always white, made of "white cotton or linen, or at most white satin" (Steele 39). Though always hidden beneath the clothes in the nineteenth century, patterns for stays were also regularly displayed in magazines such as *Godey's Lady's Book*—of course, without a female body inside them (Steele 40). One fashion magazine states, "'The corset is an ever-present monitor indirectly bidding its wearer to exercise self-restraint: it is evidence of a well-disciplined mind and well-regulated feelings'" (qtd. in Nelson 23). At the same time, the corset was considered an "unmentionable": as late as 1947 a fashion book illustrating nineteenth-century dresses shied from direct reference to it. James Laver's *Costume Illustration* (1947) explains that around 1820 the "skirt swelled out (many petticoats beginning to be worn underneath) and the *other device* adopted, to make the waist look even smaller than it was" (3, emphasis mine). Hidden, the corset nonetheless becomes evidence; encasing the body, it nonetheless signals a controlled mind and emotions. In their simultaneous status as "unmentionable" and expected, in their everyday use and literary popularity, corsets functioned as white things in the same way dishes, fashion, and houses did, with the feminine addition of disavowing its power.

RE-MOTTLED KITCHENS

The securing of a tight corset and fashionable dress could be a ritual establishing race, therefore, but one inviting certain problems for an abolitionist writer. In *Uncle Tom's Cabin*, Stowe reveals the tension in the supposed sisterhood between slaves and mistresses when Eliza appeals to Mrs. Shelby about Mr. Shelby's plans to sell her son. The novel's clothing scenes demonstrate the anxiety of femininity's resting in the hands of one not invested in it—of the dependence of femininity on the symbolic image and physical labor of the black woman, who by definition can neither participate in nor benefit from this gendered ideal. Conflicts in the novel's racialist treatment of slaves throughout can be viewed in light of the antebellum "Negro problem": how does a white woman protect femininity when it depends upon a self-willed, human support? The plot of *Uncle Tom's Cabin* is motivated largely in exploring solutions to this problem: the white woman can gain the sympathy and support of the excluded black female; she can continue to depend on her servant but keep her hidden away; or she can send her away entirely. Stowe tests the success of each of these: with the first, the supportive slave must be constantly supervised and negotiated with in order to maintain her fidelity. For the second, slaves continually unsettle the hidden-ness of their work by appearing, observing, and talking back. Stowe is left with the final alternative only—self-willed blacks must leave the country or die.[8] Stowe later voices a concern that "'the essential *animus* of the slave system still exists'" in the relationship between housekeepers and their servants; in an article called "A Family Talk on Reconstruction" in 1869, Stowe worries that the "'desire to monopolize and to dominate'" will manifest itself with domestic employees, suggesting that the mistress-slave relationship would remain a constant temptation even without its legal sanction.[9] A household "without servants" is the only solution—although, I would argue, Stowe's reformed domesticity continues to rely on the racial underpinnings of conspicuous leisure. The visible expulsion of labor by its always already being "done up" depends upon the slavery-induced flight from physicality informing femininity.

In the novel's opening scene, Eliza obtains information that her mistress is not privy to, because, as a slave, Eliza listens at the door while Mr. Shelby agrees to the sale of Tom and her son Harry. Eliza moves between the masculine realm of men discussing business in the parlor and the feminine realm of Mrs. Shelby's bedroom. Although the subject of the conversation, she is also a disrupter in the household, through her mobility among realms and her observant presence. In *Uncle Tom's Cabin*, Gillian Brown argues, slavery "undermines women's housework by bringing the confusion of the marketplace into the kitchen, the center of the family shelter" (16). The slave's presence in the household does create this disruption: that the slave conflates work and home in her person is bad, but what is worse is that her status as "ungendered" gives her a mobility that undermines the masculine and feminine realms of her owners. As Eliza tries to learn more about her son's sale, Mrs. Shelby calls her away—so Eliza can dress her. Eliza's problem is introduced to Mrs. Shelby, purportedly a "woman of a high class, both intellectually and morally," when Eliza upsets the wash pitcher and work stand, "and finally was abstractedly offering her mistress a long nightgown in place of the silk dress she had ordered her to bring from the wardrobe" (Stowe, *Uncle Tom's* 20, 18). Though she will be properly sympathetic towards Eliza when she learns the news from her husband, in this scene Mrs. Shelby is disturbed by

Eliza's attack on her femininity, as well as her momentary visibility created by her failure to do her job smoothly. The wash pitcher and work stand are feminine furnishings, marking Mrs. Shelby's class status, as cleanliness still reflected refined living, and her intellectual development, as the work stand was a feminine desk for personal rather than business letters. Mrs. Shelby is preparing for "an evening visit," and Eliza's offer of a nightgown in place of a silk dress is a shocking affront to Mrs. Shelby's modesty, class status, and awareness of time-appropriate fashions.

Her response to Eliza seeks to restore the household balance by constructing a strictly feminine sphere, where black and white women can co-exist peacefully, apart from masculine integration. She does so, however, first by over-feminizing Eliza, and then by re-establishing a racial hierarchy between the females. She denies that Mr. Shelby intends to sell Harry, exclaiming, " 'Sell him! No, you foolish girl! . . . Why, you silly child, who do you think would want to buy your Harry? Do you think all the world are set on him as you are, you goosie?' " (19). Her protests attempt at each pause even further to infantilize Eliza, from mother to "girl" to "child" to "goosie." Rhetorically rendered a toddler, Eliza cannot seriously offend: Mrs. Shelby can imagine that Eliza's foolishness rather than her distress has led her to disregard fashion and that Eliza cannot really understand what she sees when she trespasses into improper realms. Mrs. Shelby then seeks to reassure Eliza through the ritual of constructing Mrs. Shelby's own femininity: she continues, " 'Come, cheer up, and hook my dress. There now, put my hair back up in that pretty braid you learnt the other day, and don't go listening at doors anymore' " (19). Mrs. Shelby re-negotiates her servant's support here, positioning herself as mother to the "goosie" and sister to the hairdresser. As a caveat, however, she adds a command, in the position of mistress, to avoid the need for further negotiations: stay hidden and immobile when not serving—don't go listening at doors.

The novel moves from Eliza to an unshakably reliable slave, Aunt Chloe, who combines evidence of an investment in femininity and contentment with her exclusion from it. The easy intrusion into Uncle Tom's cabin as the narrator states, "Let us enter the dwelling" marks it as a slave dwelling, but also signifies the occupants' willingness to be supervised (Merish, "Sentimental Consumption"). Indeed, in the family scene following, the slaves' attention remains on the white master, Mas'r George, as he eats Aunt Chloe's cooking and corrects Uncle Tom's writing. The cabin itself displays an investment in white middle-class femininity. On the outside, flowers cover its "rough logs," leaving "scarce a vestige . . . to be seen" (28). Inside, Aunt Chloe has carved out a "*drawing room*," consisting of a piece of carpeting that for Aunt Chloe signifies "the upper walks of life" and a bed "covered neatly with a snowy spread." This portion of the "snug" cabin imitates middle-class fashion and pretensions and shows, with the flowers, Aunt Chloe's valuing of these pretensions. But it is the other corner of the cabin that is "designed for *use*." (29, italics in text). Here, there rests a "much humbler" bed, scriptural prints on the wall, a portrait of George Washington colored black. Elsewhere, for use, are a table "somewhat rheumatic in its limbs," "cups and saucers of a decidedly brilliant pattern," and a "cracked teapot" (30, 34). Aunt Chloe "uses" her white bedspread and refined articles in the same way the earlier slave used a hoop dress on Sundays—as a signal of imitation and investment in white middle-class ideology, but also as a collection of things segregated from her everyday life. Aunt Chloe's practical furnishings mark her rather as a slave, with cracked and handed-down dishes in colorful rather than white patterns.

But Aunt Chloe also displays on her person the "sentimental ideal of transparency," revealing through her skin a true portrait of her soul—the model for beauty set forth by *Godey's Lady's Book* in what Karen Halttunen calls the "cult of sincerity" (Halttunen 71; 88). Aunt Chloe has a "round, black, shining face . . . so glossy as to suggest the idea that she might have been washed over with white of eggs" (29). Her blackness, Stowe suggests, is enabled and exaggerated by the whiteness washed over it, just as her cabin is all the more clearly a slave cabin because middle-class pretensions render half of it unusable. She emphasizes for her white master her own bodily blackness and how it fits her for labor. Aunt Chloe narrates a subtle struggle for control of the kitchen when she says to Mrs. Shelby, " 'Now, Missis, do jist look at dem beautiful white hands o' yourn, with long fingers, and all a-sparkling with rings, like my white lilies when de dew's on 'em; and look at my great black stumpin hands. Now, don't ye think dat de Lord must have meant *me* to make de piecrust, and you to stay in de parlor?' " (32–33). Claiming control of a territory was one form of slave rebellion, and plantation mistresses had a particular problem supervising the kitchen against territorial cooks (Weiner). A cook for Caroline Merrick in South Carolina also invoked race as architecturally constructed to convince her mistress not to interfere with the cook's labor: she would say, " 'Yer ain't no manner er use heah only ter git yer face red wid de heat. . . . Jes' read yer book an' res' easy till I sen's it ter de dining-room' "

(Weiner 122–123). Aunt Chloe goes further, recognizing her rebellion as a necessary act in enforcing the God-directed activities allowed to femininity, and her own blackness as a declaration of her mistress's femininity. Even under the most ideal of slave environments, Stowe suggests with these early examples, labor's blackness will reveal itself and undermine a white wife and mother's domestic authority.

The supportive slave functions fairly well under Mrs. Shelby's capable hands—even George, slave to a cruel master, agrees that Eliza should obey her mistress because of Mrs. Shelby's kindness (26). The slave cook at the St. Clare plantation, Dinah, commandeers the kitchen in the same way Aunt Chloe does, but Dinah's organization is secretive and hidden, and her mistress does not supervise. While Mrs. Shelby is an "uncommon" housekeeper, Marie St. Clare is an "unsystematic and improvident housekeeper," leaving the household slaves to their own devices and lounging lazily about the parlor and breakfast-room complaining about her suffering. When Miss Ophelia begins to organize the house, "hidden things of darkness were brought to light to an extent that alarmed all the principalities and powers of kitchen and chamber" (194). Miss Ophelia finds the slave Dinah's mode of organization to be "without any sort of calculation as to time and place," so that supervision and order are impossible (195). She opens drawers containing, amidst nutmegs, onions, old shoes, and hymn-books, "one or two gilded China saucers with some pomade in them [Dinah's hair oil] . . . several damask table-napkins, some coarse crash towels," along with "a fine damask table cloth stained with blood, having evidently been used to envelop some raw meat" (196). Beyond experiencing the obvious revulsion of eating food that has commingled with shoes and hair oil, Miss Ophelia reacts against the systematic contradictions of the drawer. Dinah uses the master's display china for her private bodily attentions; she integrates the "working" towels with the dining damask napkins. Even during her " 'clarin' up times,' " when Dinah scrubs the tables "snowy white" and dons a "smart dress, clean apron, and high, brilliant, Madras turban," she can accomplish such order only by tucking "everything that could offend . . . out of sight in holes and corners" (198).

The bloodstained tablecloth encapsulates the danger of this disorder, however: that which is hidden away will continue to haunt and reappear. Revealing that it has "evidently" enclosed raw meat, the marked table cloth has failed in its purpose to hide the animal aspect of dining, and the bloodstained cloth is much more repulsive than the table it was intended to hide. It discloses its fineness as a veneer over the rawness of the bloody slave institution: in fact, Dinah pollutes the white veneer with this evidence of what has given it shape.[10] These stains, in fact, haunt the narrative, and it is appropriate that they appear on linen. Little Eva's ideal white dress "never contract[s] spot or stain," but the working household is in constant danger.

The impulse among white masters to hide slaves while yet to supervise them is seen historically in an exemplary instance of control and design in Thomas Jefferson's Monticello, which has been thoroughly documented since the nineteenth century. The design of Monticello ostensibly was to transform its owner " 'into an all-seeing I' " where Jefferson might supervise his grounds without being observed; yet he "also went to extraordinary lengths to render his enslaved workforce invisible." Outside the house, the landscape was arranged to hide slave cabins and work areas; in 1804 Jefferson cleared away wooden sheds and slave cabins along Mulberry Row and built a "ha-ha" at the base of his gardens (Epperson 70). Terrence W. Epperson refers to " 'spaces of constructed invisibility' " on Jefferson's plantation: inside the house, "Jefferson developed devices such as dumbwaiters, lazy Susans, and a *garde-robe* privy that could be emptied from the basement to minimize intimate contact with his slaves" (64, 70). The problem with such ideals of hidden-ness, as in the problems encountered at Monticello, is that the mobile, self-willed workforce will reappear. At Monticello, for example, domestic garbage could never quite be kept from view. William Kelso finds archaeological evidence that drainage from the privy probably washed out onto a carriage road (15). Slave cabins in varying degrees of decay, surrounded by deep layers of trash, and an equally strewn kitchen yard stood between the great house and the garden walks. Carriage turnarounds were paved with trash (Kelso 15–16). Like Jefferson, Miss Ophelia in *Uncle Tom's Cabin* would hide "everything that could offend," but for Ophelia the offenders would be the slaves themselves. The slave Dinah resists this strategy, talking back through the linens and dishware, controlling her realm by refusing supervision. Stowe recognizes that though Ophelia might possibly impose order on Dinah's kitchen, such organization would only deny, not destroy, the fact of slavery. A proper plantation mistress would not allow a bloodstained linen; she would have the meat cooked and placed in a white dish above the damask tablecloth. But it is only a more civilized version of the same mess.[11]

Dinah seems perfectly capable of small rebellions in the running of her kitchen, but even as she critiques the system by wrapping meat with a tablecloth, she implicates femininity in her dishwashing. Arguing over slave supervision with his sister, Augustine St. Clare asks, " 'Don't I know . . . that she washes dishes with a dinner napkin one day, and with a fragment of an old petticoat the next?' " (199). More overtly than she exposes slavery in the tablecloth, she exposes her own participation in femininity with an old petticoat. Because it is underclothing, Dinah's open use of the petticoat is at least embarrassing; but she washes the dishes with it, soiling a hidden feminine article in the process of cleansing dishes, themselves feminine items meant for display. Dinah's hand tells the tale that Monticello and other plantations tell, and Miss Ophelia's Northern home as well: that femininity is unavoidably soiled in its construction of white refinement and that the black hand that prepares both will leave neither fully white.

INSTITUTIONAL WHITES

If Dinah rebels against her mistress's tyranny by washing the dishes with an old petticoat, fashion reformers sympathized, rebelling against the tyranny of the petticoat itself. In response to the unhealthy and uncomfortable fashion of tightly laced corsets and multiple petticoats, Amelia Bloomer designed a knee-length walking dress that required no corset, but nonetheless provided for modesty by adding ankle-length pantaloons. Although for a brief period at the turn of the century, corsets fell out of fashion and classical gowns depended upon a "minimum of underclothing," the Bloomerists' rejection of stays in the 1850s signaled for detractors "immodesty and immorality" (Halttunen 73; Mattingly 67). By 1851 when Bloomer introduced her design, the corseted dress had become a mark of feminine self-control set against the unrestrained corporeality of slave women and the more flexible work clothing of lower-class women, as well as the simple limb-dividing pantaloons required for men's maneuverability in the marketplace. Therefore, although doctors and magazine editors initially praised the bloomer design as more healthy and practical, publications soon settled upon criticism and ridicule (Mattingly).

Carol Mattingly examines the progress of the dress reform movement as it was debated in popular periodicals and medical journals. Underpinning negative reactions to bloomers were medical arguments against women in pants, appeals to proper femininity, and subtle racial concerns. The simple demand for bodily comfort voiced by bloomer-wearers confronted the disembodying work of the corset and unnatural fashions; bloomers could be seen as a challenge to "femininity" in general, and a disregard for the racial and class structures used to create it. *Peterson's* magazine states that " 'Nature has decided this matter, and there is no escaping Nature. A woman, in walking, moves the lower limbs in a circular sweep. A man moves them straight forward. This any anatomist will declare' " (qtd. in Mattingly 77). Appeals to femininity entrusted all of feminine and masculine behavior on the simple corset and skirt, as various articles threatened a complementary end to "gallantry" when femininity was thus abandoned (70–72). Specific opponents attacked Bloomerists' femininity subtly by connecting them to African American women: one set of opponents made a present of " 'the Turkish costume and a gypsey hat' to a 'colored lady' in Syracuse" (73). Elsewhere, a reporter for the *New York Daily Times* describes a woman in Bloomers as " 'quite pretty, but her ungainly pantalets of purple linsey-woolsey were shocking' " (82). Linsey-woolsey, commonly understood to make up slave clothing, critiques this woman's neglect of fashion as, at least, smacking of lower-classness and, more "shockingly," suggesting an ungendering that would affiliate her with slave women. Sojourner Truth rejected the Bloomer, according to Stowe, because it resembled her slavery costume (Mattingly 110). Since slaves were allotted a standard length of "nigger-cloth" apiece, Truth's skirts never fully covered her long legs: for her, Bloomers represented not freedom from excessive material, but the paucity of dress suffered by slaves.

While Bloomer wearers were mocked in public and in print, women wearing men's clothing were often arrested. Sumptuary laws regulated slave clothing in the South, but they also influenced male and female clothing in the North. The 1850s saw several famous cross-dressers—always women dressed as men—and newspapers reported on their various arrests. Carol Mattingly reports on two famous women in the 1850s, Dr. Mary Walker and Emma Snodgrass. Dr. Mary Walker was a public speaker who had received the Congressional Medal of Honor. Even though she was able to produce a congressional letter granting her the privilege to wear men's clothing, she was repeatedly arrested for appearing in male attire for her public lectures (99). Mattingly reads a "contradictory message" in the newspaper treatments of Emma Snodgrass, the attractive young daughter of a New York police captain. Though the cross-dresser is " 'unsexed' " by her costume, she also creates " 'a sensation among romantic loving young men' " (102). In fact, the message agrees with the contemporary construction of femininity: lacking a dress and restraining corset, the young woman cannot be feminine, but femininity is characterized by purity and self-control—which are not necessarily conducive to romantic sensation.

For Confederate soldiers viewing Dr. Mary E. Walker on stage, the "unsexing" of the cross-dresser renders her not only unfeminine, but inhuman. Although their reaction is mixed, their impression is definite: "'[We] were all amused and disgusted ... at the sight of a thing that nothing but the debased and depraved Yankee nation could produce.... She was dressed in the full uniform of a Federal Surgeon.... She would be more at home in a "lunatic asylum"'" (qtd. in Mattingly 85). Women appearing as public speakers already posed a threat to notions of the "feminine realm," and most compensated by emphasizing their femininity in white gowns. These women assumed the costume of Quaker clothing, whose whiteness seemed "'incapable of receiving soil; and cleanliness in them [seemed] to be something more than the absence of its contrary'" (Charles Lamb, qtd. in Mattingly 17). Dressed as one of the "'troops of the Shining Ones,'" they could "divert attention from their bodies" to assert their femininity and thereby "ensure some consideration for their cause'" (17, 34). Although blackface minstrelsy often featured men dressed as women even as the whites portrayed blacks, such play was amusing rather than threatening. The inclination of a woman to dress as a man, however, challenged femininity: and in the mid-nineteenth century, femininity was a crucial ingredient in the material construction of whiteness. Its challenge or rejection in the form of loose-fitting pants called for institutional control to replace the self-control no longer practiced by the wearer—the prison or insane asylum.

E.D.E.N. Southworth's *The Hidden Hand or, Capitola the Madcap* (1859) approaches this threat of the institution—asylum or prison—as a means of exploring the limits of clothing's power in shaping gender identity. Joanne Dobson argues that the novel is safely able to challenge gender norms because "Cap remains in the realm of fantasy, her character and her story exaggerated to the point of remaining ... obvious and self-conscious literary constructions"—that the novel's humor allowed it to become a "compensatory fantas[y]" for its nineteenth-century readers (Dobson, "Hidden" 235, xiii). However, its own "self-conscious" construction calls attention to the humor as a safety device; the novel full of puns, doubling, and jokes never fails to explain itself. Clara Day becomes a pun soon explained—"'Clare Day—how the name suits her! ... Her face is indeed like a clear day,'" exclaims Traverse (Southworth 137). Dorky

Knight is first encountered on a dark night (277). Mrs. Condiment is Old Hurricane's housekeeper, and Mr. Breefe is his lawyer. Of course the layering of blacks—Capitola Black, Black Donald, Colonel Le Noir, Granny Raven, Herbert Greyson, Father Gray—all intimately bound up with Capitola's past and future, cannot be missed by the reader. The novel calls attention to its manipulation of gender and race in the same way: so that whatever might be hidden in their construction becomes evident. The reader is left no work to do or mystery to unveil—even the ghost that haunts Hidden House and later Clara Day's house is obviously the missing Madame Le Noir. Just as she does with the punning names, Southworth hides the constructing agents and then exposes their hiddenness—thus exposed, they cannot haunt. On her first night at Hurricane Hall, Capitola establishes a rhetorical sisterhood with her newly assigned slave Pitapat, based on the shared "pit" in their names. The similarity is architecturally expressed as well by the "pit" existing in Capitola's bedroom. When she inspects this pit, she discovers only "darkness 'visible' ": and it is the visibility of the darkness, the acknowledgement of the backgrounded slave, that defines Capitola's gendered freedom and privilege (76).

Southworth connects the color white with femininity and then explores how this construction might be manipulated; she supports this femininity with troops of blackness—servants, settings, and names—but then revels in the buoyancy their support offers. The layers of things surrounding each character determine his or her complexion and femininity, but the things can also be changed to transform identity. Such possibility for change causes anxiety in real life, expressed through sumptuary laws, Negro codes, segregating architecture: but Southworth invests her heroine with the power simply not to take them seriously, so that she can control their movement rather than be controlled. In this way, the central name game of the novel, "*capital* Capitola," enjoys the mobility offered by capitalism and its ability to confer privilege strictly through things. At the same time, the novel signals danger with its white things, marking their potential to re-fix gender, class, and race in its radiant meanings (338, italics in text). Capitola enacts her femininity not through having and pretending not to want, but by pretending to pretend not to want. She establishes her racial whiteness not by contrasting and expunging the enslaved blackness that serves her, but by openly using it and becoming stronger through that use.

The opening scene reveals the hidden-ness of the hand, and the rest of the novel continues in this revelatory mode. Hurricane Hall is a "dark, red sandstone" mansion in Virginia, occupied by Major Warfield, with "his complexion dark red" (7–8). The first scene shows him in his bed chamber, preparing for bed, and surrounded by his comforts: "Old Hurricane, as I said, sat well wrapped up in his wadded dressing-gown, and reclining in his padded easy chair." Having established his padded comfort, the narrator describes the accessories surrounding him: "On his right hand stood a little table with a lighted candle, a stack of clay pipes, a jug of punch, lemons, sugar, Holland gin, etc.... On his left hand stood his cozy bedstead with its warm crimson curtains festooned back, revealing the luxurious swell of the full feather bed, and pillows with their snow-white linen, and lambswool blankets inviting repose." Only after describing the luxury of the room and meditating on its overwhelming fluffiness does the narrator attend to the slave enabling this comfort: "Between this bedstead and the corner of the fireplace stood Old Hurricane's ancient body-servant, Wool, engaged in warming a crimson cloth nightcap" (9). Besides playing with the obvious racial standard of a woolly-headed slave in the naming of this servant, Southworth also overtly connects him with his surroundings, layering his wooliness with the lambswool, padding, wadding, and coziness. Further, she alerts us to the fact that she has elided him earlier: the narrative eye moves from Old Hurricane's left side, to his right side, and then back between them to note the hidden "hand."

Just as Southworth brings forth the hidden laboring force of the novel, she exposes the fabricated basis of gender: clothing. Scholars have noted the novel's gender play variously as a subversion of popular femininity, a reconciliation of contrasts—mainly masculine and feminine—and even a pronouncement against sex itself.[12] In fact, however, the novel is an exploration of the detachability of gender, the material basis of femininity that allows it to be removed and replaced at Capitola's convenience. Early in the story, Capitola does not assume a masculine role as a bootblack in order to earn a living; rather, she changes clothes when she "'made up [her] mind to be a boy!'" (46, italics in text). When she is arrested for her male attire, she can nevertheless take refuge in her femininity: once Old Hurricane recovers from his shock at mistaking her sex, he demands that the arresting officer "'treat her with the delicacy due to womanhood'" (39, italics in text). Capitola repeatedly sets aside her femininity in the midst of an adventure—saving a damsel in distress, fighting a duel, capturing Black Donald—but she gathers it around her when femininity might protect her.[13] She persists in referring to herself as a "hero" rather than a heroine, and she fulfills this title by saving herself and her friends repeatedly—not by virtue and moral suasion in a feminine fashion, nor " 'by the strength of [her] arm,' " the manly route, but by daring and wit (77, 308).

The upper-class women in the novel are submissive and properly white-clad, but remain powerless against their male abusers. Clara is a "fair, golden-haired, blue-eyed, white-robed angel"; Madame Le Noir is a "beautiful pale, spectral woman" "clothed in white."[14] These very white garments help to imprison them, however; Madame Le Noir appears as a ghost in her "white raiment": Clara Day must change into Capitola's riding habit in order to save her honor and to avoid suicide. Even as Clara Day escapes from danger in Capitola's nonwhite dress, Marah Rocke connects her changed clothing to her character. When Clara exhibits the spunk to suggest she work for a living, Marah accuses her of " 'contract[ing] some of [her] eccentric little friend Capitola's ways, from putting on her habit' " (326).

Southworth's critique of femininity as produced by white things becomes clear as Southworth describes Capitola's much-abused mother. She appears only near the end of the novel, having been enclosed in an attic for most of eighteen years. Small and graceful, with a "snow-white cheek" and a face of "marble whiteness," arched eyebrows and ringlets "black as midnight," Madame Le Noir languishes in an insane asylum, placed there by an evil brother-in-law eager to collect her husband's wealth (440–441). This institution, enforcing an architectural control over femininity, is in fact the only edifice in the novel that is white. As Traverse approaches the asylum, he sees a "large, low, white building, surrounded with piazzas and shaded by fragrant and flowering southern trees," which "looked like the luxurious country seat of some wealthy merchant or planter" (439). Inside, the cells of the imprisoned women have "white-washed walls, and white curtained beds and windows," and are "excessively neat" (440). Thus describing the ideal of a Southern plantation or a middle-class feminine home, Southworth deftly links femininity to an entrapping confusion of the mind.

Southworth's disassembly of femininity occurs both materially and philosophically. Having exposed some of the physical ingredients defining the feminine, she undermines its institutional agents—in a conversation, appropriately, between a planter and a minister. Soon after assuming care of Capitola, Major Warfield has cause to complain, " 'She won't obey me, except when she likes! she has never been taught obedience or been accustomed to subordination, and don't understand either!' " Major

Warfield seeks the advice of a minister to help him control his female charge, and the minister responds with a guidebook means to managing women: " 'Lock her up in her chamber until she is brought to reason' " (175). Various other suggestions—masculine "firmness," an appeal to Capitola's gratitude, and moral suasion—likewise fail because Capitola sees through their constructedness. When Capitola teases the minister with the hint that she has hidden a man in her bedroom, the minister's response reveals the devastation Capitola has wreaked upon the gender constructions so carefully built. He rushes to Major Warfield and exclaims, " 'Thrash that girl as if she were a bad boy—for she richly deserves it!' " (185). In desperation, the minister reverts to her corporeality, but Capitola can respond to this new threat by re-assuming her femininity and wondering that a gentleman would consider hitting a lady.

More directly, Capitola saves herself and her servant by removing her corset, in a scene nearly a mirror opposite of Scarlett and Mammy's. Discovering a set of armed desperados under her bed one evening, Capitola must contrive to leave the room without arousing their suspicion. She accomplishes this by abusing her slave girl and demanding a tray of food, cursing her corset properly with " 'come here this minute and unhook my dress, I can't breathe! Plague take those country dressmakers, they think the tighter they screw one up the more fashionable they make one appear! Come, I say, and set my lungs at liberty' " (193). Having lured her servant from the dangerous environs of the bed, Capitola orders Pitapat to the kitchen for more food, and then follows her because the slave is afraid of the dark. Outside the room, she covers the sound of her locking the door with "loud and angry railing against poor Pitapat" (195). Her sisterhood with this slave has been established on Capitola's first night, but this sisterhood is still one of mistress and slave. Capitola escapes the threat of the desperadoes because she knows when and how to remove her feminine "unmentionables," and she visibly performs her dependence on a slave for the process.

Southworth demonstrates in this exchange between the heroically abusive mistress and the stereotypically comic slave the power of the corset constraining them both. Her ultimate message seems to be, however, that for all its power, femininity limits those who invest in it. Femininity, as with its constituent white things, is best viewed as a tool rather than an identity it constructs. The object of Southworth's critique appears to be, then, not femininity itself, nor slavery or class distinctions: these are made into jokes but ultimately upheld. What the novel will not re-establish is the hidden-ness that enables whiteness and the whiteness that has to hide the hand. The novel's "compensatory" fantasy is based upon an appropriation and exposure of the enabling blacks and blackness. Where Stowe would hide or expel the slave's blackness, Southworth will flatten and detach it—for if the white things creating femininity can be detached, so can the black things threatening and supporting it. Her ultimate statement about slavery, sentimentality, and even clothes seems to be, then, "lighten up"—at least enough to enjoy the darkness.

VEILED THREATS

It is the detachability of femininity's ingredients that distresses the narrator of Nathaniel Hawthorne's *The Blithedale Romance*. While Capitola revels in her ability to don and divest herself of femininity, Coverdale becomes victim to it, rendered disembodied, passive, ornamental. The feminine realm of the cemetery included an increasing variety of images sculpted in stone, some identified by Susan K. Harris as part of a "code" for femininity in nineteenth-century literature—and many of these objects begin to adhere to Coverdale in his narrative. Flowers, Harris asserts, marked the "heroines' natural piety," but they also carried individual meanings that were decoded in floral dictionaries (79). Flowers were sometimes carved along the border of slate gravestones, among the geometric designs popular in the eighteenth century, but blossoms appear as the central image on nineteenth-century marble markers. The motif of the flower gathered in full bloom was a widespread romantic image for the death of a young person especially, and appears in sentimental novels and tombstone inscriptions alike (see Combs, 201–209). Other popular gravestone images included angels, grieving women, willow trees, columns, and veils. Prevalent designs include a partially veiled urn, a veiled column or obelisk, and a veiled tomb. Each of these images, by association—especially the veil—comes to symbolize or signify femininity.

In *The Blithedale Romance*, Coverdale reveals his implicit faith in specifically white things as a reliable measure of identity. Throughout the novel, the narrator never fails to describe the clothing of the ones he observes and deduce a class, gender, and moral status from it. As Zenobia first appears, she is immediately described as "dressed as simply as possible, in an American print" and "a single flower" in her hair, and Coverdale's first conversation with her is about clothing (17). Priscilla arrives "dressed in a

Veiled tomb, woman mourning with urn in white marble, Mt. Auburn Cemetery, Boston, Massachusetts. Amos and Mary Ann Binny, died 1847 and 1884, respectively. Photography by Bridget Heneghan.

poor, but decent gown, made high in the neck, and without any regard to fashion or smartness" (27). Moodie's clothes are consistently introduced; as he visits Blithedale "dressed rather shabbily yet decent enough, in a gray frock-coat, faded towards a brown hue, and . . . a broad-rimmed white hat, the fashion of several years gone by" (77). When Coverdale leaves Blithedale and returns to town, he renews his costume descriptions as he meets each character again: he himself dons a fashionable coat "with a satin cravat . . . a white vest, and several other things" (126). Coverdale describes Zenobia's and Priscilla's town dresses as well, and he suggests their power when he teases Zenobia by asking, " 'has Hollingsworth ever seen [Priscilla] in this dress?' " (156). Coverdale resents Westervelt for his fashioned superiority: "I hated him, partly . . . from a comparison of my own homely garb with his well-ordered foppishness" (86).

Clothing creates social identity for Coverdale. Even non-material designations take on import through being allied with clothing: Coverdale worries that the company's enthusiasm for the experiment might "grow flimsy and flaccid as the proselyte's moistened shirt-collar" (77). As he speaks of Christianity he describes the "One, who merely veiled himself in mortal and masculine shape, but was, in truth, divine" (112). Even at

Blithedale, costume becomes the common pastime, as the company performs "*tableaux vivants*" with "scarlet shawls, old silken robes, ruffs, velvets, furs," and later the group enjoys an outdoor festival dressed as Native Americans, mythical characters, religious and military figures, and African Americans, and dress in flowers for a May Day procession (198, 191). Coverdale does not, in fact, shun the marketplace, but trusts in materially developed identities so completely that he finds himself constantly in danger, among the fluid signifiers of Blithedale, of becoming someone else altogether. The veil that hides the Veiled Lady fully reveals her femininity, and Coverdale trusts this white thing with nothing beneath it, because it defines a feminine relationship to goods: a disembodied whiteness that can claim but not possess.

At Blithedale, it "was impossible . . . not to imbibe the idea that everything in nature and human existence was fluid, or fast becoming so," and gender roles are confused to the extent that some "that wear the petticoat, will go afield, and leave the weaker brethren to take our places in the kitchen" (18, 129). Within this fluid environment, Coverdale feels his former identity to be likewise confused and discovers that the material things of the Blithedale farm have the power to reshape his identity. The main image of the narrative, the white veil introduced by the Veiled Lady, then becomes the motivating force and symbol for Coverdale's narrative. Coverdale explains of the veil, "It was white, with somewhat of a subdued silver sheen, like the sunny side of a cloud; and falling over the wearer, from head to foot, was supposed to insulate her from the material world, from time and space, and to endow her with many of the privileges of a disembodied spirit" (6). But, as Zenobia's legend suggests, beneath this veil lies nothing; the whiteness of this signifying cloth encompasses all of its power; only an idea supports it. In Zenobia's legend, to be beneath the veil is to be in bondage "worse than death," but when Zenobia's hero lifts the veil, the pale maiden beneath it disappears. As with the idea of the "feminine," the veil contains no person, place, or thing. Similarly, Coverdale designates the (white) sexes by noun and adjective—when he returns to Blithedale and encounters a costumed parade, he encounters its participants first as voices, "male and feminine" (190). The veil then represents for Coverdale both the power of femininity and its dangers. But it also remains throughout a powerful white thing—the ultimate white thing that invests its wearer with ideal femininity.

Coverdale experiences this ideal and danger personally through an accidental accumulation of feminine things. The sickbed is the first artifact of femininity donned by Coverdale, the first morning after he arrives at Blithedale. As he lies in his sickbed, Coverdale whispers about the "magical property in the flower" in Zenobia's hair—specifically, that it signals her sisterhood to the Veiled Lady. In response, Zenobia presents him this added memento of femininity: the hothouse flower. Administered medicine enough to have "lain on the point of a needle," and fed such food as to reduce him to "a skeleton above ground," he becomes intuitive and ethereal, feminine qualities that, minus his masculine flesh, leave him susceptible to the "spheres of our companions" (44–45). The combination of feminine codings begins to tell upon him. "Zenobia's sphere," he confesses, "impressed itself powerfully on mine, and transformed me, during this period of my weakness, into something like a mesmerical clairvoyant" (45). He is transformed by this woman's sphere into a "mesmerical clairvoyant," the exact role of the Veiled Lady, that symbol of femininity.

For Coverdale's final initiation into the ranks of wispy womanhood, Priscilla enters Coverdale's sick-chamber and presents him with the emblem of pure womanhood, white garb. Approaching the weakened narrator, Priscilla holds out "an article of snow-white linen" that symbolizes a woman but is tailored for a man. The object's message is so startling that the narrator sets it off in an emphatic paragraph of its own: "It was a night-cap!" (47). After being overpowered by the feminine sphere, assuming the role of the Veiled Lady, and accepting this white clothing, Coverdale appropriately emerges from the sick-bed on May day, festival of flowers and the crowning of the May queen (230).

Coverdale's distress at assuming a feminine identity through his white clothes and things derives from his being, this once, behind the veil, and understanding costume as a performance entirely detachable from the body beneath it. His body, he repeatedly reminds his readers, is tanned and muscular, with "great brown fists [that] looked as if they had never been capable of kid gloves" (60–61). Even in this observation, his body contradicts his clothing, and Coverdale responds by anxiously reconstructing a masculine, upper-class identity in town. Preparing to leave Blithedale, Coverdale appears at the dinner table "actually dressed in a coat": "with a satin cravat, too, a white vest, and several other things that made me seem strange and outlandish to myself" (126). And when Zenobia accuses him of resuming "the whole series of social conventionalism, together with that straight-bodied coat," he can acknowledge it without regret (130). The material things that a town identity depends on are numerous and stable: Coverdale dresses in upper-class masculine clothing and retreats to town to surround himself with masculine architecture and props. If his identity is based on the things around him, as he has discovered, he must more carefully select these things to avoid the threat of a feminine construction.

Escaping the fluidity of Blithedale, Coverdale establishes himself within the solid materiality of the city, listening to the clocks ring "[h]our by hour," the traffic on the streets and in the hotel, and the sound of a diorama show (134). His view from his hotel window offers "the backside of the universe," which is more real than the dressed-up fronts of buildings because the fronts are "always artificial . . . and [are] therefore a veil and a concealment" (134). With this view, he elaborates for himself the social structures underlying gender and class in the form of a "stylish boarding-house" (137). He spends the afternoon after leaving Blithedale smoking cigars in a bachelor hotel room and begins to study the interiors of the neighboring hotel. There, he sees on the top floor "a young man in a dressing-gown, standing before the glass and brushing his hair, for a quarter-of-an-hour together" (138). The bachelor continues to dress, spending another fifteen minutes adjusting his cravat, and finally donning a dress-coat that looks new. On the floor below the bachelor's is a family: two children playing are surprised by their "papa" "coming softly behind them," and he in turn is surprised by "mamma, stealing as softly behind papa, as he had stolen behind the children." The couple then steals a kiss, unnoticed by the children, and Coverdale proclaims it "a prettier bit of nature" than he has seen even at Blithedale. On the next level down, the chambers are uninhabited, but Coverdale watches instead "two housemaids . . . industriously at work." The next day, he will see Zenobia and Priscilla in this apartment. Below them, in the "lower regions" of the building, he sees "the red glow of the kitchen-range" as the cook comes out to "draw a cool breath" and an "Irish man-servant, in a white jacket, crept slily forth and threw away fragments of a china-dish, which unquestionably he had just broken" (138). Later, Coverdale sees a "lady, showily dressed," with "what must have been false hair, and reddish-brown, I suppose, in hue" making a "momentary transit across the kitchen-window" as she supervises the preparation of food (138–139). Above all, at the peak of a dormer window, sits a dove, which flies "so straight across the intervening space, that I fully expected her to alight directly on my window-sill." She does not, however, but rather swerves aside and vanishes, "as did likewise the slight, fantastic pathos with which I had invested her" (139).

Coverdale reconstructs a social hierarchy from this scene based not upon gender roles or class, but upon a person's relationship to things. The bottommost level is lower-class and nonwhite, colored by the "red glow of the kitchen range" and by the hue of physical labor. Here, a servant sneaks into the alley and hides a piece of china that he has broken. The house mistress down here is also deceitful and nonwhite: even from a distance Coverdale can detect her false hair, "reddish-brown" in color. Directly above these lower-class laborers is the apartment of Priscilla and Zenobia, who reside within the architecture of material femininity. Their apartment is almost completely veiled by a white muslin curtain. What Coverdale sees within is, first, two maids laboring, and later, Priscilla and Zenobia. The female labor is temporally separated from the feminine leisure, and both are modestly veiled, but they do belong in the same place. The hotel's next highest apartment belongs to a husband and father, head of an economically successful and devoted family. While Coverdale declares this scene to be "natural," he also undercuts its material happiness by repeatedly using "stolen" to describe their actions. Perhaps, in fulfilling natural as opposed to social roles—man, woman, and children displaying physical affection—they are cheating the material economy, even as they invest in it enough to dress prettily and enjoy luxurious housing. Their identities are not material, he suggests, but rather "natural"—nonetheless their status appears above the feminine. At the top of the hotel architecture is the bachelor, who enjoys a clear-cut relationship with his things—he alone can have them, enjoy them, and purchase more.

Above all stands the dove, clearly significant as Coverdale invests "her" with a "fantastic pathos." The dove appears ready to fly to Coverdale, but instead veers away and reappears at the dormer window peak the next day. This dove is Coverdale's ideal femininity, divested of a material-based identity. He imagines that this spiritual whiteness has approached him on his sickbed, as he experienced femininity, and he imagines he can invest Priscilla with it in her immaterial mesmeric trance. He clings to this dove, this imaged free-floating femininity only a scant level above his own bachelor apartments, for the rest of the narrative. The symbolism that he invests in his white dove—that of disembodied femininity—he also applies to other creatures. As he leaves Blithedale, he says good-bye last to the pigs: "four huge black grunters, the very *symbols* of slothful ease and sensual comfort" and parallel portraits to the four unhappy actors in his love square (132, emphasis mine). Coverdale presents the pigs as the symbolic opposite of the feminine dove: "they were involved, almost stifled, and buried alive, in their own corporeal substance" (132). In the material world clothes and coded things signify gender and class considerations; in Coverdale's symbolic imagining, the highest status is marked by white ethereality and the lowest classes by redness and deceit or by blackness and corporeality.

When he concludes his story by revealing his "one secret," he recounts his own masculine bachelorhood, but grasps at a way of realizing his myth of white femininity. He proclaims at the end his love for Priscilla, presenting it as a hesitant, shameful confession. But in fact, the faltering dashes of the final phrase—"I—I myself—was in love—with—PRISCILLA!"—admit Coverdale's failure to settle femininity even by the end. His concluding confession admits the truth of his initial claim, that the Veiled Lady's "pretensions" "have little to do with the present narrative" (8). The lady herself, embodied in Priscilla, moves throughout the story, but her "pretensions"—her claims to an ethereal white identity that disavows class and ambition—have "little to do" with Coverdale's story. Rather, the characters in every scene are built and rebuilt by the things around them.

Femininity as demonstrated by the proper fashion, as demonstrated by the proper maintenance and management of the household, was culturally understood and established in the nineteenth century. The racial component in antebellum America required, however, a devotion to the color white, to white things that could not be tainted, because the upper- and middle-class mistress depended upon the labor of a black servant or slave, or the unrefined presence of lower-class "help." At the same time, the tension of the polarities pulling on the posture of femininity—female physicality at one side and masculine ambition on the other—produced a shimmering "sphere" that required constant negotiation, constant performance, constant renewal. The concreteness represented by the white things dependably delivered in standardized shapes offered to offset these tensions, stabilize an identity into a fixed, delimited realm. They signified an expunging of the blackness that could always undermine the constructions, a victory in the household negotiations between dark and white women. And they became yet another message to negotiate and control.

CHAPTER FOUR

SEE SPOT RUN

White Things in the Rhetoric of Racial, Moral, and Hygienic Purity

Toni Morrison's narrator, Claudia, in *The Bluest Eye* (1970) fixates upon her own convoluted relationship with white women—how she, as black, can be seen to love cleanliness and the image of white femininity represented by Shirley Temple, but how this love is in fact a self-protective "adjustment" that will keep her from dismembering the white girl. The child narrator cannot comprehend the attraction of cleanliness—"irritable, unimaginative cleanliness"—just as she cannot comprehend the elements that make a white girl or a white-girl doll so attractive to society (22). Claudia's "one desire: to dismember" the doll reflects the subdued violence of a woman told to admire white femininity but excluded from it. She would study the doll's components to discover which is the crucial, determinant physical feature that separates herself from the doll's desirability. The doll is "a most uncomfortable, patently aggressive sleeping companion" with "hard unyielding limbs" and irritating "starched gauze or lace on the cotton dress" (20). In Claudia's untrained reaction to the doll's excluding beauty—her "pristine sadism"—she "fingered the face . . . picked at the pearly teeth . . . traced the turned-up nose, poked the glassy blue eyeballs, twisted the yellow hair" and proceeded to "[b]reak off the tiny fingers, bend the flat feet, loosen the hair, . . . [r]emove the cold and stupid eyeball . . . take off the head, shake out the sawdust, crack the back against the brass bed rail" (21). Her exercise is clearly the opposite of *Gone with the Wind*'s Mammy's, even as she uses the bedpost as a weapon.

This violent investigation attempts to discover "why," but the dissected doll reveals no secrets; the exact chemical and physical composition of beauty, embodied in whiteness, cannot be measured (6). The question unanswered is ambiguously both *why* the white-girl doll is considered beautiful based on these constituent body parts and *why* Claudia should march with society in emulating and admiring an ideal specific enough to exclude most people. Failing to find an answer, she settles for "how": her evolving ability to "worship" the nation's young, feminine, white ideal of beauty and "delight in cleanliness" is only demonstration of a process, a training, "adjustment without improvement" (6, 23). Claudia, in her innocence, attacks an intact representation of the white feminine ideal built throughout the nineteenth century from white things. The tragic characters in Morrison's novel mark the beginning of their tragedy—the failure of a happy home life and the white beauty that define nineteenth-century "femininity"—with a piece of torn furniture and a decayed front tooth. In centering on these things—household furniture and white physical features—these characters draw upon the reasons for their excluded blackness: from the early nineteenth century, racial whiteness was built not only from white skin, but also from refined white things. The white things used to construct a notion of privileged racial whiteness in antebellum America were based on consumer choice. White consumers began to prefer white things that mass-production made available beginning in the late eighteenth century and continuing until the Civil War; these things included dishes, house paint, and gravestones, as well as household décor, women's clothing, and the skin of sentimental heroines. As these white things contributed to developing notions of race, class, and gender, they demanded from their users not only the wealth to afford them, but also the training to use them properly, the proper attitude in pursuing and displaying them, and the ability to maintain them. The desirability that inheres in Claudia's Shirley Temple doll focuses the central maneuvers with white things that defined racial whiteness in antebellum America. Claudia attacks the white body, which is the final locus of "whiteness," but Morrison includes in its social success the maintenance of other things—household furniture and white teeth—whose always extant failure in her fictional family marks them as ugly, unsuccessful, and ultimately doomed.

In attempting to "dismember" the white girl-doll to discover the source of her power, Claudia seeks the composition of "beauty"—which plastic part actually determines the doll to be beautiful, and what distinguishes it from Claudia's own physical composition. In doing so, Claudia addresses a formula developed during the nineteenth century that marked beauty with moral, racial, and hygienic purity and hinged these purities on visual clues from the body and its possessions, and the demonstrated care taken of them. The visual culture of antebellum America demanded that such invisible qualities as moral goodness and racial heritage be demonstrated visibly. Response to such spectatorial demands settled on the surface of things: white skin had to be undisputedly white—not tanned, or freckled, or scarred—in order to qualify for racial whiteness. Likewise, it had to be demonstrably clean to indicate an invisible and inner cleanliness. The surface of refined white things also had to remain clean and unmarred as one's identity began with the skin and extended to one's possessions. Therefore, the material markers of whiteness required special care to keep them clean, unmarked, and unbroken. Mass production helped this impulse by providing affordable replacements for damaged goods. In seventeenth-century Dutch paintings, as James Deetz notes, broken plates and bowls appear in use even in upper-class settings: replacements just were not available (Deetz, Flowerdew 30). But by the nineteenth century in America, the appearance of damaged goods or disabled furniture marked nonwhiteness. In Uncle Tom's Cabin, even Aunt Chloe's aspiring slave cabin sports a "cracked teapot" and a chair "somewhat rheumatic in its limbs" (23). Most slaves, if not issued the darker earthenware dishes, were handed down the chipped dishes no longer used by the master. In addition, white skin was necessarily a marker, but one of considerable delicacy: a white thing, but non-replaceable and non-disposable, requiring herculean (and Sysaphean) efforts in cleanliness and protection from scarring, tanning, and marking. One nineteenth-century advisor insists, " 'It were better to wash twenty times a day, than to allow a dirty spot to remain on any part of the skin' " (qtd. in Peiss 17). If whiteness was posed as a choice, white skin alone would not constitute racial whiteness.[1] Instead, white skin is another white thing: a prerequisite for whiteness certainly, but not a determinant.

For example, one could be Caucasian but forfeit his or her whiteness through many means: by being dissipated and uncontrolled in diet, by being dirty or having dirty clothes and house, by participating in uncontrolled or lower-class activities that exposed one to the sun. A person could also appear white while actually "black": numerous runaway slave advertisements, abolitionist arguments, and tales of "passing" expose the claim of visual whiteness or blackness as a fiction. The anxiety over what exactly constituted pure whiteness, and therefore desirability, was manifested in racial sciences featuring a "calculus" of black blood, in more and more scrupulous hygiene extending from upper-class to middle-class bodies and households—and eventually to cemeteries and cities—and in an intense focus on the skin's appearance, including visual clues as to race, a condemnation of false statements made by make-up, and taboos about tattoos and scars. With such a strict definition of "whiteness," the anxiety to locate its exact boundaries and the falling-off mark for lower-middle-class or nearly white citizens, appeared much the same as Claudia's operations on the doll: as a precise examination of dismembered body parts—skin, eyes, teeth, hands—as well as the white things in the household and how they contributed, an expulsion of any possible mark or dirt that became an obsession with cleanliness, and a new organization of "trash." One might have been born with a biological whiteness, and earn or inherit it in the upper-class goods delimiting class, and display it upon the body and throughout the house, but one also had to maintain it—clean it and polish it and take care not to break it—in order truly to achieve whiteness.

By the nineteenth century, America determined that racial whiteness required complete racial purity; in contrast to other nations, American law declared that "one drop" of African blood kept a person from being white and from the privileges included. In Spanish Louisiana, a legal designation and trial of *"limpieza de sangre"*—literally translated to "cleanness" or "purity" of blood—was sometimes sought for women before they entered into prestigious marriages (Spear 97). Werner Sollors recounts mathematical exercises designed to determine how many generations of interracial offspring would wash the African stain from one's blood: John Stedman in 1796 outlined a chart that designated three generations, after which the Negro heritage could no longer be detected, with $\frac{1}{16}$ African blood. Julien-Joseph Virey's system in 1801 required as little as $\frac{1}{32}$ African blood to determine "blackness." At the farthest extreme—failing the racial binary in the United States that determined blackness from "one drop" of African blood—in Santo Domingo, Moreau de Saint-Mery asserted that any more than $\frac{1}{512}$ African blood rendered a person black (Sollors 119–121).

The law demanded, in effect, a compositional purity, an unmixed white heritage, to achieve whiteness. "Purity" is essentially a description of components: an ideal of 100 percent desirable ingredient and 0 percent contaminants. For the sake of everyday life, however—for contact with strangers in an urbanizing environment—this compositional purity had to be translated into the visual realm. Translated from the scientific to the cultural, from the compositional to the visible, purity shifted in focus from meaning "unmixed" to meaning "unmarked." Proof of racial whiteness demanded, therefore, an unmarked body and collection of things: clean, unstained, undeformed skin and household items. Neatness and hygiene, notably an American obsession, developed in the beginning of the nineteenth century in part as a response to this demand for racial purity, requiring visible spotlessness for the conferring of legal privileges and social status.

At the same time, the traditional understandings of whiteness, which Melville rehearses in *Moby Dick* as "the emblem of many touching noble things—the innocence of brides, the benignity of age . . . the majesty of Justice . . . the divine spotlessness and power," linked the color white with spiritual purity. Melville mentions an ancient vision of whiteness from the Book of Revelation, where "white robes are given to the redeemed, and the four-and-twenty elders stand clothed in white before the great white throne, and the Holy One that sitteth there white like wool"; in the nineteenth century, whiteness as signaling spirituality could be transferred to white things, and those who owned or used them could claim the symbolic purity (163–164). Furthermore, in an inversion of an older puritan tradition, this godliness was next to cleanliness. In the eighteenth century, Puritan reformer Cotton Mather describes sin, or spiritual impurity, as filth; translated into visual terms, physical filth demonstrated spiritual sinfulness in the nineteenth century.[2] The *Encyclopedia of Domestic Economy* declared in 1844 that "Cleanliness . . . has moral as well as physical advantages, personal as well as domestic. . . . It evinces an absence of slothfulness; for without activity and exertion, cleanliness cannot be practised: it is an emblem, if not a characteristic, of purity of thought and propriety of conduct" (qtd. in Horsfield 23). Bronson Alcott, a reformer in spiritual as well as physical health, believes that " 'he who neglects his person and dress will be found lower in the scale of morals, other things being equal, than he who pays due regard to cleanliness' " (qtd. in Bushman and Bushman 1224). Cleanliness was considered not only morally but also socially beneficial: a mid-century domestic guidebook proclaims, "Cleanliness is an unequivocal good; and accordingly we find that it confers a species of rank on all its votaries" (qtd. in Horsfield 23).

If whiteness and white robes represented moral purity, filth was aligned with their opposite, blackness and black things. Spiritual purity became translated into visual terms as physical cleanliness; (white) racial purity was translated into whiteness of skin; the need to deny either tint or taint merged into an understanding of racial whiteness that demanded perfectly white skin that was unobstructed by dirt, freckles, or markings, and corroborated by other well-cared-for white things. For example, Bob Jones, an ex-slave interviewed after the Civil War, understood the equation of epidermal whiteness with piety. His master died in the war, and the day after Yankees visited the plantation looking for "Reb scouts," Jones saw his master's body, saying, "He had been dead so long that he had turned dark, and Sambo, a little nigger, says to me, 'I thought, Bob, that I'd turn white when I went to heaven, but it appears to me like the white folkses am going to turn black' " (Hurmence 4). A late eighteenth-century gravestone carver imprinted the same sentiment. On one of the few early stones carved for an African, one from 1780 in North Attleboro, Massachusetts, praises the deceased slave in these terms:

> Here lies the best of slaves
> Now turning into dust
> Caesar the Ethiopian craves
> A place among the Just.
> His faithful soul is fled
> To realms of heavenly light,
> And by the blood that Jesus shed
> Is changed from Black to White. (Garman 28)

Moral referents could inhere in the things one used as well. At the Magdalene Asylum for fallen women, ceramics were designed to "teach the Magdalens their social and economic, as well as their moral, place" (De Cunzo 107). Much of their tableware was outdated creamware, relegating them to the rank of servants: Magdalens uniformly belonged to the lower class. More significantly, however, the women also used locally produced redware on the dining table and at tea time, even though redware was almost never used at the table in common practice (De Cunzo 51, 70). The ever-whitening wares appearing on the tables of middle-class women associated them with purity, but those who bought for the Magdalen society denied the fallen women that association.[3]

When Lydia Maria Child addresses race prejudice, she asserts that "as slavery inevitably makes its victims servile and vicious, and as none but negroes are allowed to be slaves, we, from our very childhood, associate everything that is degraded with the *mere colour*" (*Appeal* 66, italics in text). "We" is presumably white middle-class Americans in this statement, and the victims' servility and viciousness appear from a free citizen's point of view. But she points out elsewhere that slaves' appearance falls along a "scale of complexions" depending on their purity of blood, and that runaway slave advertisements sometimes describe white people who nonetheless are called "negroes" (*Oasis* 199). The relationship between blackness as servile and servants as black, which in a binaric black and white society would be exact, slips as slaves reveal themselves to be not-black. In Child's assertion, the "*mere colour*" of Africans renders blackness despicable; Robyn Wiegman contends that Americans first had to be taught to see Africans *as* black, and to charge Africans with inherent inferiorities, before their blackness could become degraded (slaves are degraded; slaves are black; therefore black is degraded). In fact, the ideal of Caucasian white skin was also a fiction, which had to be learned and maintained in the face of varying shades of complexions. The fiction of racial whiteness was less forgiving, however, because it asserted a perfect, compositional purity; and the threat of forfeiting whiteness and its privileges was ever-present. White consumers were continually taking apart the doll, the model of white desirability, in order to locate for themselves which parts were determinant. Because racial awareness pervaded antebellum culture and the risk of losing a white status resided in so many material constructions—downward class mobility, improper attitude towards or use of or maintenance of one's refined goods, a dubious stain on the skin—white Americans had to perform constant searches to locate and expunge any of these dangerous markers. The humor of blackface minstrelsy, the seductiveness of the tragic mulatto, the taboo against tattoos or scarring or freckles or make-up, and the obsession with hygiene are the anxious return, again and again, to this troubled transitivity. If a black person could pass as white, he revealed black and white to be places on a continuum of color rather than polar opposites. Each of these popular trends became both the denial of black's ability ever to become white and, more importantly, the calculation of where, in fact, white might become black.

CHECKERED PAST

The minstrel plays and "tragic mulatto" stories, both widely popular in the years before the Civil War, investigate this concern from different angles—and the primacy or attainability of whiteness differentiates the tragic from the comic. One of the most widely known and performed minstrel shows of the nineteenth century, "Old Zip Coon," opens in the Happy Hours Company version with a blackfaced Zip sipping expensive brandy, his feet propped up, reminiscing about the joys of past "ole Jamaica" liquor and the "good old-fashioned breakdown" of slavery days.[4] After indulging in an irresistible minstrel dance, the newly elegant Zip confesses to his friend, "de massa's gone away and I got his property and married Sal [the cook], and we got a darter—black one side de face an' white todder—an' she won't touch nuffin short ob a piannum" (Engle 52). That the daughter soon appears in piebald makeup, half blackface and half white, accentuates the concreteness of blackface color. No character gives a description of Sal the cook as black or white; likely, the master's cook is a slave as well (as a house slave, possibly light-skinned). The daughter's face displays the essentialism of race—that the two races can never really mix even when found in the same body. And as the daughter enters the scene, she demonstrates that the airs she takes on as half-white are frustrated by her blackness—she cannot understand her Italian music teacher, even though she rejects any teacher less sophisticated.[5]

The challenge of locating the exact position where white might become black—the question that concerned upwardly or downwardly mobile whites—settled finally upon, and within, the body of the mixed-race slave. Possibly, a mulatto's blackness could be detected from barely discernible physical clues. A character in Mary E. Braddon's *The Octoroon* (ca. 1862) claims to be able to detect blacks passing as whites by looking at "the extreme corner of the eye, and at the root of the finger nails . . . though but one drop of the blood of the despised race tainted the object upon whom he looked" (qtd. in Sollors, 149–150). Werner Sollors identifies many novels and historical accounts where a similar claim is made: failing proof by nonwhite skin, the skeptical may examine the subject's nails, eyes, and hair to detect blackness. More telling, however, were other material markers—furniture, clothing, housing, education. In the story of the tragic mulatto, the author provides the title character with as many of these signifiers of whiteness as possible, in order to examine the limits, or the fault lines, of their signifying power. The story is for whites, and about whiteness—about locating the tainted spot within a character's material identity, her household or behavior—so that white readers might do the same in their own lives and expunge this racial and economic threat.

The formula of the tragic mulatto (or quadroon, or octoroon) remained relatively unchanged over the course of the nineteenth century: usually female, she is the daughter of a wealthy white planter and is reared in protected seclusion according to upper-class white morals and education. In Jules Zanger's summary, she discovers she is a slave, is sold into slavery, and "is victimized, usually by a lower-class, dialect-speaking slave dealer or overseer"; occasionally she is rescued by a liberal Northern lover, but more often she goes insane or "dies a suicide, or dies of shame, or dies protecting her young gentleman" (285). The scholarship on the tragic mulatto story asks, in general, two questions: what is she racially, and why were the stories so popular? In the early years of mulatto stories, argues Sterling A. Brown, "the mulatto inherits the vices of both races and none of the virtues," and "any achievement of a Negro is to be attributed to the white blood in his veins" (278–279). Later, the mulatto became an embodiment of racial conflict, with his white blood contributing intelligence, reason, and dignity, and his black blood emotionalism and savagery (279). In each of these, race remains essential and unmixed, for all that white and black are contained by the same body. The attraction of the first might be a simple reinforcement of racial superiority; in the latter, this claim can be paired with the mulatto's embodying the racial conflict taking place in society, and ultimately ending the conflict with his or her death. The mulatto is over-represented in abolitionist fiction; possibly the character is painted mostly white so that a white audience might identify with her. Possibly, the horrors of slavery can best be appreciated when the slave is white (Bullock 280). Readers may so identify with her, it has been suggested, that they fear with her that they too might discover they are slaves and become victims of sexual and lower-class aggression. The mulatto may be an embodiment of sexual immorality practiced by white planters—a living accusation of the evils of slavery. Possibly, as Sánchez-Eppler argues, the tragic mulatto succeeds in fiction because she is a white woman, only technically black, who is culturally allowed to have a black man ("Bodily Bonds").

Given the stereotypical characters and the formulaic plot, however, I would argue that the tragic mulatto is less an examination of miscegenation than an interrogation of whiteness. It is unlikely that a middle-class white reader would wonder to herself if she may indeed be black and in danger of the same tragedy; and though the mulatto's whiteness may allow some sympathy, her tragic flaw of black blood cautions readers to withhold identification with her. The formula remains the same throughout a century of tragic mulatto stories—she must die or go insane at the end. In fact, even in James Fenimore Cooper's *Last of the Mohicans* (1826), identified as having the earliest appearance of the tragic mulatto, I would argue that the audience can already anticipate her necessary death. If her life story and death are foregone conclusions, therefore, the crux of the story must lie elsewhere. Two convincing suggestions come from Werner Sollors, who argues that mulatto stories, unlike other abolitionist texts, allow a straightforward examination of race, and from Jules Zanger, who asserts that the stories may be attractive because of the threat to white audiences of downward mobility, so that they are a class story with a built-in scapegoat. More specifically, these stories are at once a reiteration of essentialized blackness, since the black blood within her body remains forever segregated and determinant, and an examination of socially earned whiteness. The story becomes an endlessly instructive game of "Find the Spot": an exercise in locating what defines the mulatto as white—her surroundings, her femininity, her skin color—and in identifying what element demands her failure.

Harriet Beecher Stowe begins Dred (1856) with such an examination of the limits of race in the quadroon couple Harry and Lisette. Harry is the enslaved brother and caretaker of the novel's sentimental white heroine, Nina, who immediately establishes the components of her attractiveness: "dancing, glittering, fluttering little assortments of curls, pendants, streamers, eyes, cheeks, and dimples!" (31). She catalogues, as Morrison's Claudia does, the essential ingredients to attractive whiteness, intermixing clothing, jewelry, and body parts.[6] As the novel continues, Stowe tests the power of these individual elements, searching in the definition of whiteness for a means to escape the degradation of blackness. Ultimately, her search ends with freedom, but mainly a freedom stolen or earned by the slaves themselves—distinguished from her earlier arguments for abolition by her mistrust of white political force. In Uncle Tom's Cabin, abolition or escape or death would free the slaves, but they would still be (as evidenced by her deportation of them) unfit for American society, still a symbol of degradation and dependence invading the domestic sphere. In Dred, Stowe continues to depend on essentialist designs; she attributes to Harry "the temper and constitution of his [white] father, tempered by the soft and genial temperament of the beautiful Eboe mulatress who was his mother" (68). In treating the tragic mulatto Lisette, Stowe also insists on the "one drop" rule of race, but claims that this inescapable inherited blackness need not be degraded, but is only made so by its legal connection to slavery.

Harry and Lisette participate in most of the economics of whiteness. In their household, Stowe examines the danger of black slavery by pushing the limits of white signification—through white things. Although Harry's race is not identified explicitly until chapter 4, his first appearance is as "a well-dressed, gentlemanly person of about thirty-five, with dark complexion and hair, and deep, full blue eyes. There was something marked and peculiar in the square, high forehead, and the finely-formed features, which indicated talent and ability; and the blue eyes had a depth and strength of color that might cause them at first glance to appear black" (32). Although casting his features in positive terms, Stowe also here reveals her racial politics. The eyes reveal a trace of black, as expected by race police in the nineteenth century; his face is both "marked" and "peculiar," marked in fact by the peculiar institution; and though well-dressed, he cannot be a gentleman—only an impersonation of one, a "gentlemanly person."

Stowe recognizes the problematic implications of a whitened slave home: it represents an investment in the ideology that excludes blacks and rationalizes their slavery. For all Uncle Tom's spiritual strength, he ultimately became a cultural symbol of submission. Even more, white things negated attempts made by legally black persons to draw themselves into the ideal. Aunt Chloe may grow flowers to hide the crude logs of her cabin, but she has no means to build herself a better cabin. In *Dred*, Harry Gordon, quadroon brother to the white heroine Nina, struggles to make an ideal home within the limits of slavery. In an early chapter, Harry's wife, Lisette, orchestrates a perfect domestic scene to greet him. Their house, a "neat log cabin" "almost enveloped in luxuriant wreaths of yellow jessamine, and garlanded with a magnificent lamarque rose," is set beside a garden full of "the finest fruits and flowers"—similar to Uncle Tom's cabin (85). Inside are two rooms, according to a wealthier standard than Uncle Tom's cabin: the inner room is properly decorated with "white window-curtains," a matted floor, and a "draped feather-bed" (89). On the other side, cream-colored roses cluster along the walls, and a table stands under a spotless tablecloth and a delicious tea setting (89). Lisette may be easily comparable to her white sister-in-law Nina in femininity as well: she wears a white linen chemisette covered by a blue basque; she inquires after the latest fashions that Harry has learned from Nina; and when Harry reveals that Nina is engaged, Lisette concedes, " '[S]he always did have lovers, just, you know, as I used to' " (96). The only items that might suggest slavery thus far are her colorful turban and the presence in her house of others' clothes: she is working on "various articles of feminine toilet, too delicate and expensive to have belonged to those in humble circumstances" (86).

Lisette trips about the room imagining how charmed her husband will be with this elegant domestic scene, but she becomes distracted by flies which "finally were seen brushing their wings and licking their feet, with great alertness, on the very topmost height of the sacred bed-curtains" (90). After chasing the flies, Lisette upsets her entire room in her hurry to arrange the tea. But she cannot expel these spots of blackness: like her own drops of black blood, they will disturb her domesticity for as long as she remains a slave. In fact, Harry's dissipated half-brother and master, Tom, soon threatens to "possess" himself of Lisette merely to antagonize Harry, and Harry knows that under slavery he can never protect his wife. The bed-curtains are the victims of both Tom's and the flies' intrusion: the odd close-up of the fly illustrates some sinister and lascivious creature. Through the image of these predatory flies, Stowe attempts to detach the cause of Lisette's tragedy from her person. Their blackness marks her slavery, but not her morality; nonetheless, they can intrude freely upon Lisette's whitened home.

The "buzzing intruders," the spots of blackness, illustrate the notion that whiteness depends upon racial purity, that black can never become white; the appearance of Dred illustrates that blackness cannot be positively developed within domestic walls or a domestic institution. Robert S. Levine argues that when the title character finally appears, nearly 250 pages into the novel, "what truly brings about the novel's transformation is the emergence of the repressed—the 'naturalized' black presence that supports both the plantation and the plantation novel"—revealing that "to this point our reading of the plantation (novel) has been thoroughly inadequate" (177). This inadequacy, he suggests, extends back to *Uncle Tom's Cabin* as well. By the time she wrote *Dred*, Lisa Whitney suggests, Stowe had become "less and less confident that the sentimental solutions offered in her earlier work would help bring an end to the crisis threatening the peace of the nation" (Whitney 152). Dred stands, I would argue, as both an embodiment of and a counter-example for enslaved blackness: the buzzing flies relocated to the swamp and magnified through self-possession. Significantly, the nearly white Harry first meets Dred after Harry is made to bear his blackness physically, when Tom Gordon "marks" his skin. Calling Harry a "damned nigger," Tom strikes him "across the face twice with his whip," proclaiming, "'Isn't that a master's mark?'" (259). Harry replies, "'You may be sure, Mr. Gordon, this mark will *never* be forgotten!'" (260). Immediately afterwards, Dred emerges from the swamp a "magnificent" personification of this mark.

Dred's skin is "intensely black, and polished like marble"; his muscles are bulging, his head is "massive"; his eyes have the effect of "unfathomable blackness and darkness which is often a striking characteristic of the African eye" (261). His things, moreover, are African rather than servile: he wears a turban and "coarse negro-cloth pants"—but he also carries a hatchet, a knife, and a rifle (261).

In the visual presentation of purity established by white things and domesticity, Stowe finds an immovable element in the inherited blackness of the slaves. Her political premises are that black and white are essentially determining and that black can never be re-formed biologically, legally, and therefore materially into white.[7] Given these premises, the negotiations with slavery attempted by white characters—the Claytons in their attempt to educate their slaves, helpers in the Underground Railroad, and even abolitionist reformers[8]—become fruitless exercises that cannot confer personhood to slaves because they do nothing to undermine a racial hierarchy. Blacks can never become white; whites cannot help blacks to improve themselves; the black population must undo the degraded condition of blackness by helping themselves. Although the novel ultimately shies away from a violent slave rebellion, it nonetheless carries the reader to this inevitable conclusion: in an oppositional economy there can be no compromise, only conflict.

SKIN FLICKS

The essentialized impossibility of Lisette's attaining whiteness was followed, by whites, with a practical difficulty in achieving true whiteness of skin. The perfect whiteness of the literary heroine would have been difficult to retain, even aided by skin bleachers and lotions. The skin, as a living artifact, was bound to wrinkles, freckles, blemishes, tanning and reddening, scarring and marking, and was therefore an unreliable while unavoidable marker of whiteness. Therefore, taboos evolved surrounding the skin and its care: taboos about permanent marking by tattoos, branding, and scarring; about temporary discolorations from neglect, such as blemishes, sunburn, redness or sallowness from immoderate diet; and against any attempts at deceit through cosmetics. Sentimental literature's simultaneous demand for a woman's skin to be an unmarked white competed with its demand that skin be "transparent," a window to her soul, and unimpeded either by a veil or by any sort of concealing make-up.

Commenting on antebellum women's fashion as developed by *Godey's Lady's Book*, Karen Haltunnen states that face paint "represented a flagrant violation of the cult of sincerity."[9] Kathy Lee Peiss has studied the use of cosmetics throughout the nineteenth century and identifies two categories for chemical skin whiteners—cosmetics and paints—although the use of either would likely have been denied by the aspiring white woman. As Peiss reports from a nineteenth-century advice book, cosmetics "'assist Nature, and make amends for her defects,'" whereas paints "masked Nature's handiwork to hide expression and truth behind an 'encrusted mould'" (12). Cosmetics, including lotions, creams, and powders, were allowed to feminine women, and skin whitening recipes regularly appeared in household guidebooks and cookbooks. Throughout the nineteenth century, "skin whiteners remained the most popular cosmetic," with white powder viewed as "the most acceptable on sanitary and practical grounds" (40).

The whiteness of skin as a class as well as a racial marker can be seen in treatment of white face-painting in literature. In general, white women who "painted" were seen as immoral, aspiring to a higher class without acquiring the wealth, discipline, or refinement to deserve it. Paradoxically, the use of "chalk" in attempts to imitate upper-class whiteness could ultimately emphasize one's nonwhiteness: the New York *Daily Tribune* jests, "Do you hear that lady talk? / See her face destroyed by chalk; / Once't was white, but now, 'tis yellow, / Coarse and rough, and dark and sallow" (qtd. in Peiss 20). Frances Trollope also comments on antebellum Americans' use of powders: "'The ladies have strange ways of adding to their charms. . . . They powder themselves immoderately, face, neck, and arms, with pulverized starch; the effect is indescribably disagreeable by daylight, and not very favourable at any time'" (qtd. in Peiss 40).

The deceit rendered visible was ridiculed, because a woman's overt attempt at whiteness in itself revealed nonwhiteness, coupled with an admiration for the ideal that excluded her. Jessie Benton Freemont wrote, "'[I]t is quite funny to see that smeared smooth white face, & red wrists emerging from one button pale gloves. But the creme de lis [a whitening paste] is sure to be on'" (qtd. in Peiss 40). After the Civil War, these usually lower-class women who painted themselves began appearing in medical records: the most popular white paint was lead-based, and sometimes the lead poisoning resulted in death. Among African Americans, painting as an attempt to Anglicize oneself was noted as early as the 1850s: women with "lips 'puckered up and drawn in,' the hair 'sleeked over and pressed under, or cut off so short that it can't curl,'" made "'[b]eautiful black and brown faces . . . assume unnatural tints, like the vivid hue of painted corpses,'" argues the *Anglo-American Magazine* (Peiss 41). Such denunciations focus on the skin as attached to a working-class or black body, emphasizing the worker's hands, or the black woman's potential for putrescence, in order to undercut the effects of a white face and to forbid femininity.

Nonetheless, the redness of the working-class skin was likely less fictional than the whiteness of the upper classes. From the beginning of the nineteenth century through the Civil War, Americans evinced a "'rage for portraits.'" For those who could afford it, professional portrait painters could be hired; for the less wealthy, folk painters produced what were criticized as "'blank, monotonous, over-fed, wretched counterfeits'" (Vlach, "Very Tasty" 179). John Michael Vlach argues that the quality of the portrait was less important than the fact of it: having one's portrait drawn was a mark of refinement ("Very Tasty"). Significantly, however, these portraits could use white paint freely in their depictions of the subject's skin, even if the subject herself could not use paint. When photography became widely available in the 1850s, photographers discovered that women too refined for face paint still demanded white complexions in their pictures. These photographs and portraits were to some extent permanent reflections of one's face, and therefore of social status. Those ladies who would "'not care to have their own faces enamelled,'" complained photographers, nevertheless wanted a "'highly-retouched fraud which represents them as marble'" (qtd. in Peiss 47). In rural areas, where "'even the pretty girls are sadly tanned by exposure to the weather,' itinerant photographers . . . discovered that customers expected a white face without wrinkles, blemishes, or freckles on their portraits" (Peiss 32). The social projection offered by photos gives an insight into the racial and class indication of one's face: one photographer experimented with a chiaroscuro technique where one side of the face is shaded, but found them rejected. One of his clients objected, "'the face looks dirty, just like a nager'" (Peiss 33).

Other bodily markings were likewise regarded as proof of lower-classness or servitude. Tattoos might have been sported by sailors or carnival performers before the Civil War: such deliberate destruction of the skin was an event and a spectacle (Govenar 212). In Europe, stories of sailors forcibly tattooed by savage captors drew widespread attention. In the United States, an Irishman named James F. O'Connell toured with

Dan Rice, father of the minstrel show, to display his tattooed body. After being rescued in 1835 from a Micronesian island where he was reportedly tattooed over his entire body, he toured the Southern and Eastern states as a sideshow for twenty years. At the same time, *A Narrative of Shipwreck Captivity and Suffering of Horace Holden and Benjamin Nute* was circulating and "went through several editions between 1836 and 1841" (Oetterman 199). In this story, Holden and his mates are reportedly tattooed over their entire bodies as well, and although Holden through pleading manages to spare his face, his mates all die from the operation. O'Connell's face was tattooed, however, and "it was said that women and children who encountered him on the road died of shock, thinking they had seen the devil incarnate" (Oetterman 199).

Herman Melville's first novel, *Typee* (1846), while based in part upon Melville's own experiences in the Marquesas from 1842, would also have been informed by these earlier popularized tales. While the novel shocked readers with an admiring description of native practices and native morals, including female nudity and female polygamy, the narrator ultimately recoils from the tribal paradise when threatened with tattooing. After watching the operation performed on another native, accomplished with a collection of strange instruments resembling dentist tools, the narrator himself attracts the tattooer's attention. "The idea of engrafting his tattooing upon my white skin filled him with all a painter's enthusiasm," Tommo explains, and the tattooer's relentless pursuit of him afterwards revives his illness and "nearly unman[s]" him (242, 254). His subsequent discovery that the islanders eat human flesh—including, "to my horror . . . that of a white man"—seems the logical next step in the narrator's disillusionment of paradise: for all that is admirable, the natives have an entirely inappropriate attitude towards the flesh.[10]

Marked skin signified an uncivilized, savage, or degraded state in antebellum America. It always, in addition, signaled a spectacle. David Brion Davis connects the practice of marking slaves in ancient societies, with "shorn heads, identification tablets, branding, and tattooing," with the later American conception of slaves as marked with blackness. Wiegman contests the continuity of this symbolism, stating that the black slave's inherent markings differ from the master-imposed brands or tattoos of earlier societies, in that the latter occur in discreet, witnessed events, whereas for black slaves, their body was the mark of slavery (*American Anatomies* 24–25). The slave's scarred skin, however, functions as proof of slavery, while his black skin functions as a rationale. Escaped slaves speaking before abolitionist audiences were requested to offer proof of their slavery by exhibiting their naked back, "displaying for all to see the permanent disfiguration caused by the overseer's and the slave driver's whips" (Baker 10). In a letter prefacing *Narrative of the Life of Frederick Douglass*, Wendell Phillips criticizes "those who stare at the half-peck of corn a week, and love to count the lashes on the slave's back" as poor reformers (*Narrative* 43).

Douglass himself claims his skin as text, although he would deny that it tells only of victimized slavery. He reports, "I was a 'graduate from the peculiar institution,' Mr. Collins used to say, when introducing me, 'with *my diploma written on my back!*'" (*My Bondage* 219, italics in text). But while Mr. Collins suggests that Douglass not become "too learned" so that he can continue to seem an uneducated slave, Douglass proceeds to read in other parts of his skin manhood and freedom. Because, he says, "[My] hands had been furnished by nature with something like a solid leather coating, and I had bravely marked out for myself a life of rough labor, suited to the hardness of my hands, as a means of supporting myself and rearing my children" (*My Bondage* 219). His leathery hands, he claims, provide as much text as his scarred back—but they offer evidence of manly responsibility rather than of brutalized slavery.

In *Moby Dick*, Melville stages his narrator's politics almost entirely on the surface of the skin. Race and commodification become epidermal issues, the subject of surface markings on which Melville shifts polarities and meanings, with illegibility as the final goal. But while the whale, the skin, color and markings must remain on the market, Ishmael will shift color codes in a skillful shell game, so that "race," finally, cannot be read from the skin. Posing a mixed-race marriage between himself and Queequeg, Ishmael upsets epidermal expectations immediately with the claim that a white man is not "anything more dignified than a whitewashed negro" (60). The whitewashed Negro, or black person painted white, was not simply the opposite of ideal white skin, but a parody emphasizing all the more pointedly the black person's distance from whiteness. Throughout *Moby Dick*, Melville encourages his readers to unlearn racial distinctions, leading the reader through a process of mistake and correction in the course of his chapters. Melville's strategy is to evoke a racist ideal based on the constructions of color, tempting the reader to invest in them, only afterwards to undercut these constructions by locating them on the fungible skin.

For example, the novel provides two entertaining blackface minstrel scenes, featuring uncritiqued stereotypes of his African American characters Pip and Fleece. While Pip enacts the blackface song and dance in

"Midnight, Forecastle," Fleece performs as a blackface end man, casting witty retorts and delivering a ridiculous stump speech in "Stubb's Supper." Few scholars have been able to redeem Fleece from appearing as a straightforward blackface portrait;[11] but the cetological chapters that follow, especially "The Blanket," can be read as a commentary on black skin and the blackface that has just amused Melville's readers. In "The Blanket," the narrator attempts to define and locate the whale's skin, and the trouble that Melville takes is illuminating. Ishmael begins by describing the outer layer of skin—"the skin of the skin"—an "infinitely thin, transparent substance" (259). This outer layer, about the thickness of parchment, begins "almost as flexible and soft as satin." When dried, it becomes "hard and brittle," but good for bookmarks. His digression gains significance when the narrator further explains, "[the skin] is transparent, as I have said before; and being laid upon the printed page, I have sometimes pleased myself with fancying it exerted a magnifying influence. At any rate, it is pleasant to read about whales through their own spectacles" (259). This stiffened and transplanted "spectacle" either marks its text, or, when read through, magnifies it. The paper-thin "skin of the skin," Ishmael suggests, is transferable, transparent: a layer of visibility encasing the actual skin. Similarly, an understanding of "race" can only be a whitewash or a blackface mask, a layer of meaning overlaying the living tissue.

Ishmael continues by asserting that this outer layer alone does not make up the "skin" of the whale. Rather, he insists that the entire blubber layer is skin. With this assertion, Melville diverges from his source, William Scoresby, Jr., from whose accounts Melville gleaned much of his cetological information. Scoresby identifies the parchment-thick outer layer as the "skin," as opposed to the blubber layer within (Vincent 239–240). That Melville struggles to include blubber, the marketable substance, as skin is important: the black skin of the whale, the slave, or the minstrel becomes commodified. Of Moby Dick, the white skin becomes so as well—except that his white skin is never detached. The skin becomes the capitalist focus of the whaling voyage and the philosophical focus of the quest: not an abstracted idea of whiteness, but rather an expansive, valuable, and white thing.

An important feature of this inner layer of "skin" is its unreadable linear marks: "In life," the narrator testifies, "the visible surface of the Sperm Whale is not the least among the many marvels he presents" (*Moby Dick* 260). Upon the whale's skin appear marks, "crossed and re-crossed . . . like those in the finest Italian line engravings," which "do not seem to be impressed upon the isinglass substance above mentioned, but seem to be seen through it, as if they were engraved upon the body itself." Ishmael describes the "numerous rude scratches" to be found on whale's "back, and more especially his flanks, [which] effaced in great part . . . the regular linear appearance." While the marked skin of the whale resembles the marked skin of a slave, Ishmael dislocates the spectacle from slavery alone by stating that although similar marks exist on the banks of the Mississippi, he surmises that the scars on the whales occur from contact with "New England rocks on the sea-coast" or "hostile contact with other whales" (260). Therefore, the whale's skin is marked by both Southern and Northern contact, as well as violence among his peers, just as the commodity of marked skin extends from slavery to minstrelsy to color prejudice within and without the black race. As the narrator of "The Blanket" attempts to understand the whale's markings, he finally must include the skin of the whale among the numerous incomprehensible texts on his voyage. The linear marks that remind him of "those mysterious cyphers on the walls of pyramids" or "old Indian characters chiselled on the famous hieroglyphic palisades on the banks of the Upper Mississippi" finally must elude interpretation, just as the doubloon, the markings on Queequeg's coffin, and Queequeg's very tattoos must.

In fact, unreadability must be the lesson drawn from interpretations of skin: as Ishmael first views Queequeg and tries to decipher the purple, yellow, and black-looking squares that cover Queequeg's face, back, and legs, he becomes frightened. Only when he ceases trying to make color signify, conceding that "It's only his outside"—only when the narrator concludes that color remains unreadable because it signifies nothing inherently, can he heal his own psychic fragmentation (29).

A CLEAN AS REAL AS IVORY

As truly white skin was largely fictional, a fiction Melville would attempt to read or "read through," it required not only an avoidance of permanent markings, but also a continual expulsion of dirt. Items in the household, floors, yards, cemeteries, and eventually cities were expected to be kept clean. Richard L. and Claudia L. Bushman study the fashion of cleanliness, which spread from European gentility to American upper and middle classes at the turn of the nineteenth century, and then perpetuated itself into new demands such as daily cleansing and the use of soap.

Before the nineteenth century, even the gentry manifested wariness towards showers and full baths; one upper-class woman in 1799 tells her journal that she is gathering the courage to use the family shower, even though she has already owned it for a year (1224). In Essex County, Massachusetts, not a single record of a washstand has been found from before 1763; but by 1850, "the basin, pitcher, and washstand were becoming standard fixtures in the middle-class bedroom" (1227). Use of the toothbrush also became common in the nineteenth century. The 1790s showed advertisements for toothbrushes and toothpowder only among other luxury items, whereas by the mid-nineteenth century use of the toothbrush was widespread (Shackel 73).

Such standards of cleanliness extended throughout the house and eventually into the landscape as the nineteenth century wore on. When the Bixbys of Massachusetts painted and improved their household and painted its outside white, they also began cleaning the yard and depositing trash in hidden pits—whereas the general practice earlier entailed scattering trash from windows and doors as a means of deposit. Around 1800, household floors came under scrutiny as a new type of broom began to circulate. Late in the eighteenth century, a Philadelphia housekeeper spoke approvingly of a " 'white floor sprinkled with clean white sand,' " and Stowe's *Oldtown Folks* reinforces the sandy ideal (Bushman 265). Describing his grandmother's comfortable kitchen from decades ago, which the family prefers over the parlor even though its members are "on tea-drinking terms with the high aristocracy of Oldtown," Stowe's narrator mentions at the outset the "white-sanded floor [which] was always as clean as hands could make it" (*Oldtown* 59, 57). But in 1797 Levi Dickinson invented a broom made not from twigs but from broom corn, which swept a floor completely clean rather than leaving a layer of silt. By 1850, sales of such brooms reached several million (Bushman 265). The accompanying increase in carpets also required that family members keep their shoes and feet especially clean.

Cleanliness and the use of clean white dish sets signaled a position along the scale of civilization. Claims an early nineteenth-century medical book, " [t]he more any country is civilized, the more they consult this part of politeness' " (qtd. in Bushman and Bushman 1225). Filthiness of any kind came to represent moral as well as social degradation, and the lowest class of citizens was associated with filth. Conversely, cleanliness could be regarded as an antidote to immorality. Refined household goods would "seduce wayward individuals into the regenerative sociability of the domestic sphere and, by inspiring purified sentiments, could draw individuals to God," while a poorly designed house could warp a child into " 'a sharp, shrewd, narrow-minded, and selfish youth; from thence into a prudent, hard, and horny manhood, and at last into a covetous, unloving, and unloved old age' " (Merish, "Hand" 487; Praetzellis and Praetzellis 77). One reformer writes in 1852 that " '[n]o man . . . could live just the life in a well-proportioned and truely [sic] beautiful dwelling that he would in a mud shanty or rude log cabin' " (qtd. in Clifford Clark 46). Pattern books offered examples of orderly houses made from rammed earth in order to emphasize that a good home could be built for little money (Wright 84). In this way, opportunistic architects worked to rationalize as well as to market the proper architecture. Their message was that the economic differences that *enabled* some to purchase or build nice homes also *resulted* from them; those that provided themselves with only a log cabin were dooming themselves to its uncivilized influences, and thus to continued poverty. The rationalization worked for slaves as well, especially if one believes in the home's influential power: slaves housed in a shed or cabin could not improve themselves and were therefore properly housed as animals or uncivilized humans.

In this light, the complaints of slave owners that their slaves insisted on living in squalor despite adequate cabins can be recognized as more than a concern for hygiene or even appearance—they are claims to the inherent savagery of their chattel. James O. Breeden reviews advice offered among slave owners in Southern journals; a primary concern was the "natural" tendency of slaves to be dirty. Slave cabins were recommended to be elevated so that trash could not collect, and many masters called for a regular "cleaning out of all the filth and trash that may accumulate there." "The habits of the negro are filthy and careless," one planter observes (124). Others agree, in matter-of-fact tones. Slaves "should not be permitted in these filthy, though very natural, propensities," a Mississippian writes; they are a "proverbially filthy . . . race" another adds (128, 134). One planter exceeds his own notions of delicacy in the attempt to convey the stench and filth associated with his slaves, finally surrendering with, "I would not if I could give you or any other friend of mine an idea of its [a slave house's] fetidness" (131). The universal squalor of slave houses and habits seems a foregone conclusion, whether the slaves are to blame or not, and the only countermeasures suggested are supervision, cleaning, or possibly a coat of whitewash. The use of whitewash, suggested by only the most progressive planters and rarely used, underscored the association of whiteness as an antidote to filth. Whitewash made the dwelling appear "neat and comfortable" and had a "cleansing and purifying effect" (121). Even so, it remained a response to the planters' offended notions of cleanliness and asserted a white control over the slave cabin—which of course actually belonged to the white planter.

In the 1850s, Southern journals printed much advice for the housing of slaves. In a collection of such advice, most contributors report their own experiments, following concerns such as "First, the health and comfort of the occupants; Secondly, the convenience of nursing, surveillance, discipline, and the supply of wood and water; and Thirdly, economy of construction" (129). Several prefer framed houses over log cabins, arguing that logs absorb the odors of the place, that slaves fill the cracks with "dirty rags, old shoes, coon skins, chicken feathers" (128). Such filth was seen to contribute to disease and threaten a planter's investment. The association of slaves with filth implicated race in the new notions of bodily and household cleanliness. The ambitious began to control, contain, and hide their garbage and bodily functions. The lowest classes became for the newly disciplined both the filthy and the filth itself—to be similarly controlled, hidden, or cast out.

Lydia Maria Child invokes the stereotype of the filthy slave in her *Freedmen's Book*, published immediately after the Civil War to encourage freed blacks and help them ease into civilized life. Among biographies of important slaves, Africans, and African Americans, she includes a chapter on hygiene. She explains that "the human body should be washed all over every day; but if circumstances render that difficult, the operation should be performed at least two or three times a week" (246). While outlining scientific theory about skin and perspiration, she gives explicit instructions as to how to bathe, including water temperature, the best time of day, and procedure: for example, "[t]he best way [to bathe] is to plunge into water when you first get up in the morning, and then rub yourself with a cloth till you feel all of a glow" (247). She never mentions soap, but she does universalize the need for her advice by remarking that "[p]eople in general are not aware how important frequent bathing is" (246).

Trash and household filth may have had cultural or resistant purposes among the slaves, however. Larry McKee argues that the accumulation of debris beneath a slave cabin may have been a way of hiding contraband, and the planters' need to clear it away was for better supervision as much as hygiene (McKee, "Ideals" 205). Ywone D. Edwards also finds many cultural uses for the "trash" found in slave houses and yards, some of them relating to African retentions. Trash immediately around the cabin, especially oyster shells, would create noise if anyone were to approach, thus warning the slaves inside. Slaves were also likely to keep tools and non-domestic articles near the cabin in order to save the time of fetching them when needed. Obviously, those with fewer resources would have made use of the items that would be discarded by upper-class consumers. Thorstein Veblen lists conspicuous cleanliness as a pretension of the leisure class, which has the time to devote to cleaning as well as the wealth to buy newer and better goods. Trash buried within the house or in specific places around the yard might also have suggested "that curing/conjuring rituals were enacted in the cabin and that the trash was related only in part to Euro-American culture" (Edwards 261). What was perceived as trash may have been part of African religious tradition; for example, "certain colors such as white and red and asymmetrical or busy patterns were methods Africans and their descendants in the New World deliberately employed to confuse evil spirits." It was believed, Edwards reports, that evil spirits had to "decipher these codes or patterns before they could harm the living." These distracting elements in a yard might then be perceived as trash to the uninitiated (252).

In an upper- or middle-class white view, filth characterized not only slaves but also the lowest class of whites, in the North and the South, complicating the qualifications for whiteness and refinement. Stowe repeatedly mentions the lowest class of whites with pity in *Dred*, having her characters lament the poor whites' helpless, degraded condition which is brought about because slavery steals work from them. In Olmsted's overview of the Southern states, he only briefly mentions the houses of whites who are not of the planting class: "[t]he more common sort of habitations of the white people are either logs or loosely boarded frames, a brick chimney running up outside, at one end: everything very slovenly and dirty about them" (31). Not least in contributing to this dirtiness are the "[s]wine, hounds, and black and white children . . . commonly lying very promiscuously together on the ground about the doors" (31). The term "common" merges its suggestion of universality with an indication of class, one that neglects necessary racial maintenance. Sharing housing types with slaves, the poor whites lie "promiscuously" with blacks just as their homes are "loosely" boarded. Everything that is "slovenly and dirty about" the houses must include their occupants, who lie "about the doors" in the dirt.

Rebecca Harding Davis's *Life in the Iron Mills* uses filth as a class and ultimately a racial measurement. Her argument depends on the conflation of types of purity— conflation which would equate racial purity with physical purity, physical purity with moral purity. Recent scholarship has attended to Davis's comparison of the mill workers to slaves, debating the issue of "wage slavery," whether Davis uses the abolitionist movement to expose the evils of factory work, or whether she uses the evils of wage slavery to critique the narrowness of antislavery reformers.[12] In fact, her concern is for the equation, and for the conditions, however produced, that disrupt this equation. In the final scene, Hugh gazes from his jail cell onto the marketplace, onto "the busy crowd of whites and blacks shoving, pushing one another," but he sees himself as excluded from both race and class distinctions (67). The "tall mulatto girl, following her mistress" through the marketplace, has a "free, firm step," and the "very vilest cur, yelping there in the gutter," is "free to act out whatever thought God had put into his brain": both have masters, but are freer than he (69, 68). On the other hand, Hugh sees Joe Hill, the lamplighter, who always jokes and is good to his sick wife. Though certainly lower-class, Joe keeps his "room so clean" that laughter abounds even in the midst of sickness and poverty (70).

In discussing a choice of titles for her story, Davis suggested "The Korl Woman," mentioning to her editor, "I would be sure to read an article with that caption in the hope of discovering some new race,—of Hottentots perhaps" (Schocket 46). Eric Schocket derives from this comment an understanding of race in the novel that treats dirt as a racial marking, creating a "new class (the working class) whose white bodies are inscribed with uncanny signifiers of blackness" (47). The African Hottentot broached by Davis was seen as the " 'lowest exemplum of mankind on the chain of being' " in scientific journals (47), providing a black base for the progressive development of civilization. Schocket reads Davis's racial politics as involved with unfixed color referents: "blackness traffics between modes of production and comes, momentarily at least, to characterize the conditions of white wage labor," while "whiteness" is a "signifying agent of class mobility" and "an internal, residual sign of an unmarked soul" (50; 54). The blackness of the worker, in his argument, is temporary, marking a slave-like condition, but covering (if one were to look beneath) an upwardly mobile white potential. This insightful reading establishes the connection between marked whiteness and blackness: but Davis neither shies from race nor shifts the issue to class in the novel.

Hugh's skin, "yellow with consumption," might mark him as nonwhite and lower class, but his filth racializes him, indeed, to the level of the Hottentots. Rather, Davis paints a "new race" as she has suggested: Hugh is apart from both the "blacks and whites" in the marketplace; he belongs, like the industrial waste sculpture that is "the very type of her class," to another caste, poor white trash (R. Davis 53).

Dirt characterizes this excluded race, just as it characterizes the setting. A "town of iron-works" is dominated by smoke (39). The air is "thick, clammy," with "foul smells," "black, slimy pools," "greasy soot," "reeking" animals, "begrimed" workers, "fog and mud and foul effluvia" (39–41). Even death promises not a park-like respite, but "a hole in a muddy graveyard" (40). The main character, Hugh, lives in a "kennel-like" room, the rented cellar to a house whose "earthen" floor is covered with "a green, slimy moss" (42–43). Although "half a dozen" factory families live in this same house, Hugh and Deborah's cellar dwelling establishes them as the lowest rank of inhabitants, according to a household hierarchy understood by middle-class readers as well as the lower classes. The bare brick walls are cobwebbed (60).

The conditions of his environment mark for Davis the tragedy of Hugh's life: they disrupt the smooth flow of transitives that connect racial whiteness with refinement and morality. Hugh witnesses each type of purity in the equation. He is Welsh, of "pure, unmixed blood"—a biological requirement for whiteness (42). His artistic sensibilities lend him a "groping passion for whatever [is] beautiful and pure" also—but these longings are frustrated by "all the vileness and coarseness of his life" (47). The upper-class men embody this frustrated purity: Mitchell, with his attractive "white hand," throws into contrast Hugh's "filthy body, his more stained soul" (51–52). Deborah finally bridges the transitive connections with the aid of a Quaker woman, whose "white fingers" deign to touch the dead mill worker (72). Deb enjoys, at the end, the "sunshine, and fresh air, and slow, patient Christ-love, needed to make healthy and hopeful [her] impure body and soul," so that at last she can look forward to the "purer" hills of heaven (73). Purity in the novel attaches to racial designation, to refinement and wealth, to cleanliness, and to morality; impurity belongs to any group denied these privileges. In fact, the denied make up their own group: Mitchell describes the mill workers as "this lowest deep—thieves, Magdalens, negroes" (57). Here, the lower-class laborers are indistinguishable from economic and sexual sinners and blacks. Negroes themselves carry the immoral implications of filth: the "negro-like river" reminds the narrator of the "stream" of mill workers, who not only have "skin and muscle and flesh begrimed," but also spend their days in "dens of drunkenness and infamy" (40).

The novel shares little concern for those necessarily cut off from whiteness, such as the mulattos or blacks, nor for those content with immorality through drunkenness or other sin. But Hugh distinguishes himself, marks his possibility, through his Korl-woman statue. Among the "things" owned by Hugh and Deb—a broken chair, a wooden bench, faded clothes and rags—Hugh displays his potential, both economic and artistic, through this white thing: a marble-like statue of "a woman, white, of giant proportions" (52). Because of this thing, Hugh is noticed by the upper-class visitors, and through this thing only can he communicate his hunger and aspirations. Davis's solution, as applied to Deb, is not so much labor reform or abolition, but rather cleanliness and a comfortable home. The Quaker woman who saves Deb has a "homely body"—an adjective evoking domesticity more than ugliness—and Deb finally becomes healthy when she resides in a "homely pine house" (73). Her former house cannot be considered a home—she spends no time in it, as content to sleep in factory ashes as in her own straw pile. This degraded environment produces her racial exclusion: not marked by either the white things of the upper classes or the dark things of slaves, Deb's house has essentially no things. But Hugh demonstrates his need for the material objects that his environment denies him: he despairs in prison only after he realizes that he can never carve korl again. At this point, he stops looking at the marketplace and begins to carve himself. Deb's cries of " 'Hugh, boy, not THAT!' " refer, we suppose, to his plan of committing suicide. But his death is nearly guaranteed in prison. Possibly her horror stems instead from an understanding that Hugh, forever forbidden to own or make new things, determines to mark his skin racially—not with the washable filth of factory soot, but with an indelible cut that releases a "black, nauseous stream of blood" (71).

Davis therefore concludes the story by returning the reader to a middle-class environment, and relocating Hugh's white statue to it as well. The narrator draws attention, finally, to the "objects which lie scattered around [her] room: . . . a half-moulded child's head; Aphrodite; a bough of forest-leaves; music; work; homely fragments, in which lie the secrets of all truth and beauty" (74). In the things, the "homely fragments," lie the truth and beauty that have escaped Hugh, and in them also are the manufacture of a middle-class environment. That Hugh's white thing, curtained to hide its coarseness, might belong to this room, also, marks the possibility and the tragedy of the novel.

BY THE SKIN OF HER TEETH

The narrator in Poe's "The Man That Was Used Up" spends the story moving from one social display to the next in his quest to find out the secret about what happened to Brevet Brigadier-General John ABC Smith. He begins at a party, gossips at church, visits a Shakespeare play, drops in on ladies playing whist, and attempts dancing as he hunts for sources of information about the man. Finally, he visits the general in person, to watch aghast as John ABC Smith assembles himself, with the help of a black servant, body part by body part. All the while, Smith provides a running advertisement for the makers of his limbs: Thomas, he says, makes a "capital" cork leg, but Bishop is better for arms; Ducrow markets a good bosom, and De L'Ormes puts out a "capital" wig. Throughout these recommendations, Smith abuses his black servant Pompey, but he saves his racial slurs for the adjustment of his false teeth, screeching, "'Now, you nigger, my teeth!'" In the course of a recent battle against the Indian tribes the Bugaboos and the Kickapoos, General Smith explains, "'I swallowed some very capital articles . . . when the big Bugaboo rammed me down with the butt end of his rifle'" (412). While the narrator has previously observed that he has never "beheld a finer set of teeth" and that the general has a mouth "utterly unequaled," Smith's teeth are the only articles that Smith believed to be "capital" before paying for the false replacements. His original teeth, in fact, are a product of the marketplace every bit as much as the cork legs and the toupee; they participate in Smith's conspicuous consumption in a number of ways—all of them understood by the narrowly defeated Bugaboo and Kickapoo tribes. The original teeth advertise the general as upper-class, industrious, and hygienic; they signal, in fact, his whiteness—the whiteness that justifies for him his assault upon the Native American tribes and his mistreatment of his black servant. As he is forced to swallow his teeth—these "capital" articles which symbolize, especially for the big Bugaboo, the invasiveness of capitalism—he ends up consuming these instruments of consumption. But the Bugaboo is ultimately frustrated, because these articles of industrialist display are readily replaced by more manufactured goods, and only the man can be "used up," but nevermore the system he supports.

The narrator begins his search for John ABC Smith's secret by asserting, "I could not bring myself to believe that *the remarkable* something distinguishing Smith could "lay altogether, or indeed at all, in the supreme excellence of his bodily endowments"—exactly the same way Claudia of *The Bluest Eye* cannot believe in beauty built from disparate parts (406). He discovers, however, that it does: the Bugaboos and Kickapoos have dismembered the man, and technology has re-membered him as fine-looking and valorous. But while the society describes Smith with epithets such as "prodigies of valor!" and "immortal renown!" the narrator takes a more negative view that nobody thus far has been able to admit—that Smith is "used up" (409). He is entirely in use, in fact: he is things made into a man, a disembodied man who has rebuilt himself through the use of capital products. He is, at the same time, dependent upon the faithful service of his slave for daily re-assembly.

But if a person's identity is built from things, and built by others—manufacturers and servants—then to whom does the identity belong really? In "Berenice," the narrator obsesses around a phrase he has provided, "*que tous ses dents étaient des idées. Des idées!*" suggesting that teeth, Berenice's teeth, support his ideas, perception, and purpose (647). Joan Dayan asserts directly that "Poe takes the mouth of a lady and turns it into the mind of a man," and that the teeth "stand for or constitute his identity" (Dayan, *Fables* 136, 145). But while Dayan establishes an intricate philosophical word puzzle wherein " 'I'/dents/ idées" becomes identity, Poe's narrator provides a more direct and socially resonant argument of his own (*Fables* 142). In describing his cousin's illness, Egaeus equates the "more startling changes wrought in the *physical* frame of Berenice" with the "singular and most appalling distortion of her personal identity" (Poe 645). Her teeth are the most dominant feature in her physical appearance, and her appearance constitutes her identity. As with the manufactured body parts of John ABC Smith, nineteenth-century white teeth participate in industrial discipline, rules of hygiene, supportive servants, and gendered ideals of beauty. Teeth are most anxiously situated white things, indeed a prime example of the antebellum white thing, because they depend upon careful care and maintenance just as white skin does, but they also participate in the animal act of eating and therefore deny the civilization that their whiteness asserts. In addition, teeth are truly personal white things, not mere rhetorical extensions of one's identity; but at the same time, they can be removed.

In a letter to the editor of the *Southern Literary Messenger* for March 1835, Edgar Allan Poe offers a backhanded apology for his story "Berenice":

"'The subject is far too horrible, and I confess that I hesitated in sending it to you as a specimen of my capabilities. The Tale originated in a bet that I could produce nothing effective on a subject so singular, provided I treat it seriously. . . . I allow that it approaches the very verge of bad taste—but I will not sin so egregiously again'" (qtd. in Dayan, "Identity" 494). In this confession, which at once admits a "sin" and exults in winning a bet, Poe confounds the "horrible" nature of the story and the money to be gained by both writing and publishing it. Possibly, the news of grave-robbers pulling teeth stimulated the bet (Dayan, "Identity" 494). In the scholarship, these teeth become everything from "the mind of a man" to the "*vagina dentata*," from the "silenced . . . female voice" of courtly love poetry to the fear of literary immortality or a twisted vampire legend.[13] These scholars fail, to a greater or lesser degree, to attend to the narrator's emphasis on the "*invariably frivolous*" nature of his subjects, and the "*attentive*" quality of his meditations (Poe 644, italics in text). "Few deductions, if any, were made," the narrator insists, "and those few pertinaciously returning in upon the original subject as a center." The teeth, for him, come to represent nothing besides themselves; they are their own problem, invariably frivolous but excessively serious. Poe's choice to win his bet by focusing on "the most ordinary objects in the universe"—not allowing deductions or departure from the surface of these things, and yet imbuing them with such destructive, distracting power—insists that we investigate the teeth themselves (644). They are nineteenth-century teeth, white things with preternatural power.

Berenice's teeth are the most active agent in the story, performing the only work of will accomplished throughout the narrative. Neither Egaeus nor Berenice act volitionally; both appear disembodied, occupying "the land of dreams." The trances suffered by both further separate their minds from their wills—the narrator slips into immobile reveries that involve "[f]ew deductions" and are "*never pleasurable*"; Berenice's resemble "positive dissolution" (643, 644). Within the narrative, Egaeus never even describes a move from his library, and Berenice's arrivals and departures go unobserved. The only actors in the story are two momentary servants who react to the spectacle, and the teeth. The *teeth* employ the active verbs: they "disclosed themselves" to the narrator's initial viewing; ever after, they "would not be driven away"; their details "brand in upon [his] memory." While the narrator remains immobile, they are active: "they were here, and there, and everywhere, and visibly and palpably before me," and he assigns them "a sensitive and sentient power," "a capability of moral expression" (646). The immobile teeth assume a "terrible ascendancy" over the human owner and spectator; they seem to be dignified, personified, even moral anchors for the indecently writhing flesh that claims them. In her premature death, Berenice is also passive as her body and things act upon her: she is "seized with epilepsy" in the morning, and at night, "the grave was ready for its tenant" (647). Likewise, the narrator watches as actions happen to him: he does not actually recall removing Berenice's teeth, but merely notes the physical evidence that it has been done—the "muddy and clotted clothes," the "indented" hand, the spade. As clues appear about the room, his body reacts without his understanding: "Why, then, as I perused them, did the hairs of my head erect themselves on end, and the blood of my body become congealed within my veins?" The "menial," "pale as the tenant of a tomb," explains the deed and guides the narrator through the clues that incriminate him. But even as revelation dawns upon him, his body does not react to his commands: he cannot open the box, and "in [his] tremor, it slipped from [his] hands." The box falls and bursts; from within it, "with a rattling sound," roll out the dental instruments and "thirty-two small, white, and ivory-looking substances that were scattered to and fro about the floor" (648).

It is no accident that these personified teeth and the briefly visible servants share the main motion of the story, nor that Egaeus finds the teeth's rootedness in Berenice's mouth ultimately unbearable. The teeth are the creators of his identity, but they are possessed by another; in the mouth of Berenice, however, they are still products of the marketplace, whitened by the work of servants and slaves, polished by industrial manners, supervised by dentists and socialites, and motivated by the danger of becoming an object. "Berenice" is a story from the perspective of the white doll that has been taken apart, afraid itself that re-assembly will not recreate the pre-existing privileged white identity; it is a story told from the viewpoint of John ABC Smith but without his valor or faith in capitalism and slaves. Egaeus cannot gain control of the makers of his identity, and therefore, he remains inactive in his ancestral home, his attention tied to these frivolous everyday white objects.

Poe wrote "Berenice" just as pressures to care for teeth became socially oppressive—around the time, one student of dentistry claims, that the "mouth with teeth" was being invented as an entity (Nettleton 88). Before the last quarter of the eighteenth century, the beginning of the "whitening" period for other artifacts, few toothbrushes existed (Shackel 6). In 1776 dental care was still relegated to the "'polite and elegant' " classes: a *Maryland Gazette* article asserts that " 'the foulness of the teeth by some people is little regarded; but with the fair sex, with the polite and elegant part of the world, it is looked on as a certain mark of filthiness and sloth' " (Shackel 73). Prior to this time, Paul Shackel explains, references to cleaning teeth only occasionally appear: Giovanni of Arcoli recommended in the fifteenth century that slivers of wood be used to clean the teeth. In the sixteenth century, Erasmus suggested a rinsing with clean water over the newly offensive habit of using napkins or tablecloth to wipe teeth. In the next century, Cardinal Richelieu ordered that knife points be rounded to keep people from picking their teeth with the points. With the advent of professional dentistry in America, a craftsman such as Isaac Greenwood was " 'an ivory turner as well as a dentist' " (Shackel 42). If ivory teeth replaced the wooden version in the last decades of the eighteenth century, false teeth as well as real ones became whiter by the nineteenth century.

The manufacture of toothbrushes signals both the popularity of dental hygiene in the nineteenth century and the discipline it demanded. From 1800 to 1860, Annapolis area toothbrushes observed by Shackel showed a decreasing variation in hole spacing, and fewer errors, because metal templates were developed for craftsmen to follow. Like ritual dining and daily cleansing, brushing one's teeth required a repetitive attention to the body, and a simultaneous disguising of its animal functions. The earliest toothbrush, consisting of the stock and the bristle, was hand-drilled freehand by a craftsman, "without benefit of a pattern." Holes were irregular and bristles were loosely packed. Increasing technology and mechanization by the nineteenth century created "a more standardized product" which could be mass-produced and therefore mass-marketed (44). Like the mass-produced ceramics of the same decades, toothbrushes demanded for their manufacture an increasing factory discipline, which created a more standard, reliable product, and in turn trained its users towards more individualized, regulated behavior. Also like the ceramics, toothbrushes were white: bristles were made from the white hair of boars and hogs, and stocks came from the bones of a cow or ox (43).

Sentimental and romantic literature reflects these new standards, as white teeth became a gauge of beauty, especially with "the fair sex." In E.D.E.N. Southworth's *The Hidden Hand*, the bachelor gentleman Old Hurricane frets at receiving a young lady into his household, claiming to know nothing of "what a young girl requires . . . combs and boxes and smelling-bottles and tooth-powder; and such" (Southworth 79).

Sentimental novels began noting the whiteness of teeth in descriptions of their heroes and heroines. The heroine in Harriet Beecher Stowe's *Dred* praises her favorite suitor in these terms: "He's tall, and rather loose-jointed—has beautiful teeth" (34). In James Fenimore Cooper's *The Last of the Mohicans*, the "surpassingly beautiful" Cora sports "a row of teeth that would have shamed the purest ivory" (489). In *Little Women*, Jo returns from a ball to report on the neighbor boy Laurie, cataloguing, "Curly black hair, brown skin, big black eyes, long nose, nice teeth, little hands and feet, tall as I am; very polite for a boy" (29). In *The Blithedale Romance*, Nathaniel Hawthorne's narrator dotes on the beauty of Westervelt— a man whose name means "Western World"—whose beauties include "remarkably brilliant" teeth (86). The narrator recoils, however, when he discovers "a gold band around the upper part of his teeth; thereby making it apparent that every one of his brilliant grinders and incisors was a sham" (88). From grudgingly admiring Westervelt's beauty, Coverdale shifts on this discovery to thinking him a "moral and physical humbug" (88). Whiteness of the teeth, like whiteness of the skin, properly signifies only if it can pretend to be inherent and at the same time signal unceasing personal discipline: make-up or false teeth are deceptions.

In speaking of the "'gospel of the toothbrush,'" Booker T. Washington asserts that "there are few single agencies of civilization that are more far-reaching" (174, 75). He emphasizes in his founding of Tuskegee that all students must have a toothbrush for this reason, even if they have no other property. In its civilizing influence, use of the toothbrush also brings about "[a]bsolute cleanliness of the body," after which may be learned finer points such as sleeping between two sheets, the use of pajamas, keeping clothes neat, and mending tears and missing buttons (175–176). It also demands individualized discipline, which Washington illustrates in a story of three girls recently arrived at the school. When he asks them if they have their toothbrushes, "one of the girls replied, pointing to a brush: 'Yes, sir. That is our brush. We bought it together, yesterday'" (175). Holding these girls up as an example of the vestigial communal attitudes of plantation life, Washington assures his readers, "It did not take them long to learn a different lesson" (175). Washington's project, narrated in 1900 about Reconstruction-era events, concerns the education of freed blacks from a communal, pre-industrial slave lifestyle to the "civilized" behavior of modern workers. His "gospel of the toothbrush" is an attempt to catch up: slaves deliberately kept from manners and "whitening" in the first half of the century had to go through the same processes as did middle-class whites at the beginning of it. The toothbrush, as Washington argues, civilizes: this civilizing discipline distinguished in the Anglo antebellum imagination the racially white from the slaves. The project of Washington specifically is not to reform ex-slaves into whites, but to undermine the social practices that limited slaves to "blackness" in the minds of whites.

Washington centers on a site fraught with meaning when he demands dental care of his ex-slave students, however. Throughout slave lore, a slave dealer's inspection of the slave's teeth becomes the final physical degradation of the auction block. Slave purchasers treated the black body overtly as a commodity, a composite of valuable parts. Determining the value of male slaves, a dealer in Olmsted's journal "grasp[s] at the man's arms, as if to feel their muscular capacity. He then examined his hands and fingers; and, last of all, told him to open his mouth and show his teeth, which he did in a submissive manner" (Olmsted 595). As Olmsted continues at the slave auction, he watches prospective buyers file past the families of slaves, each taking turns—"with no abrupt rudeness"—at "feeling their arms, looking into their mouths, and investigating the quality of their hands and fingers" (596). More than one male slave is made to undress behind a screen while "a dozen gentlemen" scrutinize his skin and hands, and "every tooth in his head [is] scrupulously looked at" before the bidding begins (598). Few other gestures can convey more powerfully to the slave his status as a thing, to be bought and sold.

Teeth are the site of an exercise of power. For slaves, their teeth marked them as marketable things. For upper- and middle-class whites, their teeth became things to be cared for, a display of personal discipline, and a new standard of beauty. When body parts enter the marketplace as products of manufactured beauty—things requiring special care and signaling social and legal status—then furniture is not a "second body" as guidebooks claimed, but the body is instead merely furniture. When Poe's narrator fixates on teeth, it is because they are the white things that construct his identity, but it is a hollow identity based upon contradictions and social fictions: disembodied femininity, dismemberable beauty, sentimental death, and civilized consumption.

Poe's narrator becomes aware, as he gazes endlessly at Berenice, that she is also a commodity and thing; in her illness, she becomes more and more clearly a composite of already interpreted parts, and these parts make up her "personal identity." More horrible than his discovery that this identity is susceptible to decay and deformation is the recognition that her identity has always been built from social commodities, and therefore his identity is too. Berenice's mouth comes under scrutiny in the same way the mouth of a slave at auction would: says the narrator, "I held [the teeth] in every light. I turned them in every attitude. I surveyed their characteristics. I dwelt upon their peculiarities. I pondered upon their conformation. I mused upon the alteration in their nature" (647). In his scrupulous attention, he seems readying to purchase these teeth— and in fact his labor demands that he possess them with or without Berenice. His frenzied description of the teeth themselves reveals the attraction of their conflicting messages. He examines them and finds "[n]ot a speck on their surface—not a shade on their enamel—not an indenture in their edges—but what that brief period of her smile had sufficed to brand in upon my memory" (646). In the first half of his description, he attributes to these teeth the ideal spotlessness and whiteness seen in the false teeth of characters such as John ABC Smith or Westervelt, the unmarred whiteness sported by a mass-produced marble gravestone tablet, and the immaculateness enjoyed by fair heroines such as Little Eva. In the second half of the sentence, however, he takes away this ideal and instead assures us that no shade or spot or indenture has escaped his notice. Thus Berenice's teeth call forth the idealized whiteness embodied in ceramics, houses, gravestones—and teeth. But he knows every spot and speck on the surface of their whiteness; his investment is in damaged goods, liable to undisciplined care especially within the diseased body of Berenice.

Berenice's story reflects the tragedy of a woman's death, but more, the travesty of the myth of the "angel in the house" and her disembodiment, which courts a symbolic afterlife but tries to ignore the physical task of living. Berenice begins as a spiritual woman, "the Berenice of a dream; not as a being of the earth, earthy, but as the abstraction of such a being; not as a thing to admire, but to analyze; not as an object of love, but as the theme of the most abstruse although desultory speculation" (645). Her illness, however, forces her body upon her, and then destroys it until it is corpse-like. She becomes a sentimental heroine, but death and disease cannot be romanticized. Her "once jetty hair" bleaches to a "vivid yellow," her "unparalleled beauty" fades to an emaciated skeleton with "very pale" skin (645–646). Her eyes, "lifeless, and lustreless, and seemingly pupilless," lose even the spot of blackness they once had (646). She changes from a woman "agile, graceful, and overflowing with energy" who enjoys the freedom of a "ramble on the hillside" to one prone to trances "very nearly resembling positive dissolution" (643). Where she once has belonged outside, the disease renders her domestic and keeps her indoors and frail, and her draping gray dress makes her outline "indistinct," completing her transformation from woman to domestic angel (646). The narrator disembodies his woman literally, demonstrating the absurdity of social fiction, and he expels every spot of blackness from her frame, revealing only a barely alive death's head.[14] He enacts this violence upon the woman because she manages the white things, and in order to be trusted with such a responsibility, she cannot maintain her own material identity.

In the end, her teeth have become merely "ivory-looking substances," "scattered to and fro about the floor" as white things. Egaeus reorders his betrothed wife's body as furniture, literalizing the popular idea of furniture as a woman's "second body." The makers of her identity, and his, have been detached from the site of their signification. The compositional purity, the tenuous links holding together antebellum ideas of beauty, domesticity, materialism, are unhinged as the model body comes apart. Poe's narrator comes to a conclusion, from his disassembled white girl, that Claudia in *The Bluest Eye* is not able to reach—since, possibly, she restrains her own violent urges: "Misery is manifold. The wretchedness of the earth is multiform. Overreaching the wide horizon as the rainbow, its hues are as various as the hues of that arch—as distinct, too, yet as intimately blended" (642). In his diseased attention to that which is frivolous, he has presumed that he can stave off identity insecurities by possessing the proper things. But he finds this possession to be too modified by the agency of a wife, and the white things that should establish a comfortable upper-class white life for him cannot be controlled. In handing white things the power of signification, the narrator finds he has handed over all his motive power, and only the servants and the things can any longer act. The promise of early nineteenth-century materialism is a fraud: misery and wretchedness appear "manifold" and "multiform" and will not be segregated to avoidable spaces in the geography. Moreover, its "hues" are various: the polar designation of black and white is meaningless if misery can encompass both; and the segregating, privileging work of white things cannot protect him, because its hues are also "intimately blended."

In antebellum stories of passing, of marked or sunburnt skin, of dirty or damaged goods, the desire to differentiate and, in effect, unblend the threats of enslavement, lower-classness, and blackness is expressed in a strict and ideally unbreachable barrier defining "whiteness." The possibilities of "white" failing to maintain its status or of racial blackness trespassing into the domain of whiteness, seemed parallel anxieties involved in tragic mulatto stories, excessive cleanliness practices, and various skin-care taboos. The cultural work of white things ultimately suggested that they could create a segregated geography that could be internalized, indeed, corporealized and controlled through exercises of self-discipline: desegregation is, perhaps, Claudia's goal when she feels urged towards dismemberment.

EPILOGUE

In 1893 the Unites States celebrated the four-hundredth anniversary of Columbus's landing by opening the Columbian Exposition World's Fair in Chicago. The intentions of its organizers were to present a modern image of the United States, to highlight its progress and mark its accomplishments, while at the same time to educate its citizens in patriotism and art. The Columbian Exposition was, as intended, a self-portrait of American values and a broad advertisement of the nation's cultural and technological achievements over the last century. Culminating in White City, the exposition laid bare the underlying messages of previous architectural and landscape fashions. Finally iterated in the last years of the century were attitudes formed by the material culture of its preceding decades. White City was a public display, a performance on the national level that echoed the many minor performances enacted in the everyday lives of upper- and middle-class white consumers before the Civil War. In a sense, the white things of White City provided a nostalgic retrospective, a romantically realized geography where the classes, genders, and races were clearly situated, labeled, and valued. In a sense, White City was also a hopeful projection—just as the everyday antebellum white things were—that attempted to expunge the problematic darker elements of society.

One of the organizers of the fair, George Brown Goode, envisioned it as an illustration of the "'steps of progress of civilization and its arts in successive centuries, and in all the lands up to the present time'" (qtd. in Hinsley 346). At the center of the exhibition was White City, a model city built of iron framework and "staff"—a white, plaster-like material. Surrounded by Greek and Roman revival architecture and staff-covered sculptures, White City housed the nation's finest technological and artistic advances. Among the displays were artifacts from Native North and

South American tribes, collected by anthropologists Frederick Ward Putnam and Franz Boas, and along the periphery of White City, living displays of native groups—Eskimos and Kwakuitl Indians—camped outside and performed everyday chores and native ceremonies for onlookers. These native groups represented the beginning of America, an imaginary view of its undeveloped origins before Columbus arrived. " 'After a stroll amid the scenes I have only briefly sketched,' " Putnam suggested, " 'one will visit the other departments of the Exposition with singular feelings and with an appreciation which could only be aroused by such contrasts' " (Hinsley 348–389).

At the "exact junction" between the Court of Honor in White City and the outlying entertainment district of the Midway Plaisance—officially within White City but confined to a separate territory—stood the Woman's Building (Fryer 23). Here were presented women's accomplishments throughout the ages, including art and philosophy as well as quilting and cooking. *Harper's* magazine announced that one could view simultaneously a woman darning a sock and a painting produced by an American woman. The report adds, however, that viewers could not expect to see "ladies" of the latter group doing work as they might observe the former; in fact, the labor of the more cultivated class would not be displayed at all—only its products. The building's architecture was described by viewers according to Victorian feminine standards, called " 'the most peaceably human of all the buildings . . . like a man's ideal of woman' " and " 'chaste and timid' " (Fryer 25).

In contrast to the seriousness of White City's displays, the Midway Plaisance featured carnival exhibits to be seen for a fee. Here was the entertainment side of White City's accomplishments, filled with carnival attractions, side shows, and a "jumble of foreignness" (Hinsley 351). The Midway included attractions such as " 'Dwarf Elephant Lily, 35 inches High,' " " 'jugglers and magicians, camel drivers and donkey boys,' " as well as " 'dancing-girls from Cairo and Algiers, from Samoa and Brazil' " and other " 'plump and piquant damsels' " (Hinsley 346, 353). The Midway as an evolutionary journey was understood. Nathaniel Hawthorne's son commented, " 'You have before you the civilized, the half-civilized and the savage worlds to choose from—or rather to take one after the other,' " and Hubert Howe Bancroft wrote, " 'All the continents are here represented, and many nations of each continent, civilized, semi-civilized, and barbarous, from the Caucasian to the African black' " (qtd. in Weddle 115–116). African blacks, representing an exotic culture with strange tools and garb, were accorded a place in the fair, although only the lowest.

African American blacks, by distinction, were "systematically excluded from the fair," except for a few contributions by black women displayed in the Woman's Building. When blacks protested this erasure, a Jubilee Day was designated for them, which they boycotted (Weddle 116). In its year-long coverage of the fair, Harper's magazine offered an official, if insulting, status for African Americans within the bounds of Chicago's Jackson Park. The journal presented numerous pictures and sketches of well-dressed white fairgoers at the exhibits, backgrounded by the striking architecture and machinery, or gazing on the strange costumes of Egyptians and Chinese. The African American family entered the fair represented by the "Johnsons," to whom a number of derogatory cartoons were devoted. In the first, a large black man with flashing white eyes and teeth accompanies his large wife and two children, speaks in exaggerated dialect, and otherwise betrays ignorance of all cultured events (Harper's 770). Their unwelcome presence at the site of America's self-definition becomes clear in the cartoon labeled, "The Johnson family visits the village of the South Sea Islanders." Here, surrounded by thatched huts and gazed upon by well-dressed white gentlemen, Mr. Johnson looks at a near-naked Islander the same shade as he is. He asks the man, "Does you speak English?" and the native replies, "Yes. Does you?" (Harper's 914).

In its messages and visual presentation, White City was only a more self-consciously staged version of the plantation mansions and middle-class dining rooms of the early nineteenth century. The successful design of White City encouraged, as it celebrated, a resurgence of whitening at the end of the nineteenth century. It signaled the culmination of the century's work, but also the beginning of its own conclusion. The whitening trend in material objects fanned out to touch other areas, die out in some, and become entrenched in others. The ideological remnants of whiteness, however, did not cease: they only began to lose their precision of form. The whiteness of houses and dishes would afterwards be overwhelmed by their commonness; the whiteness of gravestones and women would be critiqued, pushed underground, or refashioned into darker models. Louis Sullivan, teacher to Frank Lloyd Wright, complained that White City halted all architectural progress by resurrecting the fashion of white revival houses for perhaps another half century (H. Morrison 184). In 1901, Ladies' Home Journal editor Edward Bok began publishing house models by Frank Lloyd Wright, and "[t]housands of readers sent in $5 for a complete set of plans and specifications" for his white modern architecture (Wright 164). The modern buildings designed in the 1920s by Le Corbusier were starkly white, and in 1925 he could declare that " 'Whitewash is extremely moral' " (Wigley xvi). The modern middle-class house of the twentieth century, although devoid of Gothic ornamentation, nonetheless shared whiteness with its early nineteenth-century precursors. But the popularity itself rendered whiteness in houses inconspicuous—as it did with dishes. The white ceramic, finally achieved by European manufacturers at the turn of the nineteenth century, was unremarkable by the turn of the twentieth.

Suellen Hoy argues that cleanliness as a democratically applied ideal did not take hold in America until the middle of the nineteenth century, although it then surpassed European standards of cleanliness and peaked in the 1950s. Personal hygiene, arising at the beginning of the nineteenth century, radiated outward, as did home beautifying and landscaping ideals, to encompass clean cities and countrysides. Magazine advertisements marketed cleanliness as a prerequisite of good citizenship: Fels-Naptha soap addressed immigrant women's ignorance with ads entitled "Teaching Mrs. Rizzuto American ideas" and "Mrs. Zambruski doesn't quite understand" (Hoy 86). At the turn of the twentieth century cleanliness was marketed as "American," but it was still white and still economically productive. For household interiors, "[w]hite was revered as a sign of sanitary awareness. At first, concrete basements were whitewashed; then living rooms and dining rooms were whitewashed as well. Specifications for kitchen walls called for washable tiles or less expensive enameled sheet metal, lightweight oilcloth, or enamel paint—always white. Even appliances had touches of shiny white porcelain" (Wright, Building 162). Readers of *The House Beautiful* were told that "physicians who studied the effects of color on the mind considered bare white walls as effective as a rest cure."[1]

As with the kitchen itself, the food at the end of the nineteenth century became whiter: "[o]ne of the major civilizing influences in the American kitchen was widely recognized to be white sauce" (Shapiro 91). The basic white sauce, made from flour, butter, and milk, was recommended as a covering for vegetables, meats, soups, salads, and desserts. Even the choice of words used to describe the role of white sauce reveals how the message of white things could reach the minutest corners of the house: among "scientific cooks," there was "virtually no cooked food that at one time or another was not hidden, purified, enriched, or ennobled with white sauce" (91). Certainly, whiteness as a synonym for civilized, pure, rich, and noble was well established by the end of the century, if a viscous layering of it could effect such drastic ends. The "fondness for whiteness" shown by women's journals and their followers at the end of the nineteenth century rendered meals refined, nutritious, and suggestive of "harmony and order" (95). Many of the scientific dinner recipes offered meals that were "entirely white."[2]

Blanketed food served to whiten the place settings which, after the Civil War, began to change from entirely white vessels with white molded trim to white dishes with increasingly colorful decorations. As technological advances increased mass-production of ceramics, an "arts and crafts" movement also arose that valued hand-crafted and hand-painted vessels. By 1886, the author of the *Crockery and Glass Journal* proclaimed that one could no longer find an " 'American family of the great middle strata of this country that has not abolished the sepulchral white for the more pleasing and attractive decorated services for the table' " (qtd. in Blaszczyk 147).

In the final third of the nineteenth century, rural cemeteries with elaborately sculpted monuments planted among willow trees and winding paths gave way to the rolling smoothness of park cemeteries. Cemetery superintendents, promising perpetual care for the interred, preferred lawn cemeteries as easier to tend. They began regulating against enclosing fences and condemned monuments as individualistic and misdirected. Suggestions of " 'death, sorrow, or pain' " were to be eliminated in favor of a level " 'sod covered grave marked only by a single stone sunk even with the turf' " (Farrell 120, 122). By 1887, the popularity of white marble gravestone had clearly passed, when an Association of American Cemetery Superintendents speaker assumed, " 'as the most beautiful and the best in every way, that the so-called park plan will be adopted' " (Farrell 116).

The endings of a trend should be examined as well as its beginnings: what disappears may reveal more than what remains popular. An object's absence from the material record may not signal the death of an idea, but rather that idea's cultural entrenchment. By the twentieth century, the cultural work of white things had changed, as had their appearance in the material and literary record. My use of examples from twentieth-century novels to begin each chapter began as an attempt to demonstrate the vestiges of what white things wrought on racial, class, and gendered constructions. The messages of these things remained, I hypothesized, since they could signify similarly in literature of even a century after the trend's wane. Only in reviewing my examples did I discover how they ordered themselves symmetrically. Faulkner's *Absalom, Absalom!* was published in 1936, the same year as Mitchell's *Gone with the Wind*. Both are written by white Southerners born at the turn of the century (Faulkner in 1897; Mitchell in 1900); both are set in the antebellum South. Angelou's *I Know Why the Caged Bird Sings* and Morrison's *The Bluest Eye* were published in 1969 and 1970, respectively, by African American women born at the beginning of the Great Depression (Angelou in 1928; Morrison in 1931). Mitchell's and Faulkner's work, perhaps as with White City, hearken to a time when the actual landscape was integrated but the world of material things ideally imposed a social order. On the other hand, Morrison's and Angelou's stories are set in the years before World War II (or before *Brown v. the Board of Education of Topeka, Kansas*), when social and physical space was legally segregated; their young, female, black characters are aware that almost all things continue to signify racially—teeth, clothes, dishes, front yards, even dolls. Their characters attack the racial codings violently, materially, through these things.

Because race is a primary social designation for nonwhite Americans, it continues to be proclaimed loudly in everyday things; although many of the things have changed, meanings cling to previously powerful goods such as china and plantation architecture as well. One of the accomplishments of white things was that their work erased itself, for these white things to become so common as to become invisible, so standardized as to seem dependable, so obtainable as to be "normal"—so that the meaning of racial whiteness also seems inherent, inevitable, monolithic. Thus white things contributed in the early nineteenth century to the problems faced by "whiteness" scholars today–that "white" does not register as a racial designation, but rather describes the social norm, an unchallengable universal. Casting back to when these things were remarkable, we find that they were also making marks. The everyday object must be studied, because the most insignificant coffee cup might alter our behavior incrementally—but indelibly.

NOTES

INTRODUCTION

1. At slave sites on Cannon's Point plantation in Georgia, John Solomon Otto finds these coarse earthenwares to comprise almost 70 percent of the ceramic sherds found (105). Leland Ferguson finds that 70 percent of the ceramics found on 23 South Carolina slave sites to be the dark, hand-made "Colono ware" ("Struggling" 31).
2. I draw here mainly from Deetz's observations in *In Small Things Forgotten* (1977) and "Material Culture and Worldview in Colonial Anglo-America" (1988).
3. Henry Glassie's *Folk Housing in Middle Virginia* (1975) uncovers a "house grammar" which assigns specific mathematical formulas in creating house plans dating to the eighteenth and early nineteenth centuries.
4. For example, Michel de Certeau in *The Practice of Everyday Life*, translated by Steven Rendall (Berkeley, 1984), argues consumption as a form of cultural production.
5. One specific example of a product as opposed to an assemblage would be the topsy-turvy doll, which was a black woman at one end, and beneath her skirts, when flipped over, appeared to be a white woman. Shirley Samuels uses this product as an excellent illustration of the relationships between black and white women during the time of its popularity ("The Identity of Slavery"). The thing tied to a specific historical event would be, for example, the "Log Cabin" presidential campaign of 1840, which had a discrete duration and purpose (see, for example, Harry L. Watson, *Liberty and Power: The Politics of Jacksonian America*, 1990).
6. See, for example, Khalil Husni, "The Whiteness of the Whale"; Edward Stone, "The Whiteness of the Whale"; and Mary Blish, "The Whiteness of the Whale Revisited."
7. The *Pawtucket Gazette* exclaims on July 15, 1856: " 'Talking of the ladies, they are getting bigger and bigger. They fill up the sidewalks. As they brush by you, you feel bones—whalebones, I mean, for there are no others within a mile of you." The whalebone cage for skirts "reached its height of popularity in 1859" (Torrens 192).
8. In his study of recreation in the late nineteenth century, Brown sets two tasks: "The archival/archaeological task . . . consists of developing a chain of associations that

seem, retrospectively, to have converged already in the literary work. The analytical task consists in representing that convergence as an image that freshly elucidates the signifying structures and material changes of everyday life—the task, in other words, of producing the history that lingers within neglected images, institutions, and objects" (*The Material Unconscious* 4–5).

9. William Carlos Williams, in "A Sort of a Song" (1944): "through metaphor to reconcile/the people and the stones./Compose. (No ideas/but in things)" (46).

10. "Passing," entirely dependent on a social rather than a visual designation of "black," could therefore be a source of anxiety and possible violence, because seen as a way of cheating the system.

11. *Narrative* 105, 107. Douglass's stupor is immediately contrasted in this passage to the "beautiful vessels, robed in purest white"—ships in the Chesapeake—that represent freedom for him (*Narrative* 107).

12. I argue in chapter 1 that Douglass does not invest in this system, which nonetheless excludes him from the privilege of white "masculinity"; instead, he inverts the system and rhetorically takes on the master's role, while the reader is cast into a slave's perspective.

13. As Lucy Larcom claims, " 'Inanimate objects do gather into themselves something of the character of those who live among them, through association; and this alone makes heirlooms valuable. They are family treasures, because they are part of the family life, full of memories and inspirations. Bought or sold, they are nothing but old furniture' " (qtd. in Gillian Brown 46).

14. See, for example, Ann Douglas's work, *The Feminization of America* (1977), which casts ministers as among the first feminized. Emerson links scholars to clergy and asserts that the "action" of the former makes them more masculine: "I have heard it said that the clergy,—who are always . . . the scholars of their day,—are addressed as women. . . . As far as this is true of the studious classes, it is not just and wise" ("The American Scholar" 70).

15. I am aware that this mainstream understanding of crucial social categories participates in excluding many dominant groups of United States citizens; it demonstrates, perhaps, how such excluded groups continue to be overlooked. In fact, beyond a possible way of viewing antebellum social constructions, this approach to things may also help to illuminate troubling gaps in the attention of literary history.

16. See, for example, Christine Stansell's *City of Women* (1986) and Diana DiZierga Wall's *The Archaeology of Gender* (1994).

17. Michael Banton traces a history of the term "race." In the eighteenth century, the term suggested "commonality of descent or character"; in the nineteenth, it referred to nation and national character (51).

18. For example, the "No More Separate Spheres!" issue of *American Literature*, 1998.

19. As argued by David Roediger in *The Wages of Whiteness*, racial whiteness is a commodity conferring privilege for the price of industrial work-discipline and capitalist individualism.

CHAPTER 1: THE POT CALLING THE KETTLE

1. Frederick Douglass in *Narrative of the Life* describes eating from a trough (72). Writing decades later, Booker T. Washington cannot recall "a single instance during [his] childhood" when his family "ate a meal in a civilized manner." Instead, "meals were gotten by the children very much as dumb animals get theirs"—random scraps for children, perhaps a "tin plate held on the knees" for others (9).
2. Samuels claims that both pro-slavery and anti-slavery positions exhibited, "from different sides, the tension between attempts to inscribe the black-white identity of and in the body, and attempts to escape such a biologized essentialism or biological design or destiny" (160).
3. In *Folk Housing in Middle Virginia*, Henry Glassie studies Virginia's vernacular architecture from colonial settlement to the twentieth century. Deetz extends Glassie's observations to include New England as well, and Anglo-American architecture in general (*In Small Things Forgotten*).
4. Glassie sees the shift to a universal whiteness to be signify democratization, since class distinctions were no longer the basis for house color (*Folk Housing* 156). Glassie also reads in the shift from unsegmented, asymmetrical houses to the many-roomed Georgian houses a national change in mindset. Once embracing a more communal outlook, he argues, people now showed in their houses that they valued "the closed over the open, the practical over the aesthetic, the private over the public, the artificial over the natural" (*Folk Housing* 162).
5. *Folk Housing* 156. Glassie cites Richard M. Candee's *Housepaints in Colonial America* for the assertion of whiteness (2–3, 11–12). Richard Bushman also points to the evolution of houses to white in *The Refinement of America: Persons, Houses, Cities* (1992).
6. Ruskin 167. This source is indebted to Glassie's mention of it in "Folk Art" 127.
7. Deetz, "Material Culture and Worldview in Colonial Anglo-America" 223. "Assemblage" refers to the entire collection of one type of artifact from a specific site or area. Here the area is Colonial Anglo-America.
8. Outside of church graveyards in developed cities, investigating the scattered folk cemeteries of the South is time intensive and therefore limited. *Early Gravestone Art in Georgia and South Carolina* (1986) by Diana Williams Combs compares Northern traditions to the styles found in Southern churchyards; *Texas Graveyards: A Cultural Legacy* (1982) by Terry G. Jordan discusses folk cemeteries. Ruth M. Little in *Sticks and Stones: Three Centuries of North Carolina Gravemarkers* (1998) investigates rural graveyards in North Carolina; Roberta Hughes Wright and Wilbur B. Hughes III focus on African American cemeteries in *Lay Down Body: Living History in African American Cemeteries* (1996).
9. Perhaps coincidentally, in the last decades of the eighteenth century, as upper-class English women were bleaching their hands with arsenic to make them whiter, Wedgwood produced a black tea kettle. While serving tea, women could display themselves against this black vessel "to enhance the whiteness of the hands"

(Kowaleski-Wallace 29). I am unaware of a similar production for the American market. On the whole, wealthy American consumers preferred silver teapots or white ceramic sets.

10. Marion Starling, cited in Kawash 53. Kawash also notes a quilt with this design that was presented to Garrison, and transparent window blinds embossed with the scene.

11. Of course, the predominance of these types also can reflect that slaves were not allowed to earn their own money, or that if they did, they chose not to spend it on dishes. Nonetheless, the former suggests that planters might have feared their slaves' gaining a sense of individuality from ownership. The latter may also suggest that the power of the white dishes remained in the minds of the whites and not the slaves.

12. Henry Louis Gates, Jr., discusses this initial lack of knowledge suffered by Douglass as a contrast to the calendar knowledge afforded the white boys in the narrative in "Binary Oppositions."

13. Solomon Low's marker is in the Unitarian churchyard, and the latter rests in St. John's Lutheran. The name is barely legible, but may be "Sarah Gieller." These are the post-1800 slate stones I observed in my fieldwork, although they are likely not the only ones. The French Huguenot Church, the Circular Congregational Church, and the Bethel M. E. Church were inaccessible at the time I visited. I did, however, visit St. Mary's, St. Philip's Protestant Episcopal, St. Michael's Protestant Episcopal, the First Baptist, the First (Scots) Presbyterian, the Unitarian, and St. John's Lutheran Churches downtown.

14. In Savannah's historic downtown cemetery, Colonial Park, operating from 1750 to 1853, this uniformity continues, marked by one interesting phenomenon. There are only fourteen legible nonwhite stones dating from after 1800 in the cemetery. However, of the fourteen, seven are for children, and three more for related adults who died around the same time as the children. Of the four remaining, two are gray slate and proclaim the deceased's Northern origins, and one appears less professional with etching rather than engraving and initials scratched into the base. The last is a simple anomaly: William C. Mills, aged 37 years, who died in 1827, has a gray slate stone.

15. On the other hand, the inland graveyards may show more variety, since overland shipping would have added to the cost of imported stones.

16. Family gravesites, scattered and poorly preserved, may not have shown such a uniform transition to white marble—I have not evaluated research on what remains of these. Such stones, however, would have been intended less for public display, and therefore their visual message would be less insistent.

17. Black slate enjoyed a brief resurgence of popularity at Mount Auburn in the years surrounding 1900 as well.

18. Hazel Carby, for example, begins her analysis of Jacobs with the assertion, "Jacobs used the material circumstances of her life to critique conventional standards of female behavior and to question their relevance and applicability to the experience of black women" (47).

19. Yellin acknowledges Jacobs's "melodramatic confessions" as accommodations to the Cult of Domesticity, but argues that her combination of the genres of slave narrative and domestic novel creates a "new voice" (xiv). Valerie Smith believes that Jacobs's tale is limited by sentimental conventions (xxxiii). On the other hand, Hazel Carby and Claudia Tate argue that Jacobs rejects these values.

20. Although I would distinguish the narrator Linda Brent from the author Harriet Jacobs, I draw from the lives of both, which Jean Fagan Yellin has found similar enough to warrant (Yellin 223–225). Therefore, for the sake of clarity and brevity, I will refer to Jacobs's autobiographical character as "Jacobs" also.

21. An explanation of the progressive planters' perception of their slaves as filthy, and their attempts to control their slaves and better supervise them by imposing standards of cleanliness, appears in chapter 4.

22. Yellin 216. I will assume that Jacobs draws on actual experiences and manipulates their presentation to suit her ends. Therefore, diagrams of Jacobs's actual house can inform the narrative, showing the starting point from which Jacobs constructs her work.

23. Thomas B. Lovell suggests that Jacobs's view of domesticity is not antithetical to market economics as in the "sentimental tradition"; rather, as a slave, Jacobs shows that "outside of a properly organized wage system, the practice of the moral principles associated with sentimentalism is impossible" (2).

24. Ferguson, "Struggling" 31. By the middle of the nineteenth century, Ferguson notes, "most African-American slaves had stopped making earthenware," and in the South the Catawba Indians were the main producers of such unrefined earthenware (35). His arguments apply, therefore, to slave potters of the eighteenth century and early nineteenth century: the beginnings of the whitening trend.

CHAPTER 2: LIVING ON WHITE BREAD

1. Michael T. Gilmore presents a detailed social reading of "Bartleby" in *American Romanticism and the Marketplace* (1985); in addition, Wai Chi Dimock examines the narrator's conflicting use of old-fashioned and emergent capitalist attitudes when dealing with his employees ("Class, Gender, and a History of Metonymy").

2. Dimock 80–81. Bill Brown's *The Material Unconscious* (1996) discusses recreation as a serious pastime beginning only in the last decades of the nineteenth century.

3. In *The Wages of Whiteness* (1991), Roediger examines minstrel plays as a response among Northern white working-class men to the pressures of industry. While the emerging factory work emphasized regulated, disciplined behavior, these plays romanticized slave life and located carefree, sensual, and undisciplined behavior within a black skin. The bodily freedoms given up by a successful worker became part of "blackness" and slavery. Thus, Roediger argues, while "whiteness" included the undesirable abandoning of pre-industrial freedoms, it compensated white

workers by privileging whiteness ideologically. In addition, Eric Lott argues that minstrelsy's definition of "whiteness" united whites of upper and lower classes, helping to alleviate class tension while contrasting them with a distant, enslaved, black population.

4. The source areas from which Kniffen traces westward-spreading architectural trends are New England, the Middle Atlantic including Pennsylvania, and the lower Chesapeake centered from Tidewater Virginia and including the Gulf coast (10). Within these regions, two distinct "cultures" also appear: urban and rural (6).

5. Kniffen 10. In the Middle Atlantic area, the English I-house and German log construction were popular. Working with logs entails certain difficulties: logs can usually be only twenty-four or thirty feet long and remain manageable, and with notched logs, the size of the log becomes the length of the wall. Adhering to the symmetry and style of the I-house was so important, however, that dog-run and saddlebag techniques were developed to allow builders to construct I-houses despite these difficulties. In these designs, essentially two log houses were roofed over together with an intervening space. These styles spread throughout the Appalachian area, branching westward and southward to include most of the country south of New England except for the coastal South (Kniffen 12).

6. See, for example, Michael Clark's "Caves, Houses, and Temples in James Fenimore Cooper's *The Pioneers*," which includes a summary of preceding articles on architecture as well.

7. For dinner, Catharine Beecher recommends, the top plate should be placed upside-down, so as to keep off dust (*Treatise on Domestic Economy* 354).

8. Wall, *Archaeology* 148–149. After 1850, British white ironstone became popular, and its colorless relief molding was viewed as elegant in its simplicity.

9. The mistress served the soup, the first course, which Wall suggests showed her role as "family nurturer," while the master served the main meat dish, demonstrating his role as "family provider" (Wall, *Archaeology* 148).

10. Quoted from Mary Elizabeth Braddon, *Lady Audley's Secret* 222. Elizabeth Kowalski-Wallace discusses the tea-table as stage for upper-class British white women in the eighteenth century, viewing the ritual as a series of showcased poses and self-conscious statements for the female body. Her investigation of British literary tea scenes, however, reveals an emphasis on female aristocratic display that is not emphasized in nineteenth-century American counterparts *Consuming Subjects* (1997). For American women, the scene may be similar, but the woman's *use* of tea thing becomes important: her tea ritual is labor, not leisure.

11. Scholarly readings of Poe's story vary drastically with every author—from David Ketterer, who argues that Poe "is the devil in the belfry" disrupting fixed visions of the world, to Katrina E. Bachinger, who sees the story as Poe's critique of contemporary "programmed greenings of society," or Christopher J. Forbes, who sees in the story a satire of Washington Irving (Ketterer 4; Bachinger 514).

12. See, for example, Mrozowski and Beaudry 195, 197, 199.

13. Critical response to the diptych focuses on the "unhealthy sexuality" of the bachelors, and its implications on the maids' economic oppression (Karcher, *Shadow* 124). Building on a common understanding that "Paradise" explores homosexual retreats, Robyn Wiegman argues that both stories point to male bonding and patriarchal control, which depends on the exclusion of women and the lower classes ("Melville's Geography"); Philip Young notes biographically that Melville was expecting his third child while writing these stories, so they reveal the pressures of providing for a family and the terror of a seemingly unstoppable baby machine ("The Machine in Tartarus").
14. As Wai Chee Dimock and Judith A. McGaw report, Melville saw both men and women working at the Dalton paper mill he visited, so that his decision to people his fictional factory with only women was deliberate (Dimock 85).
15. "Paradise" 204. David Harley Serlin argues that this setting, identified as female, provides a heterosexual symbolism that undercuts the "dangerous, abstract sexuality" of the bachelors and their control over their cloistered world (82).
16. Kasson 137. The narrator, as Bachelor Nine, supplies an anecdote as well, entitled "The Paradise of Bachelors."
17. Karcher, *Shadow* 122. Marvin Fisher suggests that "Virginny" may be a specific girl, or the "virgin New World" (85).
18. Moseley 13. James A. Bland's "Carry Me Back to Old Virginny" was published in 1878.
19. "Tartarus" in Melville, *Great Short Works* 220. A gestational and sexual reading of "Tartarus" was nearly commonplace when Richard Chase discussed it in 1949 (*Herman Melville*). Young taunts his audience with the obviousness of this claim: "Little can be done (unless by psychiatry) for the few who have claimed there is no 'gestation symbolism' in 'Tartarus.' Those who have missed it can be helped. The problem is with those who understand well enough and think that the tale is essentially a Melvillean denunciation of the industrial revolution" (213). Wiegman also reads in the scenery and various factory mechanisms diverse male and female body parts ("Melville's Geography").

CHAPTER 3: UNMENTIONABLE THINGS UNMENTIONED

1. Among the articles in the "No More Separate Spheres!" issue of *American Literature* (September 1998) and the recent *Separate Spheres No More* (2000), the feminine sphere is variously imagined as the generic conventions and responses to women's novels; as the distinction between private versus public space, home versus market—distinctions that might be complicated by including race, class, and regional considerations; as submissive versus aggressive behavior. While no scholar disputes that an idea of a "separate sphere" indeed existed, although mainly for white, middle- and upper-class women, the projects seek to move "away from separatism to a reconciliation or a blurring of the spheres" (Elbert 9).

2. Cited in Piepmeier 215–216. In "Out in Public: Configurations of Women's Bodies in Nineteenth-Century America" (1999), Piepmeier examines the figures of Sojourner Truth, Sarah Josepha Hale, Anna Cora Mowatt, and Mary Baker Eddy as their careers placed them in the public realm, arguing that these women constructed bodily representations that worked against the common conception of domestic, disembodied femininity.

3. See, for example, Ann Douglas's *The Feminization of American Culture*.

4. On only a few stones in Charleston's historic churchyards are men seen grieving over an urn: for example, the stone of Mrs. Mary Ann Elizabeth Cogdell. This stone was carved by her own son, a Charleston sculptor, in 1827, and depicted the three Cogdell sons in classical garb (Combs 191).

5. Blumenson 23. A more detailed enumeration of the architectural and ceramic evolution of white things appears in chapter 1.

6. Roberson 3, 14. Interestingly, Roberson observes, the little black girl is able to contest Mrs. Montgomery's absolute spirituality, suggesting that her pious insistence on honesty does not take into account the starvation based on racist economics suffered by Rebecca and her mother.

7. Alice goes on to discuss France and Italy.

8. Stowe was immediately criticized for her Liberian solution offered in *Uncle Tom's Cabin*. Although she changed this stance by the time she wrote *Dred*, one might see that her expunging of the black characters is not altogether racist, but simply the final alternative after all other domestic arrangements have failed. Gillian Brown offers an excellent argument on the domestic negotiations involving slavery in *Uncle Tom's Cabin* in *Domestic Individualism* (1990).

9. Cited in Gillian Brown 53. In Brown's argument, "What begins in UTC as an anti-slavery, anti-market protest culminates in a critique of labor relations and valorization of independent housekeeping. Reliance on servants threatens Stowe's revisionary economy by perpetuating aristocratic distinctions consigning physical labor to a lower class" (53).

10. While Gillian Brown proposes Miss Ophelia's system of order as Stowe's ideal, I would argue that Stowe sees through the prevailing politics of dishware: Miss Ophelia is herself a "bond-slave of 'ought,' "—meaning that her inflexible obsession with order causes her to over-exert herself in order to produce cleanness (*Uncle Tom's* 152).

11. Rachel's kitchen might serve as another model kitchen. As Quakers were portrayed as politically neutral in the civil debate over slavery, the kitchen's decor marks it as existing outside of time and therefore beyond the influence of slavery. It is neither whitened nor blackened, but merely a homey kitchen run by a nurturing mother. It has an immaculate yellow floor, "rows of shining tin" where food has been stored, "glossy green wood chairs," and an adored rocking chair: furniture which, like Rachel's drab clothing, defies fashion (129). And of course, she does her own labor within its walls.

12. Lynette Carpenter argues that the novel exposes the similarities between contrasts, particularly male and female, white and nonwhite, house and asylum; Joanne Dobson discusses the novel as a safe subversion of mid-nineteenth-century gender norms ("The Hidden Hand"); Alfred Habegger believes that overt sexuality, rather than gender play, is problematized in the novel.

13. After shooting Mr. Le Noir in a duel, for example, Capitola rides to town and "up to the ladies' entrance" of the hotel, and in this properly feminine space confesses her "crime" (371).

14. 133, 284. Marah Rocke is also perfectly feminine, but also from the lower class and one of the "hard-working children of toil." She wears a black mourning dress with a "pure white collar around her throat" and has a "pale olive complexion" (63).

CHAPTER 4: SEE SPOT RUN

1. The thesis of whiteness as a choice is clearly and persuasively argued in David Roediger's *Wages of Whiteness*.

2. In Mather's estimation at the end of the eighteenth century, we should regard spiritual impurity with the same disgust we give physical filth: in fact, "'the most Loathsome, Dirty, Nasty Object in the World, is not so Distastful unto us, as all Wickedness is unto our God'" (qtd. in Kathleen M. Brown 79).

3. The idea of blessedness as resulting from being "unstained" rather than from accumulated good deeds or divine election may have contributed to the Cult of Domesticity's privileging of childhood. From efforts on earlier Puritans' parts to distance themselves from their children, since they often died young and their afterlife was in doubt, early Victorians turned to a cult of motherhood that fostered the mother-child and parent-child bond. In 1721, for example, Benjamin Wadsworth wrote, "'[children's] Hearts naturally, are a meer nest, root, fountain of Sin, and wickedness'" (qtd. in Stannard 15). In 1842, the Reverend John H. Morison reflects a softer sentiment: "'[t]heir angel influence shall remain unsullied by a breath from this sinful world'" (qtd. in Snyder 14). Children who died were therefore saved from any corruption of the marketplace and, unlike their Puritan foreparents, could be seen as having guaranteed sainthood. Theodore Cuyler assures grieving parents that their deceased children are now "'safe; Christ has them in his sinless school, where lessons of celestial wisdom are learned by eyes that never weep'" (qtd. in Snyder 14). This change appears in the graveyard as sculpted lambs and sleeping infants atop children's small marble tombstones, or the rare sculpted crib or child's chair (Snyder 22, 24). At Mount Auburn Cemetery, the Noll children combine several of these images: one marker from 1859 shows a young child reclining with an angel bending over him, and the other from 1856 shows an older child resting on a lamb. In Charleston, South Carolina, many children's stones have no dates, but infants can be seen kneeling and ascending through the clouds in marble relief (Unitarian Church).

4. In Gary Engle's *This Grotesque Essence* 51. Although the song "Zip Coon" was published in 1834, this version of the minstrel was copyrighted in 1874.
5. David Roediger's *The Wages of Whiteness* and Eric Lott's *Love and Theft* discuss in detail the formulation of "whiteness" through the minstrelsy tradition.
6. While she includes physical traits, of course, they are centered on the face, revealing her "sentimental" beauty but still allowing for disembodiment.
7. *Uncle Tom's Cabin*, on the other hand, does attempt to re-form Uncle Tom spiritually into white.
8. Whitney 560. Lisa Whitney argues that "In *Dred* every white adult, no matter what his or her position on slavery, participates in the system as an oppressor" (560). Stowe herself suggests that escaping slaves prolong the institution, and that the underground railroad provides an "escape-valve": "One has only to become acquainted with some of these fearless and energetic men who have found their way to freedom by its means, to feel certain that such minds and hearts would have proved, in time, an incendiary magazine under the scorching reign of slavery" (*Dred* 642–643).
9. Halttunen 88. She recounts a story appearing there, "The Fatal Cosmetic" (1839), in which a woman who paints her face allows herself other small deceits, and in telling a "white lie" ends up killing herself.
10. *Typee* 256. Samuel Otter similarly investigates Melville's attention to the skin. With the tattooing in *Typee* and flogging in *White-Jacket*, he contends, Melville examines the relationship between racial minorities and whites, and between sailors and slaves. Marked skin and legible flesh unsettle Melville's narrators because they blur the distinction between whiteness and blackness (" 'Race' in *Typee* and *White-Jacket*").
11. Only a focus on either Stubb's insensitivity or the message of Fleece's speech might save Fleece from being a mere perpetuation of "the most familiar comic distortion ever affixed to the Negro race" (Stone 359). Nonetheless, neither viewing Stubb's treatment as brutish, as Edward Grejda suggests, nor reading a moral into Fleece's speech humanizes Fleece from a blackface caricature (Grejda 125).
12. Eric Schocket concludes that though Davis's mill workers are blackened by dirt and squalor, Davis offers the hope that they may yet be redeemed to whiteness. Dawn Henwood believes that while Davis was ambivalent in her position on slavery, her exposition of factory conditions revealed the relative comfort of the slave and her "contempt for the extreme position of abolitionism" (568). Henwood interpets Davis's message to be that the slave is promised a better life (like the slavish river that will flow to greener pastures) while the mill worker is trapped.
13. According to Joan Dayan, the philosophies of Locke and Augustine combine to create "identity" from "teeth," until "the final irradiation of the teeth rattling across the floor writes out the derangement of a brain" ("Identity" 492). Joel Porte argues that the *vagina dentata* motif reveals sexual anxiety (82). Jacqueline Doyle sees a critique of courtly love poetry in "(Dis)Figuring Woman: Edgar Allan Poe's *Berenice*" (13). For Arthur A. Brown, the teeth are "the signifier and the thing itself," and therefore represent the fear of undying promised through literature (452). Hal Blythe and

Carlie Sweet argue against Twitchell's assertion that the vampire material is "just added along the way" by outlining the ways in which "Berenice" becomes a successful though mocking vampire account (23).

14. Joan Dayan writes, "If women in nineteenth-century America must bear the trappings of style, must inhabit most fully the external as essence, Poe shows how such a spectacle both exploits and consumes its participant, both men and women" ("Romance and Race" 95).

EPILOGUE

1. Wright, *Building* 162. One recalls Charlotte Perkins Gilman's critique of the sexist application of the rest cure that drives her heroine insane in "The Yellow Wallpaper" (1892). The walls play the main role in her insanity, however, and they are *not* white.

2. Shapiro 94. Shapiro describes, for example, a *Ladies' Home Journal* meal consisting of boiled cod, mashed potatoes, rice, and macaroni pudding.

WORKS CITED

Accardo, Annalucia, and Alessandro Portelli. "A Spy in the Enemy's Country: Domestic Slaves as Internal Foes." *The Black Columbiad: Defining Moments in African American Literature and Culture.* Ed. Werner Sollors and Maria Diedrich. Cambridge, MA: Harvard University Press, 1994.

Alcott, Louisa May. *Little Women.* 1868. Ed. Elaine Showalter. New York: Penguin Books, 1989.

Allen, Theodore. *The Invention of the White Race.* New York: Verso, 1997.

Ames, Kenneth L. *Death in the Dining Room and Other Tales of Victorian Culture.* Philadelphia: Temple University Press, 1992.

Amireh, Amal. *The Factory Girl and the Seamstress: Imagining Gender and Class in Nineteenth-Century American Fiction.* New York: Garland Publishing, Inc., 2000.

Angelou, Maya. *I Know Why the Caged Bird Sings.* New York: Bantam Books, 1970.

Appadurai, Arjun. *The Social Life of Things: Commodities in Cultural Perspective.* New York: Cambridge University Press, 1986.

Bachinger, Katrina E. "The Aesthetics of (Not) Keeping in Step: Reading the Consumer Mobocracy of Poe's 'The Devil in the Belfry' against Peacock." *Modern Language Quarterly* 51.4 (Dec. 1990): 513–533.

Bailey, Ronald. "'Those Valuable People, the Africans': The Economic Impact of the Slave(ry) Trade on Textile Industrialization in New England." *The Meaning of Slavery in the North.* Ed. David Roediger and Martin H. Blatt. New York: Garland Publishing, 1998. 3–32.

Baker, Vernon G. *Historical Archaeology at Black Lucy's Garden, Andover, Massachusetts: Ceramics from the Site of a Nineteenth-Century Afro-American.* Andover, MA: Roberts Peabody Foundation for Archaeology, Phillips Academy, 1978.

Banton, Michael. "The Idiom of Race: A Critique of Presentism." *Theories of Race and Racism.* Ed. Les Back and John Solomos. USA: Routledge, 2000. 51–70.

Barnes, Elizabeth. *States of Sympathy: Seduction and Democracy in the American Novel.* New York: Columbia University Press, 1997.

Baym, Nina. *Woman's Fiction: A Guide to Novels by and about Women in America, 1820–70.* Urbana: University of Illinois Press, 1993.

Beaudry, Mary C. "The Lowell Boott Mills Complex and Its Housing: Material Expressions of Corporate Ideology." *Historical Archaeology* 23.1 (1989): 19–32.

Becker, Elizabeth C. "Harriet Jacobs's Search for Home." *College Language Association Journal* 35.4 (June 1992): 411–421.

Beecher, Catherine. *Treatise on Domestic Economy.* Boston: Marsh, Capen, Lyon, and Webb, 1841.

Benes, Peter. *The Masks of Orthodoxy: Folk Gravestone Carving in Plymouth County, Massachusetts, 1689–1805.* Amherst: University of Massachusetts Press, 1977.

Berlant, Lauren. "The Female Woman: Fanny Fern and the Form of Sentiment." *The Culture of Sentiment: Race, Gender, and Sentimentality in Nineteenth-Century America.* Ed. Shirley Samuels. New York: Oxford University Press, 1992. 265–282.

Blassingame, John W., *The Slave Community: Plantation Life in the Antebellum South.* New York: Oxford University Press, 1979.

Blaszczyk, Regina Lee. "The Aesthetic Moment: China Decorators, Consumer Demand, and Technological Change in the American Pottery Industry, 1865–1900." *Winterthur Portfolio* 29.2–3 (Summer–Autumn 1994): 121–153.

Blish, Mary. "The Whiteness of the Whale Revisited." *CLA Journal* 41 (Sept. 1997): 55–69.

Blumenson, John J. G. *Identifying American Architecture: A Pictorial Guide to Styles and Terms, 1600–1945.* Nashville: American Association for State and Local History, 1978.

Blythe, Hal, and Charlie Sweet. "Poe's Satiric Use of Vampirism in 'Berenice.'" *Poe Studies* 14.2 (Dec. 1981): 23–24.

Brackner, Joey. "An Overview of the Tombstones of Nineteenth-Century Alabama and Their Makers." *Southern Quarterly* 31.2 (1993): 21–49.

Braddon, Mary Elizabeth. *Lady Audley's Secret.* 1862. New York: Oxford University Press, 1987.

Breeden, James O., ed. *Advice among Masters: The Ideal in Slave Management in the Old South.* Westport, CT: Greenwood Press, 1980.

Brown, Arthur A. "Literature and the Impossibility of Death: Poe's 'Berenice'." *Nineteenth-Century Literature* 50.4 (March 1996): 448–463.

Brown, Bill. "How to Do Things with Things (A Toy Story)." *Critical Inquiry* 24 (1998): 935–964.

———. *The Material Unconscious: American Amusement, Stephen Crane, & the Economies of Play.* Cambridge, MA: Harvard University Press, 1996.

Brown, Gillian. *Domestic Individualism: Imaging Self in Nineteenth-Century America.* Los Angeles: University of California Press, 1990.

Brown, John Gary. *Soul in the Stone: Cemetery Art from America's Heartland.* Lawrence, Kansas: UP of Kansas, 1994.

Brown, Kathleen M. "Murderous Uncleanness." *A Centre of Wonders: The Body in Early America.* Ed. Janet Moore Lindman and Michele Lise Tarter. Ithaca: Cornell University Press, 2001. 77–94.

Brown, Sterling A. "Negro Character as Seen by White Authors." *Interracialism: Black–White Intermarriage in American History, Literature, and Law.* Ed. Werner Sollors. New York: Oxford University Press, 2000. 274–279.

Brucken, Carolyn. "'In the Public Eye': Women and the American Luxury Hotel." *Winterthur Portfolio* 31.4: 203–220.

Bullock, Penelope. "The Mulatto in American Fiction." *Interracialism: Black-White Intermarriage in American History, Literature, and Law.* Ed. Werner Sollors. New York: Oxford University Press, 2000. 280–284.

Burgett, Bruce. *Sentimental Bodies: Sex, Gender, and Citizenship in the Early Republic.* Princeton, NJ: Princeton University Press, 1998.

Bushman, Richard L. *The Refinement of America: Persons, Houses, Cities.* New York: Knopf, 1992.

Bushman, Richard L., and Claudia L. Bushman. "The Early History of Cleanliness in America." *Journal of American History* 74.4 (1988): 1213–1238.

Caplan, Jane. " 'National Tattooing': Traditions of Tattooing in Nineteenth-Century Europe." *Written on the Body: The Tattoo in European and American History.* Ed. Jane Caplan. London: Reaktion Books, 2000. 156–173.

Carby, Hazel. *Reconstructing Womanhood.* New York: Oxford University Press, 1987.

Carpenter, Lynette. "Double Talk: The Power and Glory of Paradox in E.D.E.N. Southworth's *The Hidden Hand.*" *Legacy* 10(1993): 17–30.

Chase, Richard Volney. *Herman Melville; A Critical Study.* 1949. New York: Hafner Publishing Co., 1971.

Child, Lydia Maria. *An Appeal in Favor of That Class of Americans Called Africans.* Boston: Allen and Ticknor, 1833.

———. *The Freedmen's Book.* New York: Arno Press, 1968.

———. *The Frugal Housewife.* 1829. Boston: Carter, Babcock & Hendee, 1832.

———. *The Oasis.* Boston: Benjamin C. Bacon, 1834.

Clark, Christine. *Becoming and Unbecoming White: Owning and Disowning a Racial Identity.* Westport, CT: Bergin and Garvey, 1999.

Clark, Clifford Edward, Jr. *The American Family Home, 1800–1960.* Chapel Hill: University of North Carolina Press, 1986.

Clark, Michael. "Caves, Houses, and Temples in James Fenimore Cooper's *The Pioneers.*" *Modern Language Studies* 16 (1986): 227–236.

Cole, Phyllis. "Stowe, Jacobs, Wilson: White Plots and Black Counterplots." *New Perspectives on Gender, Race, and Class in Society.* Ed. Audrey T. McClusky. Bloomington: Indiana University Press, 1990. 23–45.

Combs, Diana Williams. *Early Gravestone Art in Georgia and South Carolina.* Athens: University of Georgia Press, 1986.

Cooper, James Fenimore. *Last of the Mohicans; A Narrative of 1757.* 1826. New York: Library Classics of the United States, 1983.

———. *Notions of the Americans: Picked up by a Travelling Bachelor.* 1828. Albany: State University of New York Press, 1991.

———. *The Pioneers, or Sources of the Susquehanna.* 1823. New York: State University of New York Press, 1985.

Crane, Diana. *Fashion and Its Social Agendas: Class, Gender, and Identity in Clothing.* Chicago: University of Chicago Press, 2000.

Cummins, Maria Susanna. *The Lamplighter.* Leipzig: B. Tauchnitz, 1854.

Cunningham, Patricia A. "Simplicity of Dress: A Symbol of American Ideals." *Dress in American Culture*. Ed. Patricia A. Cunningham and Susan Voso Lab. Bowling Green, OH: Bowling Green State University Press, 1993. 180–199.

Davis, David Brion. "Constructing Race: A Reflection." *William and Mary Quarterly* 54 (1997): 7–18.

Davis, Rebecca Harding. *Life in the Iron Mills*. 1861. Ed. Cecelia Tichi. New York: Bedford Books, 1998.

Dayan, Joan. *Fables of Mind: An Inquiry into Poe's Fiction*. New York: Oxford University Press, 1987.

———. "The Identity of Berenice, Poe's Idol of the Mind." *Studies in Romanticism* 23.4 (Winter 1984): 491–513.

———. "Romance and Race." *The Columbia History of the American Novel*. Ed. Elliot Emory, Cathy N. Davidson et al. New York: Columbia University Press, 1991. 89–109.

De Cunzo, Lu Ann. "Reform, Respite, Ritual: An Archaeology of Institutions; the Magdalen Society of Philadelphia, 1800–1850." *Historical Archaeology* 29.3 (1995).

De La Haye, Amy. *Defining Dress: Dress as Object, Meaning, and Identity*. New York: St. Martin's Press, 1999.

Deetz, James. *Flowerdew Hundred: The Archaeology of a Virginia Plantation, 1619–1864*. Charlottesville, VA: UP of Virginia, 1993.

———. *In Small Things Forgotten: The Archaeology of Early American Life*. Garden City, NY: Anchor Press, 1977.

———. "Material Culture and Worldview in Colonial Anglo-America." *The Recovery of Meaning*. Ed. Mark P. Leone and Parker B. Potter, Jr. Washington: Smithsonian Institution Press, 1988. 219–234.

Dethlefson, Edwin, and James Deetz. "Death's Heads, Cherubs, and Willow Trees: Experimental Archaeology in Colonial Cemeteries." *American Antiquity* 31.4 (1966): 502–510.

Dimock, Wai Chee. "Class, Gender, and a History of Metonymy." *Rethinking Class: Literary Studies and Social Formations*. Ed. Michael T. Gilmore and Wai Chee Dimock. New York: Columbia University Press, 1994. 57–106.

Dobson, Joanne. "The Hidden Hand: Subversion of Cultural Ideology in Three Mid-Century American Women's Novels." *American Quarterly* 38 (Summer 1986): 223–242.

———. Introduction. *The Hidden Hand, or Capitola the Madcap*. By E.D.E.N. Southworth. New Brunswick, NJ: Rutgers University Press, 1988.

Donaldson, Susan V., and Anne Goodwyn Jones. "Rethinking the South through Gender." *Haunted Bodies: Gender and Southern Texts*. Charlottesville, VA: University of Virginia Press, 1997.

Doolen, Andrew. "'Snug Stored Below': The Politics of Race in James Fenimore Cooper's *The Pioneers*." *Studies in American Fiction* 29 (Autumn 2001): 131–158.

Douglas, Ann. *The Feminization of American Culture*. New York: Avon Books, 1977.

Douglas, Mary. *Purity and Danger: An Analysis of the Concepts of Pollution and Taboo.* New York: Routledge, 1966.
Douglas, Frederick. *My Bondage and My Freedom.* 1855. Chicago: University of Illinois Press, 1987.
———. *Narrative of the Life of Frederick Douglass, an American Slave.* 1845. New York: Penguin Books, 1985.
Doyle, Jacqueline. "(Dis)Figuring Woman: Edgar Allan Poe's 'Berenice.'" *Poe Studies* 26.1–2 (June–Dec. 1993): 13–21.
Edwards, Ywone D. "'Trash' Revisited: A Comparative Approach to Historical Descriptions and Archaeological Analysis of Slave Houses and Yards." *Keep Your Head to the Sky: Interpreting African American Home Ground.* Charlottesville, VA: UP of Virginia, 1998. 45–271.
Elbert, Monika M., ed. *Separate Spheres No More: Gender Convergence in American Literature, 1830–1930.* Tuscaloosa: University of Alabama Press, 2000.
Elias, Norbert. *The Civilizing Process..* Vols. 1 & 2. Trans. Edmund Jephcott. New York: Pantheon Books, 1982.
Emerson, Ralph Waldo. *The Works of Ralph Waldo Emerson.* Vol. 7. Boston: Houghton, Mifflin, 1883–1887.
Engle, Gary D. *This Grotesque Essence.* Baton Rouge: Louisiana State University Press, 1978.
Epperson, Terrence W. "Panoptic Plantations: The Garden Sights of Thomas Jefferson and George Mason." *Lines That Divide: Historical Archaeologies of Race, Class, and Gender.* Ed. James A. Delle et al. Knoxville, University of Tennessee Press, 2000. 58–77.
———. "Race and the Disciplines of the Plantation." *Historic Archaeology* 24.4 (1990): 29–36.
Ettema, Michael J. "The Fashion System in American Furniture." *Living in a Material World: Canadian and American Approaches to Material Culture.* Ed. Gerald L. Pocius. St. John's: Institute of Social and Economic Research, Memorial U, 1991. 189–198.
Farrell, James J. *Inventing the American Way of Death, 1830–1920.* Philadelphia: Temple University Press, 1980.
Faulkner, William. *Absalom, Absalom!* 1936. New York: Garland Publishing, 1991.
Ferguson, Leland. "Struggling with Pots in Colonial South Carolina." *The Archaeology of Inequality.* Ed. Randall H. McGuire and Robert Paynter. Cambridge, MA.: Basil Blackwell, 1991. 28–39.
———. *Uncommon Ground: Archaeology and Early African America, 1650–1800.* Washington, DC: Smithsonian Institution Press, 1992.
Fisher, Marvin. "Melville's 'Tartarus': The Deflowering of New England." *American Quarterly* 23 (1971): 79–100.
Forbes, Christopher J. "Satire of Irving's *A History of New York* in Poe's 'The Devil in the Belfry.'" *Studies in American Fiction* 10.1 (Spring 1982): 93–100.
Forbes, Harriette Merrifield. *Gravestones of Early New England, and the Men Who Made Them, 1653–1800.* New York: De Capo Press, 1967.

Fox-Genovese, Elizabeth. *Within the Plantation Household: Black and White Women of the Old South*. Chapel Hill: University of North Carolina Press, 1988.

Frankenberg, Ruth. *Displacing Whiteness: Essays in Social and Cultural Criticism*. Durham, NC: Duke University Press, 1997.

———. "The Mirage of an Unmarked Whiteness." *The Making and Unmaking of Whiteness*. Ed. Birgit Brander Rasmussen et al. Durham: Duke University Press, 2001.

———. *White Women, Race Matters: The Social Construction of Whiteness*. Minneapolis: University of Minnesota Press, 1993.

Franklin, John Hope. *From Slavery to Freedom: A History of Negro Americans*. New York: Alfred A. Knopf, 1980.

French, Stanley. "The Cemetery as Cultural Institution: The Establishment of Mount Auburn and the 'Rural Cemetery' Movement." *Death in America*. Ed. David E. Stannard. Philadelphia: University of Pennsylvania Press, 1975. 69–91.

Fryer, Judith. *Felicitous Space: The Imaginative Structures of Edith Wharton and Willa Cather*. Chapel Hill: University of North Carolina Press, 1986.

Garman, James C. "Viewing the Color Line through the Material Culture of Death." *Historical Archaeology* 28.3 (1994): 74–93.

Gates, Henry Louis, Jr. "Binary Oppositions in Chapter One of Narrative of the Life of Frederick Douglass an American Slave Written by Himself." *Frederick Douglass's Narrative of the Life of Frederick Douglass*. Ed. Harold Bloom. New York: Chelsea House Publishers, 1988. 59–76.

Genovese, Eugene D. *Roll, Jordan, Roll: The World the Slaves Made*. New York: Vintage Books, 1972.

Gillman, Susan. "The Mulatto, Tragic or Triumphant? The Nineteenth-Century American Race Melodrama." *The Culture of Sentiment: Race, Gender, and Sentimentality in Nineteenth-Century America*. Ed. Shirley Samuels. New York: Oxford University Press, 1992. 221–243.

Gilmore, Michael T. *American Romanticism and the Marketplace*. Chicago: University of Chicago Press, 1985.

Glassie, Henry. "Eighteenth-Century Cultural Process in Delaware Valley Folk Building." *Common Places: Readings in American Vernacular Architecture*. Ed. Dell Upton and John Michael Vlach. 1972. Athens: University of Georgia Press, 1986.

———. "Folk Art." *Material Culture Studies in America*. Ed. Thomas J. Schlereth. Nashville, TN: American Association for State and Local History, 1982. 124–140.

———. *Folk Housing in Middle Virginia*. Knoxville: University of Tennessee Press, 1975.

———. "Studying Material Culture Today." *Living in a Material World: Canadian and American Approaches to Material Culture*. Ed. Gerald L. Pocius. St. John's: Institute of Social and Economic Research, Memorial U, 1991. 253–266.

Goddu, Teresa A. *Gothic America: Narrative, History, and Nation*. New York: Columbia University Press, 1997.

Gordon, Beverly. "Woman's Domestic Body: The Conceptual Conflation of Women and Interiors in the Industrial Age." *Winterthur Portfolio* 31.4: 281–301.

Gorman, Frederick, and Michael DiBlasi. "Gravestone Iconography and Mortuary Ideology." *Ethnohistory* 28.1 (1981): 79–98.

Gosden, Chris. "Postcolonial Archaeology Issues of Culture, Identity, and Knowledge." *Archaeological Theory Today*. Ed. Ian Hodder. Malden, MA: Blackwell Publishing, 2001. 241–261.

Gowans, Alan. *Images of American Living: Four Centuries of Architecture and Furniture as Cultural Expression*. Philadelphia: Lippincott, 1964.

Govenar, Alan. "The Changing Image of Tattooing in American Culture, 1846–1966." *Written on the Body: The Tattoo in European and American History*. Ed. Jane Caplan. London: Reaktion Books, 2000. 212–233.

Grejda, Edward S. *The Common Continent of Men*. Port Washington, NY: Kennikat Press, 1974.

Grossman, Jay. "'A' Is for Abolition?: Race, AuthorshiPress, The Scarlet Letter." *Textual Practice* 7.1 (Spring 1993): 13–30.

Halttunen, Karen. *Confidence Men and Painted Women: A Study of Middle-Class Culture in America, 1830–1870*. New Haven: Yale University Press, 1982.

Harper's Weekly 36 (1893).

Harris, Susan K. *Nineteenth-Century American Women's Novels: Interpretive Strategies*. New York: Cambridge University Press, 1990.

Hawthorne, Nathaniel. *The Blithedale Romance*. 1852. Ed. Seymour Gross and Rosalie Murphy. New York: W.W. Norton & Co., 1978.

———. *The House of the Seven Gables*. 1851. Columbus, OH: Merrill, 1969.

———. *The Scarlet Letter*. 1850. USA: Viking Penguin Inc., 1983.

Henwood, Dawn. "Slaveries 'In the Borders': Rebecca Harding Davis's 'Life in the Iron Mills' in Its Southern Context." *Mississippi Quarterly* 52 (Fall 1999): 567–592.

Hinsley, Curtis M. "The World as Marketplace: Commodification of the Exotic at the World's Columbian Exposition, Chicago, 1893." *Exhibiting Cultures: The Poetics and Politics of Museum Display*. Ed. Ivan Carp and Steven D. Lavine. Washington, DC: Smithsonian, 1991. 344–365.

Hitchcock, Henry-Russell. *Architecture, Nineteenth and Twentieth Centuries*. New York: Penguin Books, 1977.

Horsfield, Margaret. *Biting the Dust: The Joys of Housework*. New York: St. Martin's Press, 1998.

Hoy, Suellen. *Chasing Dirt: The American Pursuit of Cleanliness*. New York: Oxford University Press, 1995.

Hughes Wright, Roberta, and Wilbur B. Hughes, III. *Lay Down Body: Living History in African American Cemeteries*. New York: Visible Ink Press, 1996.

Hurmence, Belinda, ed. *My Folks Don't Want Me to Talk about Slavery*. Winston-Salem, NC: John F. Blair, Publisher, 1993.

Husni, Khalil. "The Whiteness of the Whale: A Survey of Interpretations, 1851–1970." *CLA Journal* 19 (1976): 210–223.

Ings, Katharine Nicholson. "Blackness and the Literary Imagination: Uncovering *The Hidden Hand*." *Passing and the Fictions of Identity*. Ed. Elaine K. Ginsberg. Durham: Duke University Press, 1996. 131–150.

Isaac, Rhys. *The Transformation of Virginia, 1740–1790.* Chapel Hill: University of North Carolina Press, 1982.

Jacobs, Harriet. *Incidents in the Life of a Slave Girl, Written by Herself.* Ed. Jean Fagan Yellin. Cambridge, MA: Harvard University Press, 1987.

Jeane, Gregory D. "The Upland South Folk Cemetery Complex: Some Suggestions of Origin." *Cemeteries and Gravemarkers: Voices of American Culture.* Ed. Richard E. Meyer. Ann Arbor: University Microfilms International Research Press, 1989. 107–136.

Johannesen, Stanley. "Invisibility, Embodiment, and American Furniture." *Living in a Material World: Canadian and American Approaches to Material Culture.* Ed. Gerald L. Pocius. St. John's: Institute of Social and Economic Research, Memorial U, 1991. 208–230.

Jordan, Terry G. "'The Roses So Red and the Lilies So Fair': Southern Folk Cemeteries in Texas." *Southwestern Historical Quarterly* 83.3 (1980): 227–258.

———. *Texas Graveyards: A Cultural Legacy.* Austin: University of Texas Press, 1982.

Joseph, J. W. "White Columns and Black Hands: Class and Classification in the Plantation Ideology of the Georgia and South Carolina Lowcountry." *Historical Archaeology* 27.3 (1993): 57–73.

Kaplan, Sidney. "Herman Melville and the American National Sin." *Images of the Negro in American Literature.* Ed. Seymour L. Gross and John Edward Hardy. Chicago: University of Chicago Press, 1966, 135–162.

Karcher, Caroline. *Shadow over the Promised Land: Slavery, Race, and Violence in Melville's America.* Baton Rouge, LA: Louisiana State University Press, 1980.

Kasson, John F. "Rituals of Dining: Table Manners in Victorian America." *Dining in America.* Ed. Kathryn Grover. Rochester, NY: University of Massachusetts Press, 1987. 114–141.

Kawash, Samira. *Dislocating the Color Line: Identity, Hybridity, and Singularity in African-American Literature.* Stanford, CA: Stanford University Press, 1997.

Kelley, Wyn. "'I'm Housewife Here': Herman Melville and Domestic Economy." *Melville Society Extracts* 98 (Sept. 1994): 7–10.

Kelso, William M. "Landscape Archaeology at Thomas Jefferson's Monticello." *Earth Patterns: Essays in Landscape Archaeology.* Ed. William M. Kelso and Rachel Most. Charlottesville: University of Virginia Press, 1990. 7–22.

Kennedy, Gerald J., and Liliane Weissberg, eds. *Romancing the Shadow: Poe and Race.* New York: Oxford University Press, 2001.

Kennedy, John Pendleton. *Swallow Barn; or, A Sojourn in the Old Dominion.* 1832. Baton Rouge: Louisiana State University Press, 1986.

Kimball, Gregg D. "African-Virginians and the Vernacular Building Tradition in Richmond City, 1790–1860." *Perspectives in Vernacular Architecture.* Vol. 4. Ed. Thomas Carter and Bernard L. Herman. Columbia: University of Missouri Press, 1991. 121–129.

Kirkland, Caroline. *A New Home, Who'll Follow?* 1839. New Brunswick: Rutgers University Press, 1990.

Klamkin, Marian. *American Patriotic and Political China.* New York: Scribner, 1973.

Kniffen, Fred B. "Folk Housing: Key to Diffusion." *Common Places: Readings in American Vernacular Architecture*. Ed. Dell Upton and John Michael Vlach. Athens: University of Georgia Press, 1986. 3–26.

Kowaleski-Wallace, Elizabeth. *Consuming Subjects: Women, Shopping, and Business in the Eighteenth Century*. New York: Columbia University Press, 1997.

Lang, Amy Shrager. "Class and the Strategies of Sympathy." *The Culture of Sentiment*. Ed. Shirley Samuels. New York: Oxford University Press, 1992. 128–142.

Lemire, Elise. "'The Murders in the Rue Morgue': Amalgamation Discourses and the Race Riots of 1838 in Poe's Philadelphia." *Romancing the Shadow: Poe and Race*. Ed. Gerald J. Kennedy and Liliane Weissberg. New York: Oxford University Press, 2001. 177–204.

Leone, Mark P. "The Georgian Order as the Order of Merchant Capitalism in Annapolis, Maryland." *The Recovery of Meaning*. Ed. Mark P. Leone and Parker B. Potter, Jr. Washington: Smithsonian Institution Press, 1988. 235–262.

Levine, Bruce C., *Who Built America?: Working People and the Nation's Economy, Politics, Culture, and Society*. New York: Pantheon Books, 1989–1992.

Levine, Robert S. "The African-American Presence in Stowe's *Dred*." *Criticism and the Color Line: Desegregating American Literary Studies*. Ed. Henry B. Wonham. New Brunswick, NJ: Rutgers University Press, 1996. 171–190.

Lewis, Kenneth E. "Plantation Layout and Function in the South Carolina Lowcountry." *The Archaeology of Slavery and Plantation Life*. Ed. Theresa A. Singleton. New York: Academic Press, 1985. 35–65.

Linebaugh, Donald W. "'All the Annoyances and Inconveniences of the Country': Environmental Factors in the Development of Outbuildings in the Colonial Chesapeake." *Winterthur Portfolio* 29.1 (Spring 1994): 1–18.

Little, Ruth M. *Sticks and Stones: Three Centuries of North Carolina Gravemarkers*. Chapel Hill: University of North Carolina Press, 1998.

Locke, Alain. "American Literary Tradition and the Negro." *Interracialism: Black-White Intermarriage in American History, Literature, and Law*. Ed. Werner Sollors. New York: Oxford University Press, 2000. 269–273.

Lott, Eric. *Love and Theft: Blackface Minstrelsy and the American Working Class*. New York: Oxford University Press, 1993.

Lovell, Thomas B. "By Dint of Labor and Economy: Harriet Jacobs, Harriet Wilson, and the Salutary View of Wage Labor." *Arizona Quarterly* 52.3 (Autumn 1996): 1–32.

Lowance, Mason I., Jr., et al., eds. *The Stowe Debate: Rhetorical Strategies in Uncle Tom's Cabin*. Amherst: University of Massachusetts Press, 1994.

Luedtke, Luther S. *Making America: The Society & Culture of the United States*. Chapel Hill: University of North Carolina Press, 1992.

Mabbott, Thomas O., ed. *Collected Works of Edgar Allan Poe*. Vol. 1. Cambridge, MA: BelknaPress, 1969.

Majewski, Teresita, and Michael J. O'Brien. "An Analysis of Historical Ceramics from the Central Salt River Valley of Northeast Missouri." *Cannon Reservoir Human Ecology Project* 2.3 (1984): 19–46.

Massey, Doreen B. *Space, Place, and Gender*. Minneapolis: University of Minnesota Press, 1994.

Mattingly, Carol. *Appropriate[ing] Dress: Women's Rhetorical Style in Nineteenth-Century America*. Carbondale: Southern Illinois University Press, 2002.

Mayo, Edith, ed. *American Material Culture: The Shape of Things around Us*. Bowling Green, OH: Bowling Green State U Popular Press, 1984.

McBride, W. Stephen, and Kim A. McBride, "Socioeconomic Variation in a Late Antebellum Southern Town: The View from Archaeological and Documentary Sources." *Consumer Choice in Historical Archaeology*. Ed. Suzanne M. Spencer-Wood. New York: Plenum Press, 1987. 143–161.

McKee, Larry. "The Ideals and Realities behind the Design and Use of 19th Century Virginia Slave Cabins." Ed. Anne Elizabeth Yentsch and Mary C. Beaudry. *The Art and Mystery of Historical Archaeology*. Boca Raton: CRC Press, 1992. 195–214.

———. Personal interview, October 1995.

———. Personal interview, April 1997.

Melville, Herman. *Great Short Works of Herman Melville*. New York: Harper & Row, 1969.

———. *Moby Dick*. 1851. New York: W. W. Norton & Co., 1967.

———. *Typee*. 1846. Boston: Routledge and Kegan Paul, Inc., 1985.

Merish, Lori. "'The Hand of Refined Taste' in the Frontier Landscape: Caroline Kirkland's *A New Home, Who'll Follow?* and the Feminization of American Consumerism." *American Quarterly* 45 (Dec. 1993): 485–523.

———. "Sentimental Consumption: Harriet Beecher Stowe and the Aesthetics of Middle-Class Ownership." *American Literary History* 8.1 (Spring 1996): 1–33.

———. *Sentimental Materialism: Gender, Commodity Culture, and Nineteenth-Century American Literature*. Durham, NC: Duke University Press, 2000.

Meskell, Lynn M. "Writing the Body in Archaeology." *Reading the Body: Representations and Remains in the Archaeological Record*. Ed. Alison E. Rautman. Philadelphia: University of Pennsylvania Press, 2000. 13–24.

Meyer, Richard E., ed. *Cemeteries and Gravemarkers: Voices of American Culture*. Ann Arbor: UMI Research Press, 1989.

———. *Ethnicity and the American Cemetery*. Bowling Green, OH: Bowling Green State U Popular Press, 1993.

Miller, George L. "Classification and Economic Scaling of Nineteenth-Century Ceramics." *Documentary Archaeology in the New World*. Ed. Beaudry, Mary C. New York: Cambridge University Press, 1988. 172–183.

———. "Marketing Ceramics in North America: An Introduction." *Winterthur Portfolio* 19.1 (Spring 1984): 1–4.

———. "Revised Set of CC Index Values for Classification and Economic Scaling of English Ceramics from 1787 to 1880." *Historical Archaeology* 25.1 (1991): 1–25.

Mitchell, Margaret. *Gone with the Wind*. 1936. New York: Warner Books, 1993.

Montell, Lynwood. "Cemetery Decoration Customs in the American South." *The Old Traditional Way of Life: Essays in Honor Warren E. Roberts*. Ed. Robert E. Walls et al. Bloomington: Trickster Press, Indiana Folklore Institute, 1989. 111–129.

Morgan, Edmund S. *American Slavery, American Freedom.* New York: W. W. Norton and Company, Inc., 1975.

Morrison, Hugh. *Louis Sullivan: Prophet of Modern Architecture.* Westport, CT: Greenwood Press, 1935.

Morrison, Toni. *The Bluest Eye.* 1970. New York: Knopf, 1993.

———. *Playing in the Dark.* 1992. New York: Vintage Books, 1993.

———. "Unspeakable Things Unspoken: The Afro-American Presence in American Literature." *Michigan Quarterly Review* 8 (Winter 1989) 1–18.

Moseley, Caroline. "'Old Virginny' in Melville's 'The Paradise of Bachelors.'" *Melville Society Extracts* 33 (1978): 13–15.

Motz, Marilyn Ferris, and Pat Browne, eds. *Making the American Home: Middle-Class Women and Domestic Material Culture, 1840–1940.* Bowling Green, OH: Bowling Green State U Popular Press, 1988.

Mrozowski, Stephen A., and Mary C. Beaudry. "Archaeology and the Landscape of Corporate Ideology." *Earth Patterns: Essays in Landscape Archaeology.* Ed. William M. Kelso and Rachel Most. Charlottesville: University of Virginia Press, 1990. 189–210.

Nakayama, Thomas K., and Judith N. Martin. Introduction. *Whiteness and the Communication of Social Identity.* Ed. Thomas K. Nakayama and Judith N. Martin. Thousand Oaks: Sage Publishing, 1999.

Neal, Avon. "Graven Images: Sermons in Stones." *American Heritage* (April 1970): 15–29.

Nelson, Jennifer Ladd. "Dress Reform and the Bloomer." *Journal of American and Comparative Cultures* 23.1 (2000): 21–25.

Nettleton, Sarah. "Inventing Mouths: Disciplinary Power and Dentistry." *Reassessing Foucault: Power, Medicine, and the Body.* Ed. Colin Jones. New York: Routledge, 1994. 73–90.

Noel Hume, Ivor. *A Guide to Artifacts of Colonial America.* New York: Alfred A Knopf, Inc., 1969.

Oettermann, Stephan. "On Display: Tattooed Entertainers in America and Germany." *Written on the Body: The Tattoo in European and American History.* Ed. Jane Caplan. London: Reaktion Books, 2000. 193–211.

Olmsted, Frederick Law. *The Cotton Kingdom.* Ed. Arthur M. Schlesinger. New York: Knopf, 1953.

Orser, Charles E., Jr. "Beneath the Material Surface of Things: Commodities, Artifacts, and Slave Plantations." *Historical Archaeology* 26.3 (1992): 95–104.

Otter, Samuel. "'Race' in *Typee* and *White-Jacket.*" *The Cambridge Companion to Herman Melville.* Ed. Robert S. Levine. Cambridge, England: Cambridge University Press, 1998. 12–36.

Otto, John Solomon. "Artifacts and Status Differences—A Comparison of Ceramics from Planter, Overseer, and Slave Sites on an Antebellum Plantation." *Research Strategies in Historical Archaeology.* Ed. Stanley South. New York: Academic Press, 1977. 91–118.

Peiss, Kathy Lee. *Hope in a Jar: The Making of America's Beauty Culture.* New York: Henry Holt and Company, Inc., 1998.

Piepmeier, Alison. "Out in Public: Configurations of Women's Bodies in Nineteenth-Century America." Diss. Vanderbilt U, 1999.

Plante, Ellen M. *Women at Home in Victorian America: A Social History.* New York: Facts on File, Inc., 1997.

Poe, Edgar Allan. *Complete Tales and Poems of Edgar Allan Poe.* New York: Vintage Books, 1975.

Porte, Joel. *The Romance in America: Studies in Cooper, Hawthorne, Melville, and James.* Middletown: Wesleyan University Press, 1969.

Potter, Parker B. "Critical Archaeology: In the Ground and on the Street." *Historical Archaeology* 26.3 (1992): 117–129.

Praetzellis, Adrian, and Mary Praetzellis. "Faces and Facades: Victorian Ideology in Early Sacramento." *The Art and Mystery of Historical Archaeology.* Ed. Anne Elizabeth Yentsch and Mary C. Beaudry. Ann Arbor: CRC Press, 1992. 75–99.

Renfrew, Colin. "Symbol before Concept: Material Engagement and the Early Development of Society." *Archaeological Theory Today.* Ed. Ian Hodder. Malden, MA: Blackwell Publishing, 2001. 122–140.

Roberson, Susan L. "Ellen Montgomery's Other Friend: Race Relations in an Expunged Episode of Warner's *Wide, Wide World*." *ESQ* 45 (1999): 1–31.

Robertson, Cheryl. "From Cult to Profession: Domestic Women in Search of Equality." *The Material Culture of Gender, The Gender of Material Culture.* Ed. Katharine Martinez and Kenneth L. Ames. Winterthur, DE: Winterthur Museum, 1997. 75–109.

Robertson-Lorant, Laurie. *Melville: A Biography.* New York: Clarkson Potter, 1996.

Robinson, Harriet H. "Loom and Spindle; or, Life among the Early Mill Girls." *Women in America: From Colonial Times to the Twentieth Century.* Ed. Leon Stein and Annette K. Baxter. New York: Arno Press, 1974. 1–216.

Roediger, David R. "Race, Labor, and Gender in the Languages of Antebellum Social Protest." *Terms of Labor: Slavery, Serfdom, and Free Labor.* Ed. Stanley L. Engerman. Stanford, CA: Stanford University Press, 1999. 168–187.

———. *The Wages of Whiteness.* 1991. New York: Verso, 1993.

Roth, Rodris. "Tea-Drinking in Eighteenth-Century America: Its Etiquette and Equipage." *Material Life in America, 1600–1860.* Ed. Robert Blair St. George. Boston: Northeastern University Press, 1988. 439–462.

Rowland, Beryl. "Melville's Bachelors and Maids: Interpretation through Symbol and Metaphor." *American Literature* 41 (1969): 389–405.

Ruskin, John. *The Stones of Venice: Volume the Second.* New York: Lovell, Coryell and Company, 1851.

Samuels, Shirley. "The Identity of Slavery." *The Culture of Sentiment: Race, Gender, and Sentimentality in Nineteenth-Century America.* Ed. Shirley Samuels. New York: Oxford University Press, 1992.

Sánchez-Eppler, Karen. "Bodily Bonds: The Intersecting Rhetorics of Feminism and Abolition." *The Culture of Sentiment: Race, Gender, and Sentimentality in Nineteenth-Century America.* Ed. Shirley Samuels. New York: Oxford University Press, 1992. 92–114.

———. *Touching Liberty: Abolition, Feminism, and the Politics of the Body*. Berkeley, CA: University of California Press, 1999.

Savage, Kirk. *Standing Soldiers, Kneeling Slaves: Race, War, and Monument in Nineteenth-Century America*. Princeton, NJ: Princeton University Press, 1997.

Saxton, Alexander. *The Rise and Fall of the White Republic: Class Politics and Mass Culture in Nineteenth-Century America*. New York: Verso, 1990.

Schocket, Eric. " 'Discovering Some New Race': Rebecca Harding Davis's 'Life in the Iron Mills' and the Literary Emergence of Working-Class Whiteness." *PMLA* 115.1 (Jan. 2000): 46–59.

Serlin, David Harley. "The Dialogue of Gender in Melville's 'The Paradise of Bachelors and the Tartarus of Maids.' " *Modern Language Studies* 25.2 (Spring 1995): 80–87.

Shackel, Paul. *Personal Discipline and Material Culture: An Archaeology of Annapolis, Maryland, 1695–1870*. Knoxville: University of Tennessee Press, 1993.

Shackel, Paul A., and David L. Larsen. "Labor, Racism, and Built Environment in Early Industrial Harper's Ferry." *Lines That Divide: Historical Archaeologies of Race, Class, and Gender*. Ed. James A. Delle et al. Knoxville: University of Tennessee Press, 2000. 22–39.

Shapiro, Laura. *Perfection Salad: Women and Cooking at the Turn of the Century*. New York: Farrar Straus Giroux, 1986.

Smith, Mark M. *Mastered by the Clock: Time, Slavery, and Freedom in the American South*. Chapel Hill: University of North Carolina Press, 1997.

Smith, Valerie. Introduction. *Incidents in the Life of a Slave Girl*. By Harriet Jacobs. Cambridge: Harvard University Press, 1987.

Snyder, Ellen Marie. "Innocents in a Worldly World: Victorian Children's Gravemarkers." *Cemeteries and Gravemarkers: Voices of American Culture*. Ed. Richard E. Meyer. Ann Arbor: UMI Research Press, 1989. 11–29.

Sollors, Werner. *Neither Black nor White yet Both: Thematic Explorations of Interracial Literature*. New York: Oxford University Press, 1997.

Sorisio, Carolyn. " 'There Is Might in Each' Conceptions of Self in Harriet Jacobs's Incidents in the Life of a Slave Girl, Written by Herself." *Legacy* 13.1 (1996) 1–18.

Southworth, E.D.E.N. *The Hidden Hand, or Capitola the Madcap*. 1859. New Brunswick, New Jersey: Rutgers University Press, 1988.

Spain, Daphne. *Gendered Spaces*. Chapel Hill: University of North Carolina Press, 1992.

Spear, Jennifer M. " 'Clean of Blood, without Stain or Mixture.' " *A Centre of Wonders: The Body in Early America*. Ed. Janet Moore Lindman and Michele Lise Tarter. Ithaca: Cornell University Press, 2001. 95–108.

Spencer-Wood, Suzanne M. "Miller's Indices and Consumer-Choice Profiles: Status-Related Behaviors and White Ceramics." *Consumer Choice in Historical Archaeology*. Ed. Suzanne M. Spencer-Wood. New York: Plenum Press, 1987. 321–358.

Spencer-Wood, Suzanne M., and Scott D. Heberling. "Consumer Choices in White Ceramics: A Comparison of Eleven Early Nineteenth-Century Sites." *Consumer Choice in Historical Archaeology*. Ed. Suzanne M. Spencer-Wood. New York: Plenum Press, 1987. 55–84.

Stachiw, Myron O. " 'For the Sake of Commerce': Slavery, Anti-Slavery, and Northern Industry." *The Meaning of Slavery in the North*. Ed. David Roediger and Martin H. Blatt. New York: Garland Publishing, 1998. 33–44.

Stamp, Kenneth. *The Peculiar Institution: Slavery in the Ante-bellum South*. New York: Knopf, 1956.

Stannard, David E. "Death and the Puritan Child." *Death in America*. Ed. David E. Stannard. Philadelphia: University of Pennsylvania Press, 1975. 9–29.

Stansell, Christine. *City of Women: Sex and Class in New York, 1789–1860*. New York: Knopf, 1986.

Starke, Barbara M. "Nineteenth-Century African-American Dress." *Dress in American Culture*. Ed. Patricia Cunningham and Susan Voso Lab. Bowling Green, OH: Bowling Green State University Press, 1993. 66–79.

Steele, Valerie. *The Corset: A Cultural History*. New Haven: Yale University Press, 2001.

Stein, Leon, and Annette K. Baxter, eds. *Women of Lowell*. New York: Arno Press, 1974.

Stone, Edward. "The Whiteness of the Whale." *CLA Journal* 18 (March 1975): 348–363.

Stowe, David W. "Uncolored People: The Rise of Whiteness Studies." *Lingua Franca* 6 (Sept.–Oct. 1996): 68–77.

Stowe, Harriet Beecher. *Dred*. 1856. Ed. Judie Newman. Halifax, England: Ryburn Book Production, 1992.

———. *Oldtown Folks*. 1869. Ed. Dorothy Berkson. New Brunswick: Rutgers University Press, 1987.

———. *Uncle Tom's Cabin*. 1852. USA: Reader's Digest Association, Inc., 1991.

Strasser, Susan. *Waste and Want: A Social History of Trash*. New York: Metropolitan Books, 1999.

Tate, Claudia. *Domestic Allegories of Political Desire*. New York: Oxford University Press, 1992.

Thomas, Julian. "Archaeologies of Place and Landscape." *Archaeological Theory Today*. Ed. Ian Hodder. Malden, MA: Blackwell Publishing, 2001. 165–186.

Thompson, E. P. "Time, Work Discipline, and Industrial Capitalism." *Past and Present* 38.1(1967): 56–97.

Tichi, Cecelia, ed. *Life in the Iron Mills*. By Rebecca Harding Davis. New York: Bedford Books, 1998.

Tompkins, Jane. *Sensational Designs: The Cultural Work of American Fiction, 1790–1860*. New York: Oxford University Press, 1985.

Torrens, Kathleen M. "All Dressed up with No Place to Go: Rhetorical Dimensions of the Nineteenth-Century Dress Reform Movement." *Women's Studies in Communication* 20 (Fall 1997): 189–210.

Trollope, Frances Milton. *Domestic Manners of the Americans*. New York: Penguin Books, 1997.

Upton, Dell. "Form and User: Style, Mode, Fashion, and the Artifact." *Living in a Material World: Canadian and American Approaches to Material Culture*. Ed. Gerald L. Pocius. St. John's: Institute of Social and Economic Research, Memorial U, 1991. 156–169.

———. "Imagining the Early Virginia Landscape." *Earth Patterns: Essays in Landscape Archaeology.* Ed. William M. Kelso and Rachel Most. Charlottesville: University of Virginia Press, 1990. 71–88.

———. "White and Black Landscapes in Eighteenth-Century Virginia." *Material Life in America, 1600–1860.* Ed. Robert Blair St. George. Boston: Northeastern University Press, 1988. 357–370.

Valverde, Mariana. "The Love of Finery: Fashion and the Fallen Woman in Nineteenth-Century Social Discourse." *Victorian Studies* 32 (Winter 1989): 169–188.

Veblen, Thorstein. *The Theory of the Leisure Class: An Economic Study of Institutions.* 1899. New York: The Macmillan Company, 1912.

Victoria and Albert Museum. *Costume Illustration: The Nineteenth Century.* James Laver, introduction. London: H.M.S.O., 1947.

Vincent, Howard P. *The Trying-Out of Moby Dick.* Boston: Houghton Mifflin, 1949.

Vlach, John Michael. *Back of the Big House: The Architecture of Plantation Slavery.* Chapel Hill, University of North Carolina Press, 1993.

———. "'In a Very Tasty Style': 'Folk' Portraiture and the Purchase of Status." *Living in a Material World: Canadian and American Approaches to Material Culture.* Ed. Gerald L. Pocius. St. John's: Institute of Social and Economic Research, Memorial U, 1991. 173–188.

———. "'Snug Lil' House with Flue and Oven': Nineteenth-Century Reforms in Plantation Slave Housing." *Gender, Class, and Shelter.* Ed. Elizabeth Collins. Knoxville: University of Tennessee Press, 1995. 118–129.

Wall, Diana DiZerega. *The Archaeology of Gender.* New York: Plenum Press, 1994.

———. "Family Meals and Evening Parties: Constructing Domesticity in Nineteenth-Century Middle-Class New York." *Lines That Divide: Historical Archaeologies of Race, Class, and Gender.* Ed. James A. Delle et al. Knoxville, University of Tennessee Press, 2000. 109–141.

Walls, Robert E., et al., eds. *The Old Traditional Way of Life: Essays in Honor of Warren E. Roberts.* Bloomington, IN.: Trickster Press, Indiana U Folklore Institute, 1989.

Walter, Krista. "Surviving the Garret: Harriet Jacobs and the Critique of Sentiment." *American Transcendental Quarterly* 8.3 (Sept. 1994). 189–210.

Wardley, Lynn. "Relic, Fetish, Femmage: The Aesthetics of Sentiment in the Work of Stowe." *The Culture of Sentiment.* Ed. Shirley Samuels. New York: Oxford University Press, 1992. 203–220.

Ware, Vron. *Beyond the Pale: White Women, Racism, and History.* New York: Verso, 1992.

Warner, Susan. *The Wide, Wide World.* 1850. New York: The Feminist Press, 1987.

Washington, Booker T. *Up from Slavery.* Williamstown, MA: Corner House Publishers, 1971.

Watson, Harry L. *Liberty and Power: The Politics of Jacksonian America.* New York: Hill and Wang, 1990.

Weddle, George E. "National Portraits: The Columbian Celebrations of 1792, 1892–93 and 1992 as Cultural Monuments." *The Cultures of Celebrations.* Ed. Ray B. Browne and Michael T. Marsden. Bowling Green, OH: Bowling Green State University Press, 1994. 111–126.

Weiner, Marli F. *Mistresses and Slaves: Plantation Women in South Carolina, 1830–80.* Urbana: University of Illinois Press, 1998.

Weinstein, Cindy. " 'A Sort of Adopted Daughter': Family Relations in *The Lamplighter.*" *ELH* 68 (2001): 1023–1047.

Whalen, Terence. "Average Racism: Poe, Slavery, and the Wages of Literary Nationalism." *Romancing the Shadow: Poe and Race.* Ed. Gerald J. Kennedy and Liliane Weissberg. New York: Oxford University Press, 2001. 3–40.

Whitney, Lisa. "In the Shadow of Uncle Tom's Cabin: Stowe's Vision of Slavery from the Great Dismal Swamp." *The New England Quarterly* 66 (Dec. 1993): 552–569.

Wiegman, Robyn. *American Anatomies: Theorizing Race and Gender.* Durham, NC: Duke University Press, 1996.

———. "Melville's Geography of Gender." *Herman Melville: A Collection of Critical Essays.* Ed. Myra Jehlen. Englewood Cliffs, NJ: Prentice Hall, 1994. 187–198.

———. "Whiteness Studies and the Paradox of Particularity." *Boundary* 2.26 (Fall 1999): 115–150.

Wigley, Mark. *White Walls, Designer Dresses: The Fashioning of Modern Architecture.* Cambridge, MA: MIT Press, 1995.

Williams, William Carlos. *The Collected Poems of William Carlos Williams.* Ed. A. Walton Litz and Christopher MacGowan. New York: New Directions, 1986.

Wright, Gwendolyn. *Building the Dream: A Social History of Housing in America.* New York: Pantheon Books, 1981.

Yellin, Jean Fagan, Introduction and illustrations. *Incidents in the Life of a Slave Girl, Written by Herself.* By Harriet Jacobs. Cambridge, MA: Harvard University Press, 1987.

Yentsch, Anne. "Access and Space, Symbolic and Material, in Historical Archaeology." *The Archaeology of Gender.* Ed. Dale Walde and Noreen D. Willows. Alberta, Canada: University of Calgary, 1991. 252–262.

———. "Engendering Visible and Invisible Ceramic Artifacts, Especially Dairy Vessels." *Historical Archaeology* 25.4 (1991): 132–155.

———. "The Symbolic Divisions of Pottery: Sex-related Attributes of English and Anglo-American Household Pots." *The Archaeology of Inequality.* Eds. Randall H. McGuire and Robert Paynter. Cambridge, MA: Basil Blackwell, 1991. 192–230.

Yentsch, Anne, and Mary Beaudry. "American Material Culture in Mind, Thought, and Deed." *Archaeological Theory Today.* Ed. Ian Hodder. Malden, MA: Blackwell Publishing, 2001. 214–240.

Young, Philip. "The Machine in Tartarus: Melville's Inferno." *American Literature* 63.2 (June 1991): 208–224.

Zanger, Jules. "The 'Tragic Octoroon' in Pre–Civil War Fiction." *American Quarterly* 18.1 (1966): 63–70.

Zierden, Martha A., and Bernard L. Herman. "Charleston Townhouses: Archaeology, Architecture, and the Urban Landscape, 1750–1850." *Landscape Archaeology: Reading and Interpreting the American Historical Landscape.* Ed. Rebecca Yamin and Karen Bescherer Metheny. Knoxville: University of Tennessee Press, 1996. 193–227.

INDEX

abolitionists, 5, 13–14, 27, 31, 51, 80, 84, 90, 109, 131, 138, 141, 144, 152, 174 n, 180 n
Absalom, Absalom!, 44–46, 170
Africanisms, African retentions, 29, 41–43, 151
Alcott, Bronson, 133
Alcott, Louisa May, 160
Alger, Horatio, 48
angel. *See* cherub
Angelou, Maya, 3–4, 170
anti-slavery. *See* abolitionists
Appeal in Favor of that Class of Americans Called Africans, An, 5, 134–35
architecture, xii, xiv, xvi, 7–9, 18, 20, 38, 40, 44, 46, 52–56, 65, 74, 76, 79, 102, 114, 118, 120, 126–27, 136, 148–49, 153, 165, 167–70, 173 n, 175 n, 176 n, 178 n, 179 n
aristocratic, xxii, 23, 63, 71, 119, 148, 178 n

"Bartleby, the Scrivener," 47, 175 n
basement, 56, 96, 114, 126, 153, 168
beauty, xxvii, 129–30, 155, 162
bedroom, 65, 86, 96, 110, 148
Beecher, Catharine, 70, 91, 176 n

"Berenice," xxvii, 156–64, 180 n, 181 n
Bible, 99–100, 133
Big House, 17, 22–23, 45–46, 118, 120
blackface, xiv, 35, 73, 79, 80, 117, 135–36, 144–46, 175 n, 176 n, 177 n, 180 n
"blackness," 5–7, 51, 74, 85, 101, 128, 130, 133, 152, 175 n
Blithedale Romance, The, xi, xv, xvii, xxvi, 104, 122–28, 160
Bloomer, Amelia, 115
bloomers, 115
Bluest Eye, The, 129–31, 156, 163–64, 170
body, xvii, xxii, 6, 24, 40, 46, 60–61, 83, 85, 88–94, 100, 107–15, 122, 127–32, 136, 138–43, 150–56, 161–64, 166
Boott Lowell Mills, 49, 72, 74. *See also* factory
Brown v. Board of Education of Topeka, Kansas, 170

Cannon's Point Plantation, xii, xiv, 7, 20, 171 n

200   INDEX

cemetery, 87, 92, 169. *See also* churchyard; folk cemeteries; graveyard; rural cemeteries
ceramics, xi, xii, xvi, 3–4, 7, 9–17, 34, 41, 46, 57–64, 67, 87, 94–95, 113–15, 130–34, 159, 162, 169–70, 175 n, 178 n
cherub, 66, 120, 162–63, 179 n
cherub design, xiii–xiv, 11, 25–26, 67, 87, 92–94, 122, 179 n
Child, Lydia Maria, 5, 7, 69, 134–35, 150
china. *See* ceramics; porcelain
churchyard, 11, 27, 94, 174 n. *See also* cemetery; graveyard
cleanliness, xiii, 20, 79, 104, 117, 130–31, 156, 160, 168. *See also* filth
clocks, 70–74, 78
clothing, xii, xiv, xvi, xxvi, 4, 13, 48–49, 66–67, 72–73, 76, 86–128, 129, 133, 136, 139, 158, 171 n, 179 n. *See also* fashion; slave clothing
clothing laws, 116, 118. *See also* slave laws
Colono Ware, 41, 171 n, 175 n
columns, 9–10, 22, 28, 94, 122
complexion. *See* skin
Cooper, James Fenimore, xxi, xxvi, 53–60, 71, 84, 137–38, 160
corset, xxvi, 86–87, 89, 92, 108–09, 115, 121
cosmetics. *See* make-up
creamware, xi, 12, 14–15, 47, 61, 134
Cult of Domesticity, 40, 62, 82, 162–63, 175 n, 179 n
cult of mourning, 35–36, 92, 94, 179 n
Cummins, Susanna Maria, xxvi, 65–69, 84

Davis, Rebecca Harding, 152–55, 180 n
death's-head motif, 11, 25–26, 93, 163

"Devil in the Belfry, The," 71–74, 176 n
dining ritual. *See* etiquette
dining room, 17, 34, 96, 167
disembodiment. *See* body; spirit
dishes. *See* ceramics; slave ceramics; table settings; tea
Douglass, Frederick, xii, xxvi, 5, 16, 21–25, 32, 70, 145, 172 n, 173 n, 174 n
Dred, xxvi, 138–41, 151, 160, 180 n
dress. *See* clothing; fashion

earthenware, xi–xii, 12–13, 15, 171 n, 175 n
Emerson, Ralph Waldo, 6, 71, 172 n
etiquette, xii, xiv, xvi, 9, 16–17, 28, 33, 52, 57–58, 60–61, 63, 76–81, 102, 160, 177 n, 180 n

factory, xxii, xxvi, 48–50, 61–62, 71–72, 74–76, 81–85, 90, 103–04, 153, 177 n
fallen women, xxiii, 105, 134
fashion, 86, 89, 94–95, 101–04, 110
Faulkner, William, 44–46, 170
female, xxiii, 87–91, 98, 107–08
feminine, xiii, xvi, xxii–xxvii, 32, 34, 36, 46–49, 50, 62, 64–66, 76, 82, 85, 86–128, 129–30, 143, 172 n, 177 n, 179 n
feminine sphere, xxv, 62, 87, 117, 125, 128
Fern, Fanny, 71, 75
fieldstone gravemarker, 11, 30, 47
filth, 37–38, 43, 46, 52–53, 65–67, 75–76, 79, 87, 114, 129, 132–33, 143, 147–56, 179 n, 180 n. *See also* cleanliness
floors, 36–37, 42, 65
flowers, xiv, 10, 24, 45, 52, 65, 100, 112, 122, 124–25, 139
folk cemeteries, 29–30, 153, 173 n

food, 33–34, 57–58, 60, 168–69, 181 n
forks, xi, 3, 16, 60, 65
Franklin, Benjamin, 48
Freedmen's Book, The, 150
front hall, 52, 96
frontier, xxvi, 53, 64–65
Frugal Housewife, The, 69
Fugitive Slave Act, 7
furniture, xvi, 94–99, 102, 110–11, 130, 136, 148, 154, 161, 163, 178 n. See also slave furniture

gender studies, xxiv–xxv, 46
Georgian architecture, 8–9, 24, 53
Godey's Lady's Book, xiv, xvi, 54, 87, 91, 94, 102–04, 109, 112, 142
Gone with the Wind, 86–87, 129, 170
Gothic Revival architecture, 95, 168
graveshelter, 29–30
gravestone motifs, 24–25, 93–94
gravestones, xiv, xvi, 4–5, 7, 10–11, 26–31, 46, 56, 70, 87, 91, 93, 95, 122, 130, 134, 162, 169, 173 n, 174 n
graveyard, 26, 28–29, 35–36, 39, 46, 173 n, 174 n, 178 n, 179 n. See also cemetery; churchyard
Greek Revival architecture, 9, 13, 23, 164, 167
guidebooks, xiv, 9, 60–61, 69–71, 78–79, 96, 100, 102, 109, 133, 142, 149–50, 161, 168–69, 176 n. See also Godey's Lady's Book

Hale, Sarah Josepha, 87, 91, 178 n. See also Godey's Lady's Book
"hand," 61, 71, 119
Harper's magazine, 166–67
Hawthorne, Nathaniel, xi, xv, xvii, xxii, xxvi, 6, 104, 122–28, 160, 166
heaven, 92, 134, 179 n

Hidden Hand, The, 84, 117–22, 159, 179 n
historical archaeology, xv–xix, xxvi
House of the Seven Gables, The, xxii
house paint, xv–xvi, 4–8, 21–22, 46–47, 52–54, 87, 130, 148, 162, 173 n
housing. See architecture; lower-class housing; middle-class housing; slave housing
hygiene. See cleanliness; filth

I Know Why the Caged Bird Sings, 3–4, 170
idleness, 48, 65–66, 70, 127. See also leisure
I-house, 30, 53, 176 n
Incidents in the Life of a Slave Girl, 31–40, 174 n, 175 n
insanity, 117, 137, 179 n, 181 n
interior decor, xii, xiv, 4, 52, 112, 119, 130, 139, 148, 168

Jacobs, Harriet, xxvi, 31–40, 174 n, 175 n
jewelry, 13–14

keeping-room, 55
Kennedy, John Pendleton, xxvi, 16–18
Kirkland, Caroline, 64–65
kitchen, 17, 19–20, 33–36, 43, 55, 96, 99, 110, 112–15, 148, 168, 178 n

labor, xxii, 39, 48, 85–89, 91, 96–99, 102, 109–10, 113, 126, 152, 154, 166, 176 n
Lamplighter, The, 65–69, 84
landscape design, xii, 8, 22–24, 28–29, 45, 52, 74–75, 114, 148, 165, 168, 176 n
Last of the Mohicans, The, 60, 137–38, 160
leisure, xxii, 108–09, 151, 176 n. See also idleness
Life in the Iron Mills, xxvii, 152–55, 180 n

linsey-woolsey. *See* slave clothing
Little Eva, 84
Little Women, 160
local ceramics, 9, 14–15
L'Ouverture, Toussaint, 27
lower-class, xi–xiv, xxi, xxiii, 12, 44–51, 66, 73, 75, 81–85, 88, 116, 126–28, 137, 142–43, 163, 176n, 177n, 178n
lower-class housing, 44–47, 66–67

make-up, 135, 141–43, 180n
"Man that Was Used Up, The," 155–56
manners. *See* etiquette
marble, xv, 5, 11, 14, 26, 30–31, 56, 93, 95, 154, 169, 174n
masculine, xxi–xxvii, 46–48, 64, 77, 82, 85, 88, 95, 98, 102, 110, 126–28, 172n
material culture studies, xv–xx
Mather, Cotton, 133, 179n
Melville, Herman, xvi, xix, xxvii, 6, 47, 76–84, 133, 144–47, 175n, 177n, 180n
middle-class, xiii, 31, 54, 63, 74–75, 85, 96, 126–28, 132, 134, 151, 161, 165, 168
middle-class housing, 53
mill. *See* factory
minstrelsy. *See* blackface
Mitchell, Margaret, 86–87, 129, 170
Moby Dick, xix, xxvii, 6, 133, 145–47, 180n
Monticello, 38, 114. *See also* plantations
Morrison, Toni, xxiv, 129–31, 156, 163–64, 170
Mount Auburn, 26, 28–29, 92, 174n, 179n. *See also* rural cemeteries
mulatto, 132, 136, 154. *See also* tragic mulatto
My Bondage and My Freedom, 16, 21–24, 145

Narrative of Shipwreck Captivity and Suffering of Horace Holden and Benjamin Nute, 144
Narrative of the Life of Frederick Douglass, xii, xxi, 21, 24–25, 70, 145, 172n, 173n, 174n
Native American, 41, 53–58, 155, 166, 171n, 175n
"Negro codes." *See* slave laws
"Negro-cloth." *See* slave clothing
New Home, Who'll Follow?, A, 64–65
Notions of the Americans, xxi

Oasis, The, 135
"Old Virginny," 79–81
"Old Zip Coon," 136
Oldtown Folks, 148
Olmsted, Frederick Law, 19, 22–23, 30, 106–07, 151, 161
overseers, 19–20, 75

"Paradise of Bachelors and Tartarus of Maids," xxii, 76–84, 177n
parlor, 17, 36, 39, 46, 52, 69, 95–96, 110, 113, 148
"passing," 131–32, 136, 163, 172n
pearlware, xi
petticoat, 108–09, 115
Pioneers, The, 53–59, 71, 84
plantation layout, 19–20, 22–23, 44. *See also* landscape design
plantation mansion. *See* Big House
plantations, xiii, 20, 38, 41, 106, 114, 167
Poe, Edgar Allan, xxvi–xxvii, 73, 71–74, 155–64, 176n, 180n, 181n
"Poor Man's Pudding and Rich Man's Crumbs," 78
"poor white trash," xxiii, 46, 75, 151
porcelain, xi–xv, 10, 11, 59, 62, 168
portraits, 25, 94, 112, 143
"Predicament, A," 71
pro-slavery, xxi, 17, 37, 50, 149–50

purity, xiii–xiv, xxv–xxvi, 28, 67, 84, 132–35, 150–53
purity of blood, 131–34

Quaker, 67, 89, 117, 153, 154, 178 n

redware, 12, 134
riots, 73
Roman Classical, 45, 94
Roman Revival, 9, 165, 167
rural cemeteries, 26, 28–29, 92, 169, 174 n, 179 n. *See also* Mount Auburn

scar, 135, 140, 144–47, 154, 180 n
Scarlet Letter, The, 6
segregation, 3, 5, 20, 34, 55, 58, 87, 102, 164, 166, 170
sentimental, xvi, xx, 4, 35, 62–63, 84, 97–98, 120, 140–41, 172 n, 175 n, 180 n
sentimental literature, xx, xxii, xxvi, 63–69
sewing, 37, 91, 97, 103, 106
sheds, xiii, 19–20, 34, 38–39, 99, 114
skin, xii, xvi–xvii, xxi–xxvii, 5–7, 34, 46, 51, 55, 59, 68, 82, 87, 105, 112, 119–20, 129–55, 179 n
slate gravestones, 5, 10–11, 26–27, 93, 122, 174 n
slave auction, 161
slave ceramics, 15–16, 41, 112, 131, 174 n. *See also* slave dishes
slave clothing, 4, 33, 50, 105–07, 116, 141
slave dishes, xii–xiii, 15–16, 40, 131. *See also* slave ceramics
slave furniture, 105–06, 112, 131
slave graves, xiii, 30–31, 35, 43
slave housing, xiii, 5, 17–24, 37–38, 40–45, 107, 111–12, 139–40, 149–50
slave laws, 48, 106, 118, 132, 138

slave resistance, 21–25, 27, 31–43, 48, 110–14, 115, 150–51
Snodgrass, Emma, 116
Southworth, E.D.E.N., 84, 117–22, 159, 179 n
spirit, 91, 93–94, 100, 153
spirit faces, 25
Staffordshire, 10, 12, 14
stoneware, xi, 12
Stowe, Harriet Beecher, xxvi, 97, 104–06, 109–15, 116, 131, 138–41, 148, 151, 160, 178 n
sumptuary laws. *See* clothing laws
Swallow Barn, 16–18

table setting, xv, 4–5, 12, 15, 17, 54, 57, 60, 63, 67–68, 134
tablecloth, 16, 33, 57, 60, 68, 99, 113–14, 139, 159
tattoos, 135, 143, 144, 147, 180 n
tea, xi, xvi, xxvi, 12, 15, 33–34, 63–67, 139, 148, 173 n, 174 n, 176 n
tea ritual. *See* tea
tea setting. *See* tea
teeth, 72, 129, 130, 155–64, 180 n
"thing," xv–xxv
time, 3, 70–72
time-discipline, 4, 33, 46, 69, 70, 72, 74, 83–84, 103, 111
toothbrushes, 148, 158–60
tragic mulatto, 135–41, 164
Transcendentalist, xii, xxiii
transvestite, 116–20
trash. *See* filth
Treatise on Domestic Economy, 70, 91, 176 n. *See also* guidebooks
trencher, xii, 5, 41
Truth, Sojourner, 90, 91, 116, 178 n
Turner, Nat, 35, 48
Typee, 144, 180 n

Uncle Tom's Cabin, xxi, 97, 104–06, 109–15, 131, 138–40, 178 n, 180 n
Up from Slavery, xiii, 5, 160–61, 173 n
upper-class, xi, xiii, 61, 65, 74–81, 85, 96, 126–28, 132, 142, 151, 159, 165, 176 n
urn-and-willow design. See willow-and-urn design

veil, 104, 122–28, 141
vernacular architecture, 53
Vesey, Denmark, 39, 48
visual economy/visual culture, xvi, xx, 7, 38, 131–33, 172 n

wage slavery, 50–51, 84, 90, 152
Walker, Dr. Mary, 116–17
Warner, Susan, xxvi, 63–64, 97–102
Washington, Booker T., xiii, 5, 160–61, 173 n
Wedgwood, 10, 13–14, 90, 173 n
White City, 165–68, 170
white ironstone, xii, 12, 95, 176 n
white slavery. See wage slavery
white things, miscellaneous, 67–69, 81–83, 99, 124, 154
"whiteness," xv, xxv, 6, 7, 46, 51, 80, 164, 170, 175 n
whiteness studies, xxiii–xxv, 170
whiteware, xi
whitewash, 6, 81, 120, 145–46, 149–50
Wide Wide World, 63–64, 97–102, 178 n
willow, xii, 27, 59, 95, 122, 169
willow-and-urn design, xiii, 11, 25, 27, 93–95
wooden gravemarkers, 30, 31, 35
work-discipline, xxii, 4, 47–48, 61–62, 63–66, 69, 71, 80, 99, 156, 159–61, 164, 172 n, 175 n. See also time-discipline
working-class, 61, 67, 175 n, 177 n. See also lower-class
World's Columbian Exposition, 165–68

yellowware, xi, 13, 59

www.ingramcontent.com/pod-product-compliance
Lightning Source LLC
Chambersburg PA
CBHW051056230426
43667CB00013B/2326